Giant
Book of
Card Games

♠ ♣ ♦ ♥

Sheila Anne Barry
Alfred Sheinwold
&
William A. Moss

Sterling Publishing Company, Inc.
New York

10 9 8 7 6 5 4 3 2 1

Published In 1998 by Sterling Publishing Company, Inc.
387 Park Avenue South, New york. N.Y. 10016

Material in this collection was adapted from
101 Best Family Card Games © Alfred Sheinwold
10-Minute Card Games © William A. Moss
World's Best Card Games For One © Sheila Anne Barry

Distributed in Canada by Sterling Publishing
c/o Canadian Manda Group
One Atlantic Avenue, Suite 105
Toronto, Ontario, Canada M6K 3E7

Distributed in Great Britain and Europe by Chris Lloyd
463 Ashley Road, Parkstone, Poole,
Dorset, BH14 0AX, United Kingdom

Distibuted in Australia by Capricorn Link (Australia) Pty Ltd.
P.O. Box 6651, Baulkham Hills, Business Centre
NSW 2153, Australia

Sterling ISBN 0-8069-4809-4

Contents

SECTION 1
Family Games

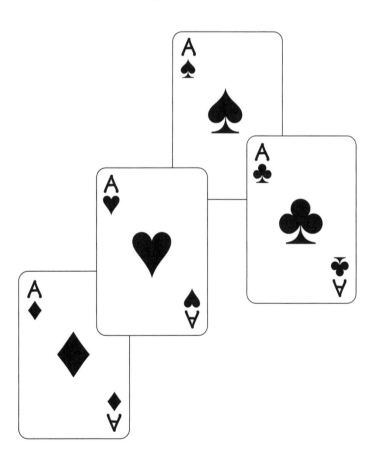

Why Family Card Games?

My own experience makes me feel that every family will benefit from playing card games together.

It is, first of all, fun—and a splendid way to enjoy spending time in each other's company. It's also a great way to get to learn how each other's mind works, which can be important to both parent and child.

Then, too, it's a healthy experience for a child to play with grownups as an equal. It adds to a child's self-esteem when he or she feels included and part of the fun— to say nothing of the implied supposition that the child is intelligent enough to learn the games and worthy of playing them with experienced competitors.

Another major benefit is that the child gets practice in losing without squawking and winning without crowing. (Many adults could use some of this practice, too!)

A young child also can learn about numbers and easy arithmetic from card games. And people of any age can exercise their brain by the logical thinking needed in the more advanced games.

—Alfred Sheinwold

1

For the Family with Very Young Children

These games are for children who are too young to think—and for grownups who would rather *not* think! Sometimes it's hard to tell whether the children or the grownups laugh harder!

Pig

This is a very hilarious game for children or for adults to play with children. Anybody can learn it in two or three minutes, and one extra minute makes you an expert!

Players: 3 to 13—5 or 6 make the best game.

Cards: 4 of a kind for each player in the game.
For example, 5 players would use 20 cards:
4 Aces, 4 Kings, 4 Queens, 4 Jacks, and 4 10s.
For 6 players you would add the 9s.

The Deal: Any player shuffles and deals four cards to each player.

To Win the Game: Get four of a kind in your own hand, or be quick to notice it when somebody else gets four of a kind.

The Play: The players look at their cards to see if they were dealt four of a kind. If nobody has four of a kind, each player puts some unwanted card *face down* on the table and passes it to the player to the left, receiving a card at the same time from the player to the right.

If, still, nobody has four of a kind, each player once again passes a card to the left and gets a new card from the right.

The play continues in this way until one player gets four of a kind. That player stops passing or receiving cards. Instead, he puts his finger to his nose.

The other players must be quick to notice this, and each of them must stop passing in order to put a finger to his nose. The last player to put a finger to his nose is the *Pig.*

Strategy: In trying to put together four of a kind, you usually start with a pair. For example, suppose you are dealt two Kings, one Queen, and one Ace. Keep the two Kings, and pass either the Queen or the Ace. As soon as you get another King, save all three of them, and pass your fourth card. Sooner or later your fourth King will come in.

Don't get so interested in looking for your own four of a kind that you are blind to what the other players are doing. Keep one eye on everybody else, particularly on those who look very eagerly at the cards they are receiving. The eager player probably has three of a kind and is just waitng for the fourth.

The best *Pig* player I know is a seven-year old girl who doesn't try very hard to make four of a kind. She always tries to look excited, and talks and squeals as she gets each card, just as though she had three of a kind. While doing all of this, she watches the other players to see which of them are most interested in her and which are interested in their own hands.

She knows that the players who are interested in *her* have *bad* hands, but that those who are thinking about the *game* have *good* hands. So little Lisa knows which players to watch, and she is never caught!

Donkey

This is the same game as *Pig*, except that when you get four of a kind you put your hand face down on the table quietly instead of putting your finger to your nose. You still get a card from your right, but you just pass it along to the left, leaving your four of a kind untouched on the table.

As the other players see what has happened, they likewise put their cards down quietly. The idea is to keep up the passing and the conversation while some player plays on without realizing that the hand has really ended.

If you're the last player to put your cards on the table, you lose the hand. This makes you a D. The next time you lose, you become a D-O. The third time you become a D-O-N. This keeps on, until finally you become a D-O-N-K-E-Y.

The D-O-N-K-E-Y loses the game, and the winner is the player who has the smallest number of letters.

Donkey Buttons

Equipment: Buttons—one less than there are players.

This is the same game as *Donkey*, except that when you get four of a kind, you shout, "Donkey!" and quickly grab a button from the middle of the table. There is one button less than there are players, so the last player to grab doesn't get a button—and becomes a D. The game continues in this way until somebody becomes a D-O-N-K-E-Y.

At the end of the game, the D-O-N-K-E-Y has to bray *"heehaw"* three times.

My Ship Sails

Players: 4 to 7—4 or 5 make the best game.

Cards: 7 for each player.

The Deal: Any player shuffles and deals seven cards to each player.

To Win the Game: Get seven cards of the same suit.

The Play: Each player looks at his hand and passes one card to the left, receiving at the same time one card from the right. The play goes on in the same way as in *Pig* or *Donkey*. The only difference is that you are trying to collect cards that are all of the same suit.

There are many different ways of ending a hand. When you get seven cards of the same suit, you put your cards down immediately and say, "My ship sails!" Another way is to say nothing but to put your finger to your nose as in *Pig*.

If it takes too long to finish a hand, try one of the shorter games—*My Bee Buzzes* or *My Star Twinkle*s (page 12).

Strategy: Begin by trying to collect the suit that you have most of. For example, if you have four or five hearts, pass the other cards and try to collect more hearts.

You may run into trouble if some other player tries to collect the same suit that you are collecting. To guard against this, start collecting a second suit if you don't have any luck with the first. If you can get three cards in a second suit, you can then start to pass the cards of your first suit and switch your plan.

For example, suppose you start with three hearts, two spades, one club, and one diamond. Keep passing the clubs and diamonds until you get another heart or another spade. If you get one more—or a third spade before any heart is passed to you, you may suspect that somebody else is saving the hearts. Your best bet is to break up your hearts and to try to get seven spades instead.

If you have four or more cards in the same suit, it doesn't pay to break. Sit tight and hope that one of the other players will break first and pass the cards that you need.

My Star Twinkles

This is the same as *My Ship Sails* except that you need only five cards of the same suit (and two odd cards) to win a hand. In this game it takes only two or three minutes to play a hand.

My Bee Buzzes

This is the same as *My Ship Sails* except that you need only six cards of the same suit to end the hand. Each player gets seven cards, but needs only six cards in the same suit (and one odd card) to win the hand. It takes less time to finish a hand in this game than in *My Ship Sails*.

Through the Window

Players: 3 to 13—the more the merrier.

Cards: 4 to each player.

The Deal: The dealer shuffles and deals four cards to each player.

To Win the Game: Win the most cards.

The Play: The dealer begins by saying, "I looked through the window and saw . . . ." Just at this moment, and not before, he turns up one of his four cards so that all the players can see it.

Then, each player (including the dealer) must try to say an animal or thing beginning with the same letter of the alphabet as the card that has been turned up. For example, if the card is an Ace, you might call out "Ant," "Alligator," "Alaska," or anything else that begins with the letter A. If the card is a Nine, you might call out "Nachos" or "Nut."

The first player to call out a correct word takes the card and starts his pile of captured cards separate from the four cards that were dealt to him. Then the person to the left of the dealer says, "I looked through the window and saw . . . ," turning up one of her cards. The game continues in the same way, in turn to the left, until all the cards originally dealt have been turned up and captured. Each person keeps his own pile of captured cards, and the one who captures the most wins the game. The captured cards have nothing to do with each player's original four cards, since each player had exactly four chances to turn up a card.

As soon as a word has been used to win a card, no player can use that same word again. For example, if you have used the word "Stone" to capture a Seven, neither you nor any other player can use the word "Stone" to capture any other card beginning with an S.

Concentration

Players: Any number at all—the more the merrier.

Cards: 1 pack.

The Deal: Spread the cards face down on a table. Don't bother to put them down neatly, but just jumble them up, making sure that no two cards overlap.

To Win the Game: Capture the largest number of cards.

The Play: Before play begins, the players should be told what their turn is, so that they know whether they are first, second, third, and so on.

The first player turns up any card and then turns up any other card. If the two cards match (for example, if they are two Aces or two Kings), the first player captures them as her pair. She then has another turn and proceeds to turn up two more cards in the hope of finding a pair. When she turns up two cards that are not a pair, she must turn them face down again in the same position. It now becomes the turn of the next player.

Strategy: The trick is to remember the cards that have been turned up and exactly where on the table they are. For example, suppose a player turns up a King and a 10. He had to turn those cards face down again. You do your best to remember exactly where that King is and where that 10 is. Then, when it is your turn, you turn up a card on an entirely different part of the table, hoping to find another King or another 10. If you find another King, you can go right to the first King like a homing pigeon and you'll have a pair of Kings to capture. If you find another 10, you can go right to the first 10 and capture those cards, too.

If you try to remember too many cards, you may forget them all. It is much better to begin by trying to remember only two or three cards. When you find that you can do that easily, try remembering four cards. In this way you can gradually increase your skill until you can accurately remember the whereabouts of seven or eight cards at a time. This should be enough to win almost any game.

Tossing Cards into a Hat

Players: Any number, but the game is best with two or three.

Cards: 1 old deck—or 2 old decks if playing with more than 3 people.

Equipment: An old felt or straw hat. A sheet of newspaper.

The Deal: Divide the cards equally among the players.

To Win the Game: Toss the largest number of cards into the hat.

The Play: Place the hat on a sheet of newspaper at the other end of the room, with crown down and brim up.

Standing the whole length of the room away from the hat, each player in turn flips one card towards the hat, with the object of landing the card inside the hat.

Each player keeps track of the cards he has landed inside the hat. If a card lands on the brim, it counts as only one-half a point. If a card on the brim of the hat is knocked in by any player, it counts a full point for the player who originally threw it.

Strategy: The trick is to hold the card between your thumb and fore-finger with your wrist bent inwards towards your body. If you then straighten out your wrist suddenly with a flick and release the card at the same time, you can make it sail all the way across a very long room and you can control it pretty well.

Although strength isn't important in this game, small children may have trouble in getting the knack. Allow them to stand several paces closer to the hat.

Special Advice: Be sure to place the hat near a blank wall, and far away from a piano, or a sofa, or any other heavy piece of furniture. Cards that land under a piano are very hard to recover.

Treasure Hunt

Players: Any number.

Cards: 2 packs.

Preparation: Before the players arrive, hide some of the cards from one deck in one of the rooms that you devote to the game. Take out of the second deck cards that match the ones you have hidden. Make sure to hide as many red cards as black ones. A hidden card should be findable without the seeker having to move anything to get to it. For example, if you hide a card in a bookcase, it should be sticking out in some way and not hidden inside any book. Every hidden card should be well within the reach of even the youngest child. It is perfectly fair to put a card under the pedals of a piano, but not on top of the piano where a small child would be unable to see it.

The Play: When the players arrive, appoint two captains and let them choose sides. One team is to find red cards (Hearts and Diamonds), and the other team black cards (Spades and Clubs).

Give each player a card from the second deck and explain that he is to find a duplicate of it, hidden somewhere in a particular room or in two or three rooms, depending on how much space you have for the game. As soon as a player finds the card he is looking for, he is to bring it back to you and get another card to look for. The first team to find all of its hidden cards wins the game.

Be sure to explain that it isn't necessary to move anything in order to find the cards. Mention, also, that anybody who finds a card that she isn't looking for should replace that card in exactly the same spot and tell no one about it. Somebody else will be looking for it, or she herself may be looking for it later on.

This is a good game to play in somebody else's house!

2
The War Family

Most games of the War family call for the players to keep their eyes open and their brains sharp but don't require great skill in the play of the cards. Skillful players usually win, but even the youngest player has a good chance.

Slapjack

Slapjack is one of the most entertaining games that you can play with a deck of cards. It is one of the very first games that my grandfather taught me, and he didn't complain when I won from him regularly.

Players: 2 to 8. The game is best for 3 or 4 players.

Cards: 1 pack.

The Deal: One at a time to each player until all the cards have been dealt out. It doesn't matter if they don't come out even. The players square up their cards into a neat pile face down in front of them without looking at any cards.

To Win the Game: Win all the cards.

The Play: The player to the dealer's left begins by lifting the top card of her pile and dropping it *face up* in the middle of the table. The next player (to the left of the first player) does likewise—that is, he lifts the top card of *his* pile and drops it face up in the middle of the table, on top of the card that is already there. The play continues in this way, each player in turn lifting the top card of his pile and dropping it face up in the middle of the table.

As soon as any player turns up a Jack, the fun begins. The first player to slap that Jack wins the entire pile of cards in the middle of the table! If more than one player slaps at the Jack, the one whose hand is at the bottom wins the pile.

This means that you have to keep your eyes open and be pretty quick to get your hand down on a Jack. Sometimes your hand is pretty red when you're so quick that another player slaps your hand instead of the Jack, but it's all in fun. Hopefully, grownups are careful not to play too roughly!

I used to beat my grandfather all the time because he would lift his hand high in the air before bringing it down on a Jack, while I would swoop in sideways and could generally snatch the Jack away before his hand even hit the table. Grandpa never seemed to learn!

Whenever you win cards, you must put them face down underneath the cards you already have.

The play goes on until one player has won all the cards. As soon as a player has lost his last card, he may watch for the next Jack and try to slap it in order to get a new pile for himself. If he fails to get that next pile, he is out of the game. Sooner or later, all the players except one are "knocked out" in this way, and the cards all come to one player, who is the winner.

False Slaps: A player who slaps at a card that is *not* a Jack must give the top card of her pile to the owner of the card that she slapped. If the false slapper has no cards to pay the penalty, she is out.

How to Turn Cards: At your turn to play you must lift the top card of your pile and turn it *away* from you as you drop it face up in the middle of the table. This is to make sure that you don't see the card before the others do. Also, make sure that you let the card go as you drop it on the table.

Strategy: Naturally, you don't want the other players to have a big advantage, so turn the card over very quickly. Then you will see it just about as soon as they do.

Most players use the same hand for turning the cards and for slapping at Jacks. It's a more exciting game, however, if you agree that the hand used for slapping will not be the same hand used for turning the cards.

Some players use the right hand to turn over the card with a quick motion, and they swoop down on the Jack with the left hand. Other experts, since they are much swifter at swooping with the right hand, turn the card over with the left hand. You may have to try it both ways to see which is better for you.

The important thing to remember is that it's better to be a swift swooper than a slow slapper.

Snap

Players: 3 to 8—4 or 5 are best.

Cards: 1 pack.

The Deal: Any player deals one card at a time, until all the cards have been dealt. They don't have to come out even.

To Win the Game: Win all the cards.

The Play: As in *Slapjack*, each player turns up one card at a time at his turn to play. The card must be turned away from the player and dropped on the table, except that each player starts a pile in front of himself for his turned-up cards. For example, in the game for four players, after each player has had a turn, there will be four piles of face-up cards and the four packs of cards face down that were dealt at the beginning.

When a player turns up a card that matches a face-up card on any other pile, the first player to say "Snap!" wins both piles and puts them face down under her own pack.

A player who says "Snap!" at the wrong time, when the turned-up card does not match one of the other piles, must give the top card of his pile to the player who just turned up her card.

As in *Slapjack*, a player who runs out of cards may stay in for the next "Snap!" in the hope of getting a new pile. If she does not win that "Snap," she is out. A player who cries a false "Snap" is out if he has no cards to pay the penalty.

Strategy: Players have to keep looking around to make sure they know which cards are on top of the piles, since these keep changing as the game goes on. They must be ready at all times to shout "Snap!" If two or more players begin the word at the same time, the player who ends the word first, wins. This is no game for a slow talker!

My grandmother used to play this game with me. We had to make a special rule once because one little girl who was playing with us said "Snap!" every time a card was turned. She had to pay a penalty card most of the time, but this was more than offset because she won every single pile. Grandma said this wasn't fair, so we adopted the rule that after three false "Snaps" a player was out.

War

Players: 2.

Cards: 1 pack.

To Win the Game: Win all the cards.

The Play: Each player puts his stack of cards face down in front of him and turns up the top card at the same time. The player who has the higher of the two turned-up cards wins both of them and puts them face down at the bottom of his stack of cards. The King is the highest card, and the Ace is the lowest. The full rank of the cards is:

(Highest)   **(Lowest)**

Sometimes *War* is played with the Ace high.

If the two turned-up cards are of the same rank, the players have a "war." Each turns one card face down and then one card face up. The higher of the two new face-up cards takes both piles (a total of six cards).

If the newly turned-up cards again match, there is *double* war. Each player once again turns one card face down and one card face up, and the higher of these two new face-up cards wins the entire pile of ten cards.

The game continues in this way until one player has all of the cards.

This is a good game to play when you have a lot of time and no-where to go.

War for Three

The Deal: When three players want to play *War*, take any card out of the deck and give 17 cards to each.

The Play: For the most part, the play is the same as in two-handed *War*, but when two cards turned up are the same, all three players join in the war by turning one card face down and one card face up. If two of the new turned-up cards are the same, all three players must once more turn one card down and one card face up. As usual, the highest card wins all cards that are used in the war.

If all three turned-up cards are the same, the players must engage in double war. Each player turns two cards face down and then one card face up. If the result is a tie, all three players engage in single war.

Beat Your Neighbors Out of Doors

Other Names: Beggar My Neighbor, Strip Jack Naked

Players: 2.

Cards: 1 pack.

The Deal: Give each player half the deck.

To Win the Game: Win all the cards.

The Play: The non-dealer puts a card *face up* in the middle of the table. If it is an ordinary spot card (from the deuce up to the 10), the dealer covers it with a card from the top of his pile. This process continues, each playing one card in turn on top of the pile, until one of the players puts down an Ace, King, Queen, or Jack.

The moment an Ace or picture card appears, the other player must pay out the proper number of cards, one at a time, face up:

> **For an Ace, four cards.**
> **For a King, three cards.**
> **For a Queen, two cards.**
> **For a Jack, one card.**

If all the cards put down for payment are spot cards, the owner of the Ace or picture card takes up the entire pile and puts it at the bottom of his stack. This is the way the cards are won, and the object of the game is to win all of them.

If, however, you turn up an Ace or picture card while you are paying out to your opponent, the payment stops and he must now pay *you* for the card that you have put down. This process continues, since either player may turn up an Ace or picture card while making a payment. Eventually, however, a player turns up only spot cards in payment, and then the entire pile is lost.

Animals

Players: 3 or more. The best game is for 5 or 6.

Cards: 1 pack.

The Deal: One card at a time until the entire deck has been dealt. It makes no difference if the cards don't come out even.

To Win the Game: Win all the cards.

The Play: Each player takes the name of an animal, such as pig, kangaroo, rhinoceros, hippopotamus.

When everybody fully understands which player represents which animal, the play begins. The player to the dealer's left turns up a card and then each player in turn turns up a card. As in *Snap*, the action takes place when a card that has just been turned up matches some other card that is face up on somebody's pile.

The players who own the matching cards must each call out the animal that the *other* represents. The first to say the other's animal name three times wins both piles.

For example, suppose three players have adopted the names Goat, Pig, and Elephant. The first turns up a Queen, the next turns up a 10, and the third turns up a Queen. The first and the third go into action, but the second must keep silent. The first shouts, "Elephant, Elephant, Elephant!" and the third shouts, "Goat, Goat, Goat!" Both piles are won by the player who finishes talking first.

Play continues until one player has all the cards.

Strategy: When some other player is about to turn up a card, make sure that you have firmly fixed in your mind the card that is at the top of your turned-up pile. And be ready to call out the other person's animal if he matches it.

When it is your own turn to turn up a card, make sure that you have looked at each of the other turned-up cards so that you can instantly spot it if you match one of them. Nine-tenths of the skill in this game lies in being alert.

As you may have noticed, it takes longer to say "Elephant, Elephant, Elephant!" than it does to say "Goat, Goat, Goat!" For this reason, it always pays to give yourself a long animal name rather than a short one. The longer it takes an opponent to say it three times, the better for you.

Good names to use are: hippopotamus, rhinoceros, elephant, mountain lion, boa constrictor, and so forth.

Farmyard

This is the same game as *Animals*, except that the players go by the noises made by a few farmyard animals instead of by the names of the animals themselves. For example, a player who chose Cow would be called "Moo-Moo-Moo" rather than "Cow, Cow, Cow." A player who chose a Duck would be called "Quack-Quack-Quack," and a player who chose Cat would be called "Meow-Meow-Meow," and so on.

I Doubt It

Other Name: Cheat

Players: 3 or more.

Cards: Use a single pack for 3 or 4 players.
Shuffle 2 packs together for 5 or more players.

The Deal: Two or three cards at a time are dealt so that each player gets an equal number of cards. When only a few cards are left, deal one at a time as far as the cards will go

To Win the Game: Get rid of all your cards.

The Play: The player to the dealer's left puts from one to four cards face down in the middle of the table, announcing that she is putting down that number of Aces. The next player puts down one to four cards and announces that he is putting down that number of deuces. The next player in turn does the same thing, stating that he is putting down that number of 3s. The play proceeds in this sequence:

(Starting)   (Ending)

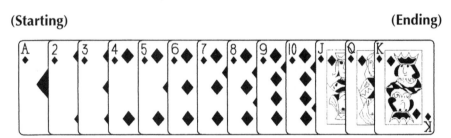

When any player puts down cards and makes his announcement, any other player may say, "I doubt it." The doubted cards must immediately be turned face up. If the statement was true, the doubter must take the entire pile into his hand. If the statement was false, the player who made the false statement must take the pile.

When the players are using two packs shuffled together, a player may put down any number of cards from one to eight.

When a player puts his last cards on the table, some other player must say, "I doubt it," since otherwise the game ends automatically. If the statement turns out to be true, the player wins the game.

A player who has no cards at all of the kind that she is supposed to put down is not allowed to skip her turn. She must put down one or more cards anyway and try to get away with her untruthful announcement. If somebody doubts her claim, she will have to pick up the pile.

If two or more participants say "I doubt it" at the same time, the one nearest the player's left wins the tie; that is, he picks up the pile if the statement turns out to be true after all.

Three-Card I Doubt It

The Deal: The cards are dealt out equally as far as they will go. Put any remaining cards face down in the middle of the table.

The Play: Each player in turn puts down exactly three cards. Instead of starting with Aces automatically, the first player may choose any denomination at all. For example, she may say, "Three 9s." The next player must say, "Three 10s," and so on. When a player has one or two cards left, he must draw enough cards from those put face down in the middle of the table to make up a total of three.

3
The Authors Family

In all of these games the object is to *match* cards in pairs or sets of four of a kind. A good memory will help you in some of the games, but you can have a hilarious time even if you can hardly remember your own name!

Go Fish

Players: 2 to 5.

Cards: 1 pack.

The Deal: If only two play, deal seven cards to each. If four or five play, deal five cards to each. Put the rest of the pack face down on the table, forming the stock.

To Win the Game: Form more "books" than any other player. A book is four of a kind, such as four Kings, four Queens, and so on.

The Play: The player to the dealer's left begins by saying to some other player, "(Jane), give me your *9s*." He *must* mention the name of the player he is speaking to, and he *must* mention the exact rank that he wants (Aces, Kings, Queens, and so on), and he *must* have at least one card of the rank that he is asking for.

The player who is addressed must hand over all the cards he has in the named rank, but if he has none, he says, "Go fish!"

When told to "go fish," a player must draw the top card of the stock. The turn to ask then passes to the player to his left.

If a player succeeds in getting some cards when she asks for them, she keeps her turn and may ask again. She may ask the same player or a different player, and she may ask for any rank in her new question.

If a player who has been told to "go fish" picks a card of the rank he has asked for, he shows this card immediately before putting it into his hand, and his turn continues. (In some very strict games, a player's turn would continue only if the card he fished for completed a book for him.)

Upon getting the fourth card of a book, the player shows all four, places them on the table in front of him, and continues his turn.

If a player is left without cards, she may draw from the stock at her turn and ask for cards of the same rank as the card that she has drawn. After the stock has been used up, a player who has no cards is out of the game.

The game ends when all 13 books have been assembled. The player with the most books wins.

Strategy: When a player asks for cards and gets them but does not put down a completed book, you can tell that he has either two or three of that rank. For example, suppose John requests Queens and gets one Queen from the player he has asked. John does not put down a book of Queens, but asks some new question and is told to "go fish." You now know that John held at least one Queen to give him the right to ask for Queens. He has received a Queen, which gives him a total of either two or three Queens.

In the same way, you know something about a player's hand when she asks for a card and gets nothing at all. For example, suppose Laura asks somebody for 9s and is told to "go fish" at once. You know that Laura must have at least one 9 in her hand.

Little by little, you can build up information about the cards the other players are holding. If you know that another player has Queens, but you have no Queens yourself, the information does you no good. If you have a Queen yourself, however, you are then allowed to ask for Queens, and if you ask the right person because of the information you have, you may get as many as three cards and be able to put down an entire book in front of you.

Fish for Minnows

This is a simpler way of playing *Go Fish*, and it is especially good for very young players.

The Deal: Deal out all the cards, not worrying about it if they don't happen to come out even.

To Win the Game: Accumulate the most pairs.

The Play: At his turn, a player asks for a rank, and the player who has been asked must hand over one such card, if he has one. The object is to form pairs instead of books of four. As soon as a player gets a pair, he puts them face down in front of him.

Authors

This game is a lot like *Go Fish*, but it can be played very seriously and with great skill.

Players: 2 to 5.

Cards: 1 pack.

The Deal: All 52 cards are dealt out, even though they may not come out even.

To Win the Game: Win more books than any other player. A book is four cards of the same rank.

The Play: At her turn, a player asks for a single card by naming both its rank and its suit. For example, she might say, "Bill, give me the Jack of Spades." Her turn continues if she gets the card she asked for, but it passes to the left as soon as she asks for a card that the player doesn't hold.

Old Maid

Other Name: Queen of Spades

Players: 2 or more.

Cards: 51, including only 3 of the 4 Queens.
Remove 1 Queen from the pack before beginning
the game.

The Deal: One card at a time is dealt to each player, as far as the cards will go. It doesn't matter if the cards don't come out even.

To Win the Game: Avoid getting "stuck" with the last unpaired Queen.

The Play: Each player sorts his cards and puts aside, face down, all cards that he can pair—two by two. For exanple, he might put aside two Kings, two Queens, two Jacks, and so on. If he had three Queens and three Jacks, he would be allowed to put two of them aside, but the third Jack and the third Queen would stay in his hand.

After each player has discarded his paired cards, the dealer presents her cards, fanned out but face down, to the player at her left. The player at the left selects one card (blindly, since the hand is presented face down) and quickly examines it to see if it pairs some card still in his hand. If so, he discards the pair. In any case, this player now fans his cards out and presents them face down to the player at his left.

This process continues, each player in turn presenting his hand, fanned out and face down, to the player at the left. Eventually, every card will be paired except one of the three Queens. The player who is left with the odd Queen at the end of the hand is the "Old Maid."

Whenever a player's last card is taken, he drops out. He can no longer be the "Old Maid."

Strategy: *Old Maid* can be learned in about one minute, and nothing you can do will improve your chance of winning. The player who is stuck with an odd Queen during the middle of the play usually looks worried and will often squeal with delight if the player to his left selects the Queen. If you keep alert, you can usually tell which player at the table has an odd Queen as the play is going on.

If you have the odd Queen, put it somewhere in the middle of your hand when you present it to the player at your left. Most players tend to pick a card from the middle rather than the ends. Make use of this same principle to defend yourself if you think that the player at your right has the odd Queen when he presents his hand for you to make your choice. He will usually put the Queen in the middle somewhere, and you can usually avoid choosing it by taking one of the two end cards instead.

It isn't bad to get an odd Queen toward the beginning of the play, for you will have many chances to get rid of it. It will then probably stay in some other player's hand or move only part of the way around the table.

If you like to cause a little confusion, act worried when you don't really have the Queen in your hand. Another idea is act delighted when the player to your left picks some perfectly harmless card. This will make the other players in the game believe that he has taken the odd Queen from you. You yourself will usually know where the odd Queen really is, but the other players may be in considerable doubt.

4

The Stops Family

The many games of the *Stops* family are all good fun, all easily learned, and all suitable for mixed groups of children and adults.

The simplest game of the group has no Stops at all, but it belongs in the family as a sort of great-grandfather of the other games. This game, called *Sequence*, is excellent for very young children.

Sequence

Players: 2 to 10—4 or 5 players make the best game.

Cards: 1 pack.

The Deal: One card at a time to each player until the deck is used up. It doesn't matter if some of the players are dealt more cards than the others.

To Win the Game: Get rid of all of your cards.

The Play: The player to the dealer's left puts down his lowest card in any suit he chooses. The rank of the cards is:

(Highest)   **(Lowest)**

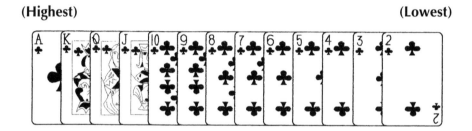

After the first card has been put down on the table, whoever has the next highest card in the same suit must put it down. This process continues until somebody finally plays the Ace of that suit.

For example, suppose that the first player's lowest Spade is the 4. He puts the 4 of Spades down on the table. Somebody else plays the 5 of Spades, and another player puts down both the 6 and the 7 of Spades (it doesn't matter if the same person plays two or more cards in a row.) This process continues until somebody finally plays the Ace of Spades.

When the Ace is reached, the one who plays it must begin a new suit. As before, the player who begins the suit must begin with her lowest card in that suit.

Sooner or later, one of the players will get rid of all of his cards. He wins the hand, and the other players lose one point for every card they still have when the hand comes to an end. (A simpler method is to forget the scoring by points and just play to win the hand.)

Strategy: Practically no skill is required for this game. It is wise, though, to begin with the deuce of some suit when it is your turn to begin a play. If you have no deuce, begin with a 3, or with the lowest card of any suit in your hand. If you don't follow this policy, you my eventually get stuck with a deuce or a 3 in your hand.

The great value of this game for very young children is that it is very easy to teach and children get practice in recognizing numbers and learning how they follow each other in sequence. For especially young children, you may want to remove the picture cards from the deck and use only the cards from 1 to 10. In this case, of course, the Ace is the lowest card, and 10 is the highest card of each suit.

Newmarket

Players: 3 to 8.

Cards: 1 pack, plus 4 special "pay cards" from another deck: the Ace of Hearts, the King of Clubs, the Queen of Diamonds and the Jack of Spades.

Equipment: A bunch of counters—poker chips, matchsticks, toothpicks, beans, etc.

Preparation: Place the pay cards in the middle of the table, where they remain throughout the game. Give each player the same number of counters. Each player puts one counter on each of the pay cards.

The Deal: The dealer gives one card at a time face down to each player, but also deals one extra hand, as though there were one more player at the table. It doesn't matter if some hands have one extra card in them.

To Win the Game: Win counters from the other players. You do this by getting rid of all your cards or by playing a pay card so you can win the counters that are placed on it.

The Auction: The dealer looks at his own hand and announces whether or not he will auction off the extra hand. If the dealer wants the extra hand himself, he puts his own hand aside, face down, and plays the extra hand in its place. If the dealer likes his own hand, he is allowed to auction off the extra hand to the player who bids the most counters for it. If two players make the same bid, the first one to speak wins. If both speak at the same time, the one who would play first going around to the left from the dealer wins the tie. Once the dealer says he is going to sell the extra hand, he is not allowed to change his mind.

The Play: The player to the left of the dealer must put down the lowest card of the suit he chooses. The player with the next higher card in the same suit continues, and the play proceeds as in *Sequence*. When any player puts down a card that is the same as one of the pay cards in the middle of the table, he collects all the counters on that card. It is therefore an advantage to hold one of these pay cards in your hand.

If a player reaches the Ace of a suit, she must start a new suit and play the lowest card she holds in that suit.

There is an important difference between this game and *Sequence*. You cannot always proceed up to the Ace of a suit, because you are sometimes stopped by the missing cards that are in the discarded hand. When no one is able to continue with a suit, the person who made the last play must begin again with a new suit, beginning (as always) with the lowest card he has in this new suit.

Sooner or later, some person plays the last card in his hand. He then collects a counter for every card left in the other players' hands.

Strategy: There is skill both in the auction and in the play. A good hand contains one or more pay cards. Even if you have no pay cards, you may still have a good chance to play out quickly if your hand contains few very low cards. It usually isn't hard to reach Queens, Kings, and Aces, but it is often very hard to get rid of deuces and 3s.

As the dealer, you may be satisfied with your hand if you have one or more pay cards, or if you have a hand that contains practically no deuces or 3s. If you have a bad hand—no pay cards and two or more very low cards—exchange your hand for the extra hand.

Follow the principle if some other player is the dealer and offers to auction off the extra hand. The extra hand isn't worth a single counter to you if you already have a good hand. If you have a bad hand, however, it is worth bidding up to three or four counters for the extra hand. If very few players are interested in bidding for the extra hand, you may get it for only one or two counters, but it probably won't be worth much. If the other players are satisfied with their hands, it is probably because they have pay cards, which means that there will be none left in the extra hand. However, there will still be an advantage in exchanging your original hand, because you will be the only player in the game who knows what cards are in the discarded hand.

In the play of the cards, it sometime helps a great deal to know when a suit is going to be stopped. For example, suppose you know that the 9 of Spades is in the dead hand. If you have the 8 of Spades in your new hand, you can safely begin Spades rather than some other suit. When you eventually play your 8 of Spades, the suit will be stopped, and you will then be able to switch to some new suit. This gives you two chances to play, so it is always an advantage to be the one who switches to a new suit.

When it is up to you to start a new suit, it is usually a sound idea to begin a suit in which you have a pay card. This is your best chance to get the pay card out of your hand and to collect the counters for playing it.

Snip, Snap, Snorem

Players: 3 or more—the more the merrier.

Cards: 1 pack.

The Deal: One at a time to each player, until the entire pack is used up. It doesn't matter if some players have more cards than the others.

To Win the Game: Get rid of all your cards.

The Play: The player to the dealer's left puts any card face up on the table. The next player to the left matches the play with the same card in a different suit, saying "Snip." The next player to the left continues to match the original play with the same card in a third suit, saying "Snap." The next player follows with the fourth card of the same kind, saying "Snorem." If a player is unable to follow with a matching card, he says "Pass," and his turn passes to the next player to the left.

For example, let's say the first player puts down a 6 of Hearts. The next player to the left has no 6 and therefore must say "Pass." The next player has the 6 of Diamonds and puts it down, saying "Snip." The next player to the left has both of the remaining 6s and therefore puts them down one at a time, saying "Snap" for the first one and "Snorem" for the second.

The player who says "Snorem," after putting down the fourth card of a kind, plays the first card of the next group of four. If he has more than one of a kind, he must put down as many as he has instead of holding out one of the cards for "Snorem." For example, if you have two Kings, you must put both of them down if you decide to play a King. You are not allowed to put down just one of the Kings and wait for the other two Kings to appear before showing your remaining King for a "Snorem."

The first player to get rid of his cards wins the game.

The Earl of Coventry

This is the same game as *Snip, Snap, Snorem* except that different words are used. The exact word depends on whether the player is young or grownup.

Young children always use the same words when putting down their cards. For example, suppose a young player puts down a five. He says, "There's as good as 5 can be." The next young player to put down a 5 can say, "There's a 5 as good as he." The next player says, "There's the best 5 of all the three." The fourth player would say triumphantly, "And there's the Earl of Coventry!"

Grownup players need to make a different rhyming statement as they play their cards. For example, an adult who plays a 5 might say, "Here's a 5 you can have from me," or "The best 5 now on land or sea," or any other rhyme.

If a grownup fails to make an acceptable rhymed statement when he plays his card, he is not allowed to begin a new play. The turn passes to the player at his left.

Jig

This is the same as *Snip, Snap, Snorem* or *The Earl of Coventry*, except that the players put down four cards in sequence instead of four of a kind.

For example, suppose that the player to the left of the dealer begins by putting down a 5. The next player must put down any 6 or must pass. The next player must put down any 7 or pass. The play is completed by the next person who puts down any 8. The one who completes the play with the fourth card in sequence then begins the new series.

The game may be played by saying "Snip, Snap, Snorem," or with rhymes, as in *The Earl of Coventry*.

Crazy Eights

Other Name: Rockaway

Players: 2 to 8. The game is best for 2, 3, or 4. In the 4-handed game, the players who sit across the table from each other are partners.

Cards: 7 to each player in a 2-handed game; 5 to each player when more than 2 are playing.

The Deal: After the correct number of cards is dealt to each player, put the rest of the cards on the table face down as the stock. Turn the top card face up to begin another pile.

To Win the Game: Get rid of all your cards. The first player to get rid of all his cards wins.

Sometimes a hand ends in a block with nobody able to play, and with nobody having played out. The hand is then won by the player with the smallest number of cards. If two or more players tie for this honor, the hand is declared a tie.

The Play: The player to the left of the dealer must match the card that has been turned up. That is, he must put down a card of the same suit or of the same rank.

For example, suppose that the card first turned up is the 9 of Spades. The first player must put down another Spade or another 9.

The newly played card is placed on top of the turned-up card. It is up to the next player to match the new card either in suit or in rank.

The four 8s are wild; that is, you may play an 8 at any time, when it is your turn. When putting down an 8, you are allowed to call it any suit at all, as you please. For example, you might put down the 8 of Hearts and say "Spade." The next player would then have to follow with a Spade.

If, at your turn, you cannot play, you must draw cards from the top of the stock until you are able to play or until there are no more cards left.. You are allowed to draw cards from the stock, at your turn, even if you are able to play *without* drawing. This is sometimes a good idea.

Strategy: The most important principle is not to play an 8 too quickly. If you waste an 8 when you are not really in trouble, you won't have it to save you when the going gets tough.

The time that you really need an 8 to protect yourself is when you have *run out of a suit*. For example, after several Spades have been played, you might not be able to get another Spade even if you drew every single card in the stock. If you are also unable to match the rank of the card that has been put down, you may be forced to pick up the entire stock before your turn is over. From here on, of course, it will be very hard for you to avoid a disastrous defeat. An 8 will save you from this kind of misfortune, since you can put it down in place of a Spade, and you may be able to call a suit that does for your opponent what the Spade would have done for you!

If you're lucky, you won't have to play an 8 at the beginning, and you can save it to play as your last card. If you're not quite as lucky as this, it is sensible to play the 8 as your next to last card. With a little luck, you will then be able to play your last card when your next turn comes—and win the hand. To play an 8 with more than two cards in your hand is seldom wise. It is usually better to draw a few cards from stock in order to find a playable card.

The best way to beat an opponent is to run her out of some suit. If you have several cards in one suit, chances are your opponent will be short in that suit. As often as you get the chance, keep coming back to your long suit until your opponent is unable to match your card. Eventually, she will have to draw from stock and may have to load herself up badly before she is able to play.

Hollywood Eights

Equipment: Paper and pencil for scoring.

This is the same as the original game of *Crazy Eights*, except that a score is kept in points with pencil and paper. When a hand comes to an end, each loser counts up his cards as follows:

Each 8	**50**
Each King, Queen, Jack, or 10	**10**
Each Ace	**1**
Each other card	**its face value**

The winner of a hand gets credit for the total of all points lost by the other players.

For example, suppose you have an 8, a 9, and a 7 when a hand ends. The 8 counts 50 points, the 9 counts 9, and the 7 counts 7. The total is 50 + 9 + 7, or 66 points.

Hollywood Scoring: Three separate game scores are kept. The first time a player wins a hand, his score is credited to him in the first game score. The second time a player wins a hand, he gets credit for his victory both in the first game and also in the second game. The third time a player wins, his score is credited to him in all three games. He continues to get credit in all three games from then on.

Sometimes the game runs on until everybody feels like stopping. In this case, the three game scores are added whenever everybody wants to stop. The winner is the player with the biggest total for the three scores.

Suppose you win five hands in a row, with scores of 10, 25, 40, 20, and 28 points. Your score would look like this:

FIRST GAME		SECOND GAME		THIRD GAME	
	10		5		40
(+25)	35	(+40)	65	(+20)	60
(+40)	75	(+20)	85	(+28)	88
(+20)	95	(+28)	113		
(+28)	123				

100 Scoring: A more popular method is to end a game as soon as any player's score reaches 100. When this happens in the first of the three games, the other two games continue. In the later hands, the score is entered on the second game and third games, but no further entry is made in the finished first game. Sooner or later, some player reaches a score of 100 in the second game, and this likewise comes to an end. Eventually, also, some player reaches a score of 100 in the third game, and then all three games have ended.

The winner is the player with the highest total score when all three game scores have been added up.

Go Boom

Players: 2 or more.

Cards: 1 pack.

The Deal: Seven cards are dealt to each player. The rest of the pack is put face down in the middle of the table.

To Win the Game: Get rid of all of your cards.

The Play: The player to the left of the dealer puts any card on the table. The next player to her left must follow by matching the suit or rank of that card. Each player in turn after this must match the previous card in suit or rank.

For example, suppose the first player puts down the Jack of Diamonds. The next player may follow with any Diamond or with another Jack. If the second player decides to follow with the Jack of Clubs, the third player may then match with a Club or with one of the two remaining Jacks.

When a player cannot match the previous card, he must draw cards from the stock until he is able to play. If a player uses up the stock without finding a playable card, he may say "Pass," and his turn passes to the next player.

When everybody at the table has had the chance to play or say "Pass," the cards are examined to see who has played the highest card. The cards rank as follows:

(Highest)   **(Lowest)**

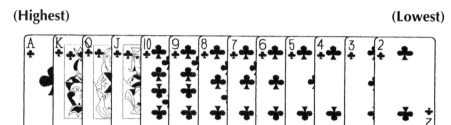

The player who put down the highest card has the right to begin the next play. If there is a tie for first place among cards of thr same rank, the card that was played first is considered higher.

The play continues in this way until one player gets rid of all of her cards. That player wins the hand.

If none of the players is very young, you might want to use a system of point scoring. When a hand comes to an end, each loser counts the cards left in his hand as follows:

Each picture card	**10**
Each Ace	**1**
Each other card	its face value

The winner of the hand is credited with the total of all points lost by the other players.

Strategy: The strategy in *Go Boom* is much the same as in *Crazy Eights.* You try to run your opponent out of a suit in hopes that he will not be able to match your play with a card of the same suit or the same rank.

In the early stages of play, it is useful to play as high a card as possible in order to have the best chance to win the privilege of beginning the next play.

Hollywood Go Boom

This is the same as *Go Boom*, except that the scoring is Hollywood style (three games at a time). As in *Hollywood Eights*, three game scores are kept for each player. The first time you win a hand, you get credit only in your first game score. The second time you win a hand, you get credit both in your first game score and in your second game score. After that, you get credit in all three game scores.

   The first game ends when any player reaches a score of 100. Later hands are scored only in the second and third games. The second game also ends when any player reaches a score of 100. Thereafter, the scores are entered only in the third game score, and when some player reaches a score of 100 in that game all the scores are totalled to see who wins.

Fan-Tan

Other Names: Card Dominoes, Sevens, Parliament

Players: 3 to 8.

Equipment: A bunch of counters—poker chips, matchsticks, toothpicks, dried beans, etc.

The Deal: One card at a time to each player until all the cards have been dealt. It doesn't matter if some players get more cards than others. Give an equal number of counters to each player.

To Win the Game: Get rid of all your cards.

The Play: To open, the player to the left of the dealer must play any 7, if possible. If not, the first player with a 7 opens. After the 7 is played, the next player to the left may play a 7 or any card in the same suit and in squence with the card previously played.

   For example, suppose that the player to the dealer's left put the 7 of Spades on the table. The next player may put down a new 7 or may play the 8 of Spades so that it covers half of the 7 of Spades. The second player, instead, might have chosen to play the 6 of Spades, putting it down also so that it just covered half of the 7 of Spades. If the 8 of Spades were played, the next player would have the right to put down the 9 of Spades. If the 9 of Spades were played, the next player would have the right to put down the 10 of Spades.

This process continues. At any turn, a player my put down a new 7 or may continue a sequence that builds up in suit from a 7 to a King or down from a 7 to an Ace. The King is the highest card that may be played on a sequence and the Ace is the lowest. If a player does not have an appropriate card, he must put a counter into the middle of the table.

The play continues until one player gets rid of all of his cards. That player then collects all the counters in the middle of the table. In addition, each loser pays out one counter for every card left in her hand.

Strategy: It is usually easy to get rid of cards of middle size, such as 8s, 9s, 6s or 5s. It is usually hard to get rid of very low or very high cards, such as Aces and deuces or Queens and Kings.

The best tactic is to force the other players to build up to your high cards or down to your low cards. You can't always carry it off, but you can try.

If you have the 8 of Spades, nobody can play the 9 of Spades or any higher Spade until you have first put down your 8. If a player who has high Spades finds no chance to play them, he must play something else at his turn. This other play may be just what you need to reach your own very low cards or your own very high cards.

This shows you the general strategy. Play as much as possible in the suit that will lead to your very high cards or to your very low ones. Wait as long as possible before playing in the suits in which you have only middle-rank cards. With just a little luck, you will get rid of your very high cards and your very low cards fairly early. You will then be able to get rid of your middle-rank cards in the last suit, catching the other players while they still have the very high and very low cards in that suit.

Liberty Fan-Tan

This is the same game as *Fan-Tan*, except that it isn't necessary to begin a suit by playing the 7. Nobody can start a new suit until the previous suit has been finished.

The player to the left of the dealer begins by playing any card of any suit. The next player must follow with the next higher card in the same suit or must put one counter in the middle of the table. The third player must continue with the next card in sequence or must put one counter in the middle of the table. This process continues, building up past the King with the Ace, deuce, and so on, until all 13 cards of the suit have been played. The one who plays the 13th card of the first suit may begin with any card in a new suit. Then the same process continues with a second suit.

The first player to get rid of all of her cards takes all the counters from the pool.

Strategy: Your chance of winning is best when you can determine which suit will be played last. If you have very few cards in this suit, you have an excellent chance to win all the counters since you will get rid of your cards while the other players still have cards of that suit left.

The time to choose the last suit does not come after the third suit has been played, since at that point there is no choice. The choice is made after the second suit has been played, since then two suits remain. The player who chooses the third suit automatically fixes the other suit as the fourth.

If you happen to end the second suit, by good luck, you will then begin the play of the third. Naturally, you should play your longer suit, saving your shorter suit for last.

If the two suits are almost equal in length, it is sometimes wiser to play the shorter suit third and save the other suit for the last. The time to do this is when you have two cards in sequence in the shorter suit. If you start with the higher of these two cards, you will naturally be the one to finish the suit when yoy play the lower card.

For example, suppose you have a hand with Spades:

You notice that the 9 and 8 are in sequence. Following the principle just mentioned, you would begin the suit by playing the 9. Other players would follow with the 10, Jack and Queen, allowing you to play the King. Then someone would play the Ace and you would follow with the 2. The others would then play on until your eight would complete the suit. Having completed the suit, it is up to you to start the next suit, and this is exactly what you had in mind.

Use the same strategy of starting the second suit with the higher card if you have two cards in sequence. This will allow you to end the second suit and choose the third

Five or Nine

This is the same as *Fan-Tan*, except that the first player may put down a 5 or a 9 (instead of a 7). The card chosen by the first player sets the pattern for the rest of that hand. If he puts down a 5, for example, the other three suits must also begin with 5s; and if the first player begins by putting down a 9, the other three suits must be started by 9s.

Regardless of how the play begins, each suit builds up to a King as its top card and down to an Ace.

Commit

Players: 4 or more.

Cards: 1 pack.

Equipment: A bunch of counters—poker chips, matchsticks, toothpicks, dried beans, etc.

The Deal: Remove the 8 of Diamonds from the pack. Deal the cards one at a time as far as thay will go evenly. Put the remaining cards face down in the middle of the table. Give an equal number of counters to each player.

To Win the Game: Get rid of all your cards.

The Play: The player to the dealer's left may put any card down on the table. She and the other players can then build up in sequence in the same suit.

For example, suppose that Gina begins with the 7 of Clubs. Any player who has the 8 of Clubs puts it face up on the table. Then it is the turn of any player who has the 9 of Clubs. This continues until someone plays the King of Clubs or until the sequence is stopped because the next card is one of those face down in the middle of the table —or the 8 of Diamonds, which has been removed.

When the play stops for either of these reasons, the person who played last begins a new sequence with any card in his hand.

The 9 of Diamonds is a special card in this game. You can of course play it when you end a sequence and it is your turn to begin a new one. But you can also play it in the middle of any sequence. When the 9 of Diamonds is played, each player in turn has the chance to proceed either with the 10 of Diamonds—continuing the Diamond sequence— or with the sequence that was interrupted by the 9 of Diamonds.

For example, suppose that Avery begins a sequence with the 3 of Spades. Barbara puts down the 4 of Spades and then follows it with a 9 of Diamonds. Chris, the player to the left, then has a choice to make. She may continue with a 10 of Diamonds, or go back to the 5 of Spades. If she has neither card, the turn passes on to the left until somebody plays either the 10 of Diamonds or the 5 of Spades, which determines how the sequence will continue.

When you play the 9 of Diamonds, you collect two counters from every player in the game. If anyone gets rid of all of his cards before you have played the 9 of Diamonds, you must *pay* two counters to every player in the game.

When a player wins the game (by playing all his cards), the remaining players must show their hands. Any player who has a King must pay one counter to every other player in the game.

Strategy: As in the game of *Newmarket*, the best strategy is to begin with your lowest card in your longest suit.

It is helpful to remember the stops. At the beginning of a hand, the only stop you are sure of is the 8 of Diamonds. It pays to begin with a low Diamond if you have the 7 of Diamonds in your hand, for then you will probably build up to that 7 and have the chance to begin the next sequence.

Rolling Stone

Players: 4 to 6.

Cards: When 4 play, use the Ace, King, Queen, Jack, 10, 9, 8, and 7 of each suit. If there is a fifth player, add the 6s and 5s. If there is a sixth player, add the 4s and 3s. There must be 8 cards for each player.

The Deal: One card at a time until each player has eight cards. This uses up the pack.

To Win the Game: Get rid of all your cards.

The Play: The player to the dealer's left begins by putting down any card he pleases. Then the play moves to the left and the next player puts down another card in the same suit. The turns continue, always moving to the left, with the other players following with another card of the same suit, if they can, playing high or low, as they please.

If all the cards in a suit are played, the person who put down the highest card leads again. And all the cards that were played to the first "trick" (sequence of cards) are turned over and put aside.

When a player cannot put down a card of the same suit when it is her turn to play, she must pick up all the cards previously played in that sequence. This ends the trick, and the player who picks up the cards then begins the next trick by leading with any card she chooses.

The process continues. In most games a player picks up the cards several times. Eventually, one player will get rid of all his cards, and win the hand.

For the purpose of winning a trick, the cards rank as follows:

(Highest)   **(Lowest)**

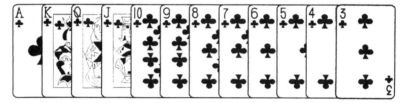

Play or Pay

Players: 3 or more.

Equipment: **A handful of counters—poker chips, matchsticks, toothpicks, dried beans, etc.**

The Deal: One card at a time to each player, until the pack has been used up. It doesn't matter if some players get more cards than others. Give an equal number of counters to each player.

To Win the Game: Get rid of all your cards.

The Play: The player to the left of the dealer may put down any card from her hand. The player to her left must follow with the next highest card in the same suit—or must put a counter into the middle of the table. This process continues, with each player in turn either putting down the next card or paying one counter.

The cards in their proper sequence are:

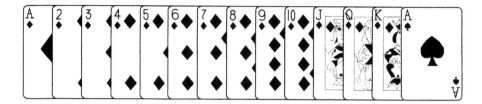

and so on.

The player who puts down the 13th card of a suit makes the first play in the next suit.

Keep on playing until someone wins by getting rid of all his cards. Each player then puts one counter in the middle of the table for each card left in his hand. The winner takes all the counters from the middle of the table.

Strategy: There is no skill in following suit; you either have the card or you don't. The only skill is in choosing the right card with which to begin a play.

If you have two cards in sequence in any suit, begin with the one that is higher in rank. Eventually, you will end that suit by playing the lower card of the sequence. This will give you the right to begin the next suit.

When possible, try to get rid of your long suits first.

5
The Casino Family

Games of the Casino family have been favorites of adults and children for hundreds of years. They are especially recommended by educators because they teach painlessly the first lessons in arithmetic.

Casino

Players: 2 to 4—best for 2.

Cards: 1 pack.

The Deal: The deck of 52 cards is used up in six deals. In the first deal:

> The non-dealer receives two cards face down.
> Then two cards are put face up on the table.
> Then the dealer gives himself two cards face down.

And the process repeats, so that each player and the table have four cards each. In the remaining five deals, the dealer continues to give each player four cards—two at at time—but does not give any additional cards to the table.

To Win the Game: Get the highest number of points. You get points by capturing the most cards, the most Spades, Aces, the 10 of Diamonds (Big Casino) and the 2 of Spades (Little Casino). See "Scoring."

The Play: Beginning with the non-dealer, each player in turn must play one card from her hand, until all four of her cards are gone. If she can find no better use for it, she simply lays her card face up on the table. This is called *trailing*. Whenever she can, though, she uses her card to capture cards from the table.

Pairing: You may win cards in various ways. The simplest is by pairing. You may capture a card on the table by another of the same rank from your hand—a 5 with a 5, a Jack with a Jack, and so on.

With a picture card—a Jack, Queen or King—you may capture only one card, but with a card of lower rank, you may take two or three of the same kind at the same time. If there are two 7s on the table and you have a 7 in your hand, for example, you can take all three 7s.

Each player keeps captured cards in a pile, face down.

Building: All the lower cards, Ace to 10, may be captured by building. Ace counts as 1. Each other card counts as its own value. Cards on the table may be taken in by higher cards to equal their sum.

For example, you may take a 5 and a 2 with a 7—or an Ace and a 9 with a 10. You may, at the same time, take additional cards by pairing. Suppose that the cards on the table are 9, 8, 5, 4, Ace. You could take them all with a single 9, since the 9s pair, 8 and 1 make 9, and 5 and 4 make 9.

Leaving a Build: Suppose that you have 8 and 3 in your hand and there is a 5 on the table, You may put the 3 on the 5 and say, "Building 8." Your intention is to capture the build with your 8 on your next turn. You cannot build and capture in the same turn, because you are allowed to play only one card from your hand at a time.

If your opponent has an 8, she can capture your build. That is the risk of leaving a build. Yet the risk is usually worth taking, because in building, you make it harder for your opponent to capture the cards. She cannot take the 5 or the 3 by pairing or by making a build of her own.

Of course, you may not leave a build unless you have a card in your hand that can take it. You *are*, however, allowed to duplicate your build before taking it in. Suppose you have two 8s in your hand. After building the 5 and 3, you could on your next turn simply put one 8 on the build, and take it with the other 8 on your third turn.

Or suppose after you build the 5 and 3, your opponent trails a 6, and you have a 2 in your hand (besides the 8). You may take your 2 and put it—with the 6— on the 5-3 build and wait until your next turn to take in the duplicated build.

An important rule is that when you have left a build on the table, you must deal with it at your next turn—take it in—or increase or duplicate it. You are not allowed to trail or to take in other cards instead.

Increasing a Build: Suppose that your opponent has laid a 4 from her hand on a 5 on the table and called out, "Building 9." You have an Ace and a 10. You may add the Ace to her build and say, "Building 10." You are allowed to increase a build of your own, in the same way.

But there are two restrictions on increasing a build. First, you may increase only a *single* build, such as the 5-4, not one that has been duplicated in any way, such as 5-4-9. Second, the card you use to increase it must come from your hand; you are not allowed to use a card from the table.

55

Scoring: After the last card of the sixth deal is played, any cards remaining on the table go to the player who was last to capture cards. Then each player looks through his captured cards and counts his score, as follows:

Cards, for winning 27 or more cards	3 points
Spades, for winning seven or more Spades	1
Big Casino, the 10 of Diamonds	2
Little Casino, the 2 of Spades	1
Aces, each counting 1, total	<u>4</u>
	11

The first one to reach a total of 21 or more points wins.

Spade Casino

This is *Casino* with a different count for Spades. Instead of getting one point for having seven or more Spades, the Spades score as follows;

Jack	2
Little Casino	2
Other Spades	1 each

There are 24 points to be won. The game is usually set at 61 and scored on a Cribbage board.

Sweep Casino

This is *Casino* with the additional rule that a player scores one point for each *sweep*. You can earn this by capturing all the cards that are on the table at any one time. To keep track of sweeps, turn the top card of each sweep face up.

    Winning the cards left on the table after the last deal does not count as a sweep.

Pirate Casino

The "pirate" feature is that you are allowed to make any play you please at a time when you have left a build on the table. You may take in other cards, or even trail.

Stealing Bundles

This is *Casino* for the very young. Cards may be captured only by pairing, but any number of the same kind may be taken at a time. Captured cards must be kept in a pile face up, and you can capture your opponent's entire pile by matching its top card with a card from your hand.

To Win the Game: Win more than half the cards.

Royal Casino

Children often prefer this colorful elaboration on the basic game. Since *Royal Casino* is more complicated, young children should learn the basic game before attempting it.

In this game you may capture face cards as well as lower cards two, three, and four at a turn. Furthermore, they can be used to capture builds:

Jack counts	**11**
Queen counts	**12**
King counts	**13**
Ace counts	**14 or 1, as you please**
Big Casino	**10 or 16**
Little Casino	**2 or 15**

Sweeps are scored, as in *Sweep Casino*.

Partnership Casino

Players: 4, the two opposite being partners.

Cards: 1 pack.

The Deal: The deck is used up in three deals. In the first, each player receives four cards and four are dealt face up on the table. For the other two deals, each receives four more cards, but no more are dealt to the table.

Otherwise, this game is played just like *Casino* (basic or *Royal*), except that you may duplicate a build left by your partner without you yourself having a card that can take it.

For example, if Tom builds 10, Nellie, his partner, may in turn put a 6 from the table and a 4 from her hand on the build, without having a 10 in her hand.

Draw Casino

You can play either basic *Casino* or *Royal Casino* in "Draw" style. After you deal, place the rest of the pack face down in the middle of the table. Each time you play a card, draw the top card of this stock, so that you keep four cards in your hand throughout the game. After the stock is exhausted, play out the hands as usual.

6
The Rummy Family

Rummy is the most widely played of all card games. Many different forms of the game are played, but all have a very strong family resemblance, Once you have learned to play the basic game, you can pick up any variation in a few minutes.

Basic Rummy

Players: 2 to 6.

Cards: 10 each when 2 play.
7 each when 3 or 4 play.
6 each when 5 or 6 play.

Equipment: Pencil and paper for keeping score.

The Deal: Deal the appropriate number of cards to each player and then put the rest of the cards face down in the middle of the table, forming the stock. Turn the top card face up, starting the discard pile.

In a two-handed game, the winner of each hand deals the next hand. When more than two play, the turn to deal passes to the left exactly as the cards are dealt out.

To Win the Game: Win points from your opponents. You usually keep track of these points with a pencil and paper score.

In order to win points, you must match up your cards. One way to match is to get three or four of a kind. For example, you might have three Kings or four 10s and so on.

A second way to match is to get sequences—cards that are next to each other in rank and are in the same suit. The rank of the cards in *Rummy* is:

(Highest)   (Lowest)

A typical sequence is:

60

Another typical sequence is: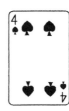

You need at least three cards for a sequence.

The Play: Each player at the table plays in turn, beginning with the player to the dealer's left. During your turn to play, you do three things

> **You draw.**
> **You meld (if you wish to do so).**
> **You discard.**

When you draw, you may pick up the top card of the stock or the top card of the discard pile. You add this card to your hand.

You meld by putting a group of matched cards down on the table. For example, you might put down three of a kind or four of a kind, or a sequence. You might even put down two groups of matched cards, if you are lucky enough to have them in your hand. You are not required to expose your meld if you don't wish to do so. You can keep it in your hand.

After some other player has melded, you may add to his meld when it's your turn. For example, if some player has put down three Kings, you may add the fourth King at your turn to play. If some player has put down the 6, 7 and 8 of Diamonds, you may add the 9 and 10 of Diamonds, or just the 9 or the 5 or 5 and 4, or any such card or group of cards. You may add to a meld that has been put down previously by any player at the table—including yourself.

After you have drawn and melded (or after you have declined to meld), it is your turn to discard. You take any card from your hand and put it on top of the face-up pile in the middle of the table. This completes your play.

When, at your turn to play, you manage to meld all your cards, you win the game. You must begin your play with a draw, thus adding one card to your hand, and then you must meld either all the cards in your hand or all but one. If you meld all but one card, that last card is your discard.

61

If no player has melded all his cards (called *going out*) by the time the stock is used up, the next player may take either the top card of the discard pile or the top card of the new stock that has been formed by turning the discard pile over. In either case, play continues as before until somebody does go out.

Scoring: The winner of a hand scores points by counting up the hands of all the other players in the game. Each loser counts his cards according to the following scale:

Picture cards	**10 points each**
Aces	**1 point each**
Other cards	**their face value**

A loser does not count cards that he has previously melded on the table, but he does count any cards that remain in his hand—*whether or not these cards match!*

A player goes "Rummy" when he melds all his cards in one turn, without previously melding or adding to anybody else's meld. A player may go "Rummy" by melding all his cards after the draw, or he may meld all but one and then discard that last card. Whenever a player goes "Rummy," he wins double the normal amount from each of the other players.

A score is kept on paper with a column for each player in the game. Whenever a player wins a hand, the amounts that he wins from the other players are put into his winning column.

Some players agree on a stopping time when they play *Rummy*. The winner of a game is the player who has the highest score when the agreed-upon time comes.

Other players end a game when any player reaches a certain total score, such as 500 points.

The score for each player is added up at the end of each hand.

Strategy: In all games of the *Rummy* family, you try to build up your hand by keeping cards that match and by discarding cards that do not match.

For example, if you drew the 10 of Spades, you would tend to keep it if your hand contained one or more 10s, or the Jack of Spades or the 9 of Spades. In such cases, your 10 of Spades might be a useful card. Even if it did not immediately give you a meld, it would probably bring you closer to one.

If you drew a card that did not match anything in your hand, you would either discard it immediately or wait for a later chance to do so.

If the player to your left picks a card from the discard pile, this gives you a clue to his hand. If, for example, he picks up the 9 of Diamonds, you know that he must have other 9s or other Diamonds in the neighborhood of the 9. If convenient, you would avoid throwing another 9 or another Diamond in that vicinity onto the discard pile. This is called *playing defensively*. You don't need to bother with defensive play against anybody but the player to your left, since your discard would be covered up by the time any *other* player wanted to draw.

The advantage of melding is that you cannot lose the value of those cards even if some other player wins the hand.

The advantage of holding a meld in your hand is that nobody can add to the meld while it is still in your hand. A second advantage is the possibility of going "Rummy" all in one play.

It sometimes pays to hold up a meld, but most successful *Rummy* players make it a habit to put melds down fairly quickly. It is usually safe to hold ip a meld for one or two turns, but after that it becomes dangerous. If another player goes out before you have melded, you will lose those matched cards just as though they were unmatched.

Block Rummy

This is the same as *Basic Rummy*, except that the discard pile is not turned over to begin as stock again. When the stock has been used up, the next player has the right to take the top card of the discard pile. If she does not wish to take it, the hand ends immediately. This is called a *block*.

When a block occurs, each player shows his hand. The player with the lowest number of points in his hand wins the difference in count from each of the other players. If two or more players tie for the low number of points, they share the winning equally.

Boathouse Rummy

This is like *Basic Rummy*, except that sequences go "around the corner." For example, you may meld:

as a sequence. But you are not allowed to meld anything at all until you can meld your whole hand and go out. When you go out, you win points from every other player according to his *unmatched* cards—that is, the cards in his hand that he has not matched up in groups of three or four or in squences.

Scoring: There are two methods. One is to count one point for each unmatched card.

The other is to count

11	for an unmatched Ace
10	for a face card
face value	for all other cards

One other peculiarity of *Boathouse Rummy* is in the draw. When you begin your turn, if you draw the top card of the discard pile, you may then draw a second card—from the discard pile or the stock, whichever you please. If you begin by drawing from stock, however, you don't get a second card.

Contract Rummy

Other Name: Liverpool Rummy

Players: 3 to 8.

Cards: 2 packs of 52 cards plus 1 Joker, for 3 or 4 players.
3 packs plus 2 Jokers, for 5 or more players.

Equipment: Paper and pencil for keeping score.

The Deal: Deal 10 cards to each player, except in Deal 7, when each player receives 12. Put the rest of the cards face down in the middle of the table, forming the stock. Turn the top card of the stock face up beside it, starting the discard pile.

To Win the Game: Get rid of all the cards in your hand by melding them.

Melds: The melds are as in *Basic Rummy:*
>*groups* of three or four cards of the same rank, such as Queens;
>*sequences* of three or more cards of the same suit, such as:

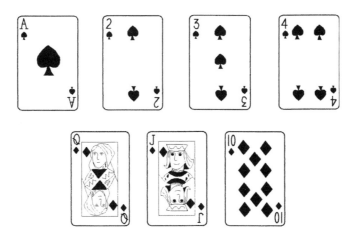

The Contract: A game consists of seven deals. In each deal, a player's first meld must be a combination of two or three sets according to this schedule:

Deal 1:	**two groups**
Deal 2:	**one group and one sequence**
Deal 3:	**two sequences**
Deal 4:	**three groups**
Deal 5:	**two groups and a sequence**
Deal 6:	**one group and two sequences**
Deal 7:	**three sequences**

When you meld in Deals 1—6, you may put down only three cards per set. If you have additional matching cards, you may put them down at any later turn.

In Deal 7, however, you must meld all 12 cards at once, thus going out.

The Play: As in *Basic Rummy*, a turn consists of a draw, melding (if you wish), and a discard.

If you, the first player, decide not to draw the top card of the discard pile, you must say so. Then any other player who wants it may take it. If two or more want it, the person nearest you (to the left) is entitled to it. He must pay for the privilege of taking the discard out of turn, though, by drawing the top card of the stock also. He must then await his regular turn before melding or discarding. Then you resume your turn, drawing the top card of the stock.

Your first meld of any kind must be the *contract.* After that, you are not allowed to meld any new sets, but you may add matching cards to any sets on the table—yours and the other players'.

A peculiarity of the game is that a sequence may be built to the Ace both ways, making a set of 14 cards. (Of course, this rarely happens.)

Wild Cards: The Joker is wild. You may call it any card you please, to help you get rid of cards by melding. You must say, though, what card it represents.

For example, if you put the Joker down with the 7 of Spades and the 7 of Diamonds, you must say either "7 of Hearts" or "7 of Clubs." The reason for this is shown by the next rule. A player who holds the named card may, in her turn, put it down in place of the Joker, thus getting the Joker for her own use.

Many players like to have additional wild cards, to make it easier to form sets for the contract. Deuces are often used as wild, but a deuce cannot be captured, as a Joker can. However, if a deuce is melded in a sequence, any player may put the natural card in its place and move the deuce to either end of the sequence.

Ending Play: Play continues until somebody goes out. If the stock is exhausted, the discard pile is turned over without shuffling.

Scoring: The player who goes out scores zero—which is good! Each other player scores the total of the cards left in his hand. Aces and wild cards count 15 each, picture cards are 10, other cards count their face value. The player with the *lowest* total score after Deal 7 wins the game.

Knock Rummy

Players: 2 to 6.

Cards: 10 cards to each player when 2 play.
7 cards to each player when 3 or 4 play.
5 cards to each player when 5 or 6 play.

Equipment: Paper and pencil for keping score.

The Play: The play follows *Basic Rummy*, but there is no melding until somebody knocks. To "knock" means to lay down your whole hand face up, ending the play. You may knock in your turn, after drawing but before discarding. You do not have to have a single meld to knock—but you had better be convinced that you have the *low* hand.

When anybody knocks, all players lay down their hands, arranged in such melds as they have, with the *unmatched* cards separate. What counts is *the total of unmatched cards.*

If the knocker has the lowest count, he wins the difference of counts from each other player.

If he lays down a *rum hand*—one with no unmatched card—he wins an extra 25 points from everybody, besides the count of unmatched cards held by the others.

If somebody beats or ties the knocker for low count, that player wins the difference from everybody else.

When the knocker is beaten, he pays an extra penalty of 10 points.

It's best to keep score with paper and pencil. Each item should be entered twice—*plus* for the winner and *minus* for the loser.

Tunk

Players: 2 to 5.

Cards: 1 pack with 2 or 3 players.
2 packs with 4 or 5 players.

The Deal: Each player receives seven cards.

The Play: The rules follow *Basic Rummy*, and the object is to go out.
Deuces are wild and may be used in place of natural cards to form melds.

To go out, you don't need to meld all your cards, but merely reduce the total of your unmatched cards to five or less. Before going out, you must give notice by saying "Tunk," in your turn—and that is all you can do in that turn. A tunk takes the place of draw-meld-discard. Then the other players unload all that they can from their hands, and on your next turn you lay down your hand, ending the play. You may at any time add cards to your own melds, or to a tunker's melds after the tunk, but not on another player's.

The tunker scores zero, and the others are charged with the count of all cards left in their hands. When a player reaches 100, he is out of the game, and the others play on until there is only one survivor.

Gin Rummy

Gin is one of the best and also one of the most popular of the *Rummy* games.

Players: 2.

Cards: A regular pack of 52. The ranking is:

(Highest)   (Lowest)

Equipment: Pencil and paper for keeping score.

The Deal: Each player receives 10 cards, dealt one at a time. Place the rest of the deck face down in the middle of the table to form the stock. Turn over the top card of the stock beside it. This *upcard* starts the discard pile.

The Play: The non-dealer plays first. If she wants the upcard, she may take it, but if she doesn't want it, she must say so without drawing. Then the dealer may take the upcard, if he wishes, and discard one card from his hand, face up. After he has taken or refused it, the non-dealer continues with her turn, drawing one card—the top card of the stock or the new top of the discard pile. Then she must discard one card face up on the discard pile. The turns alternate and there are no further complications.

To Win the Game: Reduce the count of your unmatched cards.

A "matched set" in *Gin* is the same as a "meld" in *Basic Rummy*—three or four cards of the same rank, or three or more cards in sequence in the same suit.

71

For example, here are two matched sets:

Since, in *Gin*, Aces rank low:

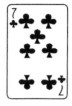     

This is a sequence.   **This is not.**

The point values are:

Ace:	1
Picture cards:	10
Other cards:	face value

Knocking: All melding is kept in the hand until some player brings matters to a halt by laying down all his 10 cards either by "ginning" or by "knocking."

To gin, you lay down all your cards in melds. When you knock, you have unmatched cards whose total is 10 or less. You may knock only when it is your turn to play, after drawing and before discarding. The final discard is made *face down*, thereby indicating the intention to knock. If you simply place the card face up, intending to lay down your hand, you could be stopped, because—according to the rules—the face-up discard ended your turn.

As you play, you arrange your cards in matched sets with the un-matched cards to one side. It is customary to announce the total count of your unmatched cards by saying something like, "Knocking with five," or "I go down for five." Your opponent then exposes her hand, arranged by matched sets and unmatched cards. She is entitled to lay off cards on your sets, provided that you don't have a *gin hand*—all 10 cards matched.

Knock Hand

For example, if you had the hand shown, your opponent could lay off the fourth Jack, and the 10 and 6 of Hearts, if she had any of these cards.

Scoring: Your opponent counts her remaining unmatched cards, after laying off what she can on your hand. If this count is higher than yours, you win the difference. If your opponent has the same count that you have—or a lower one—she scores the difference (if any), plus 25 points for *undercutting* you.

If you lay down a gin hand, your opponent may not lay off any cards on it. You win the opponent's count, plus a bonus of 25 points. This bonus cannot be won when you knock. Suppose, for example, you play 'possum with a gin hand until your opponent knocks with one point or more. You would win her count, plus 25 for undercutting, but you don't get the bonus for a gin hand.

Keepng Score: Keep score with pencil and paper. Enter the net result of a hand in the column under the winner's name, draw a line below the item, and then write the running total. The lines between items are important, to keep track of how many hands were won by each player.

The first player to reach a total of 100 or more wins the game. You score a bonus of 100 for winning and an additional 100 for a *shutout*—also called "whitewash," "skunk," "Schneider," "goose-egg," etc.—if your opponent has not scored a single point. Then each player is credited with 25 pints for each winning hand. This is called the *line* or *box* score. The winner then carries forward the difference between his own grand total and his opponent's.

Hollywood Gin

This is *Gin* with Hollywood scoring (see pages 42-43).

Oklahoma Gin Rummy

This is simply *Gin*, except that the upcard determines the maximum number with which you may knock.

For example, if you turn up a 3 from the stock, it takes 3 or less to knock in that deal.

If you turn up a 10 or a picture card, the game is no different from regular *Gin*. Some players like to pep up the game with additional rules, such as: The hand counts double when the upcard is a Spade.

Around-the-Corner Gin

This is *Gin* again, except that sequences may go "around the corner."

For example, this sequence is a matched set.

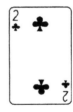

An unmatched Ace counts as 15 points. The person who doesn't knock may lay off cards even on a gin hand. The game is usually set at 125 points.

500 Rummy

The chief feature of *500 Rummy* is that you score for melding as well as for going out.

Other Name: Sequence Rummy

Players: 3 to 8.

Cards: When more than 4 play, use 2 packs of 52 shuffled together.

Equipment: Paper and pencil for keeping score.

The Deal: Seven cards go to each player. The deal passes to the left.

The Play: As in *Basic Rummy*, you may begin your turn by drawing the top card of the stock or the discard pile. But you have a third choice of drawing *any* card in the discard pile, no matter how deeply it is buried. You must immediately meld this card. You must also pick up all the cards that cover it and add them to your hand. You then proceed to meld all the cards you wish to. Your turn ends when you discard.

Discards are not stacked in a pile as in most Rummy games, but are spread out in an overlapping fan so that all the cards can be seen. It is of course important not to mix up the order in which they lie. When you "dig deep" into the discards, courtesy requires that you leave cards on the table for awhile to give the other players a chance to see what you're getting.

Melds are made as in *Basic Rummy*. You may add cards to your own melds and also to those belonging to other players.

Play ends when some player gets rid of all his cards, with or without making a final discard. If nobody goes out by the time the stock is exhausted, play continues as long as each player in turn draws from the discard pile, but it ends as soon as any player fails to do so.

Scoring: When play ends, each player counts up the difference between the cards he has melded and the cards left in his hand. This difference (which may be plus or minus) is added to his running total score, which is kept on paper.

The cards count as follows:

Ace	**15 or 1, if it was melded in a low sequence**
Picture cards	**10 each**
Other cards	**face value**

The first player to score 500 points wins the game.

Strategy: Much more is won by melding than by going out. Try to meld as much as possible, and to meld high cards rather than low ones. For this purpose, you'll want to get as many cards into your hand as you can. The deeper you have to dig into the discard pile, the happier you'll be!

If you are dealt a low meld, such as three deuces, discard one of them as soon as you can. Then, after the discard pile has grown to 10 or 12 cards, reclaim your deuce to meld it—and get some booty! Just don't be too greedy; if you wait too long, somebody else may take the pile, for you can be sure that the others will "salt" the pile too, if they have the chance.

At the beginning of a game, try to avoid making it too easy for another player to take the discard pile. You may make it easy if you discard a card that pairs with another already in the pile, or that is in suit and sequence with one in the pile. Of course, there comes a time when you have no more safe discards. Then follow the principal of doing the least damage. Discard a card that may let another player take a *few* cards, rather than a great many.

As a rule, don't meld unless you have to in order to dig into the discard pile. Keeping a meld of high cards in your hand, especially Aces, puts the fellow who has the fourth Ace on the spot. If he discards it, he gives you a chance to pick up the pile; if he holds it, he may get stuck with it. If you meld your Aces, his troubles are over. If you are too lavish in melding, you may help another player go out.

You need to be quick to switch your tactics, however, when the stock is nearly gone or when another player reduces his hand to only a few cards. That's the time to meld your high cards, to be sure that they will count *for* you instead of against you.

7
Trump Games

A trump suit is one that is given a special privilege: it can take all the other suits. For example, if Spades are trumps, a Spade will win over any Heart, Club, or Diamond. The deuce of Spades then can take the Ace of Hearts, although the Ace of Hearts can win over any lower Heart.

In some games, the trump suit is determined by turning up a card from the deck—its suit becomes trump. In other games, the right to name the trump suit is decided by the players *bidding*. It goes to the player who is willing to pay most for that right. Players *bid* what they are willing to pay—a number of counters to be put in a pool, for example. Usually, each bidder names a number of points or tricks that she hopes to win. The one who names the trump must win at least what she has bid, in order to advance her score. If she fails, points are taken away from her or her opponent's score (according to the particular game). Failing to make a bid goes by different names in different games—"set," "euchre," "bate," and so on.

Linger Longer

A good way to start learning trump games.

Players: 4 to 6.

Cards: Each player receives as many cards as there are players in the game. For example, with 5 players, each receives 5 cards.

The Deal: The last card dealt, which goes to the dealer, is shown to all the players. It decides the trump suit for that trick. The rest of the deck is placed face down in the middle of the table, forming the stock.

The Play: The player to the left of the dealer makes the first *lead* (play), putting down in the middle of the table any card in the trump suit, if he can. Otherwise, he may put down whatever card he pleases. The other players must *follow suit*, putting down any cards in their hand that match the suit of the first lead.

The cards are played in "tricks." Each player tries to capture the trick of four cards by playing the highest trump, or, if there is no trump, by the highest card played of the suit that was led.

When a player wins a trick, he "owns" those cards and draws the top card of the stock. That card determines the trump suit for the next trick. When a player is left without any cards, he has to drop out of the game, and the others play on.

To Win the Game: To get all the cards and be the last player left when everyone else has dropped out. If two or more players are down to one card each at the end, the winner of the last trick wins the game.

Napoleon

Other Name: Nap

Players: 2 to 6.

Cards: A regular pack of 52.

Equipment: A handful of counters—poker chips, matchsticks, toothpicks, dried beans, etc.

The Deal: Each player receives five cards, one at a time. Give out the counters, the same number to each player.

The Bidding: The player to the left of the dealer has the first turn. He "bids" (predicts) the number of tricks he will take if he is allowed to name the trump suit. Each player has one turn in which he may pass or may bid from one to five. A bid of five tricks is called "nap."

The Play: The highest bidder names the trump suit and makes the first lead, which must be a trump.

The cards are played in tricks. The players must *follow suit* to the lead card if they can. Otherwise, there is no restriction on what they may play or lead.

The winner of each trick leads to the next trick—playing any suit—and everyone continues to follow that lead. The trick is won by the highest card. The bidder tries to win the number of tricks she has named. All the other players combine forces against her. Play stops the moment the outcome is sure—success or defeat for the bidder.

Scoring: When a bidder wins, she collects from each other player the same number of counters as her bid. If she is defeated, she pays this number to each player.

The bid of nap" for all the tricks is special. If you make it, you collect 10 counters from each player, but if you fail, you pay five to each one.

Loo

Players: 5 to 8 (6 is best).

Cards: A regular pack of 52.

Equipment: A handful of counters—poker chips, matchsticks, toothpicks, dried beans, etc.

The Deal: Each player receives three cards, one at a time. An extra hand of three cards is dealt just to the left of the dealer. This is the *widow*. If the player to the left of the widow does not like her hand, she may throw it away and take the widow instead. If she is satisfied with her hand, though, she must say so and stick with it.

Then each player in turn has a chance to take the widow, until somebody takes it or all refuse it.

Give the same number of counters to each player.

The Play (Single Pool):   After the matter of the widow is settled, the player to the left of the dealer makes the opening lead. You must always *follow suit* to the lead when you can; you must *play higher* than any other card in the trick, if you can. Later, once trump is declared and a plain suit is led of which you have none, you must *trump*, if you can.

The highest trump, or, if there is no trump, the highesy card of the suit led, wins the trick. Aces are high.

You must keep the tricks you have won face up on the table in front of you as you play.

Trumps: Play begins without any trump suit and continues that way so long as everybody follows suit to every lead. When somebody fails to follow suit, the top card of the undealt stock is turned over. This card decides the trump suit. The trick just played is examined and if a card that has been played turns out to be trump, that card wins the trick.

Scoring: To start a pool, the dealer must *ante up* three counters. When the pool contains no more than these three counters, it is a *single*, and play takes place as described above. After the play, the pool pays out one counter for each trick won. Players who have not won a trick must pay three counters into the next pool, making it a *double*—or jackpot.

Double Pool: This is formed by the dealer's ante of three plus any payments for *loo* (not winning a trick in the previous hand). After the deal, the next card of the deck is turned up, deciding the trump suit. After checking out their hands, the players must say in turn whether they will play or drop out. If all but the dealer drop out, he takes the pool. If only one player ahead of the dealer decides to play, the dealer must play, too. He may play for himself—in which case he cannot take the widow—or he may play to "defend the pool," in which case he must throw away his hand and take the widow. When the dealer plays merely to "defend the pool," he neither collects nor pays any counters; the pool settles with his opponent alone.

The nearest active player to the left of the dealer leads first. The other rules of play are the same as in a single pool.

The double pool pays out one-third of its contents for each trick won. A player who stays in and does not win a trick must pay three counters to the next pool.

To Win the Game: Win the largest number of counters.

Rams

Players: 3 to 5.

Cards: A pack of 32. Discard all 2s to 6s from a regular pack of 52. The cards rank:

(Highest)   (Lowest)

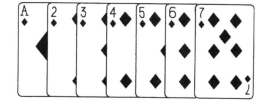

Equipment: A handful of counters—poker chips, matchsticks, toothpicks, dried beans, etc.

The Deal: Each player receives five cards in batches of three and two. An extra hand or *widow* is dealt, as in *Loo*. The last card belonging to the dealer is exposed to determine the trump suit.

Give the same number of counters to each player.

Declaring: After looking at their hands, the players in turn must declare whether they will play or drop out. If they play, they must undertake to win at least one trick. Any player in turn may discard the hand and take the widow instead (if it has not yet been taken).

Any player may declare *rams*—undertake to win *all* the tricks. This declaration may be made either before or after taking the widow, but it must be made before the next player has declared. In a *rams* game, everybody must play; players who have dropped out must pick up their hands again. If the rams player has not taken the widow, each player who has not refused it gets a chance to take it.

The Play: The player who declared rams makes the opening lead. Otherwise, it is made by the first player to the left of the dealer.

You must follow suit when you can, and you must play higher than any previous card in the trick, when you can. If a plain suit is led, you have to trump if you are able to, even if the trick has already been trumped. You must trump higher if you can. A trick is won by the highest trump in it, or, if no trump, by the highest card of the suit led.

Scoring: The dealer antes up five counters. The pool may contain counters left from the previous deal.

Each player who has stayed in the game takes one counter (or one-fifth of all the counters) from the pool for each trick he wins. Players (as in *Loo*) who win no tricks must pay five counters into the next pool.

In a rams, however, the settlement is different. If the rams player wins all the tricks, she wins the whole pool plus five counters from every other player. If she loses a trick, the cards are at once thrown in; she must pay enough counters to double the pool and five counters to every player.

If everybody ahead of the player to the right of the dealer passes, this player must pay the dealer five counters if he wishes to drop. In this case, the pool remains undivided. If only one player other than the dealer decides to play, the dealer must play to defend the pool. In this case, he takes the trump card and discards another face down.

Sixty-Six

Players: 2.

Cards: 24 cards: Ace, King, Queen, Jack, 10 and 9 of each suit. (Discard all 2s to 8s). The cards in each suit rank:

(Highest)   (Lowest)

The Deal: Each player receives six cards, dealt three at a time. Place the rest of the pack face down in the middle of the table, to form the stock. Turn the top card of the stock face up and place it partly underneath the stock. This is the *trump card* and it decides the trump suit.

Early Play: The non-dealer leads first. The cards are played out in tricks. A trick is won by the higher trump or by the higher card played of the suit led. The winner of a trick draws the top card of the stock, and the opponent draws the next card. In this way, each hand is restored to six cards after each trick.

   During this early play, you do not have to follow suit to the lead. You may play any card. The early play ends when the stock is exhausted.

To Win the Game: You try to meld marriages (see below), win cards in tricks and win the last trick. The first player to reach a total of 66 or more points wins a game point. The first one to score seven *game points* wins an overall game.

Marriages: A marriage is meld of a King and Queen of the same suit. In the trump suit, a marriage counts 40. In any other suit, it counts 20. To score a marriage, you must show it after winning a trick, then lead one of the two cards.

If the non-dealer wants to lead a King or Queen from a marriage for an opening lead, she may show the marriage and then do so. But she may not score the marriage until after she has won a trick.

Trump Card: A player who has the 9 of trumps may exchange it for the trump card—to get a higher trump. He may make this exchange only after winning a trick, before making the next lead.

Closing: At any turn to lead, a player may turn the trump card face down. By doing that he closes—that is, stops—any further drawing from the stock. The hands are played out as in *Later Play* (see below), except that marriages may still be melded.

Later Play: After the stock is exhausted, you play out the six cards in each hand. In this part of the game, you must follow suit to the lead, if you can.

Counting Cards: Cards won in tricks are counted as follows:

Each Ace	**11**
Each 10	**10**
Each King	**4**
Each Queen	**3**
Each Jack	**2**
For winning the last trick	**10**

Scoring: Marriages are scored on paper whenever melded. Points taken in tricks are not entered on paper until a hand is finished, but it is important to keep mental track of these points and your opponent's points as they are won. In your turn to play, you may claim thast you have reached 66. Then stop play at once and count. If you're right:

- **you score one *game point***
- **or two if your opponent has less than 33**
- **or three game points if he has not even won a trick.**

If you are wrong, and you don't have 66:

- **your opponent scores two game points**

The reason it's so important to realize when you have won a game—and to claim it—is that you may lose by playing out the hand. If you and your opponent both get more than 66, or if you tie at 65, neither of you wins. But the winner of the next hand gets one additional game point.

Usually, at least one game point is won by somebody in each deal. As mentioned earlier, you win by scoring seven game points in an overall game.

Three-Hand Sixty-Six

Players: 3.

Cards: Same as in *Sixty-Six*: 24 cards, Ace down to 9.

The Deal: The dealer gives six cards to the other two players, but deals none to himself.

The Play: The non-dealers play regular *Sixty-Six*.

Scoring: The dealer scores the same number of game points as the winner of the deal. If both players get 66 or more—or tie at 65 (without a claim—they score nothing and the dealer scores one. But a player is not allowed to win the overall game (seven points) when he is the dealer. If the usual scoring would put him up to seven points or over, his total becomes six, and he must win that last point as an active player.

Four-Hand Sixty-Six

Players: 4.

Cards: 32 cards from a regular pack. Ace, King, Queen, Jack, 10, 9, 8, and 7 of each suit. (Discard 2s through 6s.)

The Deal: Each player receives eight cards. The last card, turned face up for trump, is shown to each player, and then taken into the dealer's hand.

The Play: Players sitting opposite each other are partners. There is no melding. At all times you must follow suit to a lead, if possible, and also must, if possible, play higher than any card already played to the trick. When a plain suit is led and you have none, you must trump or overtrump if you can.

Scoring: Play out every hand. There is no advantage in claiming to have won. The winning side scores:

> **1 game point for having taken 66 to 99 or**
> **2 game points for 100 to 129 or**
> **3 game points for every trick (130).**

If the sides tie at 65, one extra game point goes to the side winning the next hand.

8
The Whist Family

Back in the 1890s the games editor of an English magazine received a letter to this effect:

"My son, aged nine, has seen his elders playing *Whist* and now wishes to learn the game. Can you recommend to me some simple game I can teach him that will serve as an introduction to *Whist?*"

The editor replied, "Yes, I can recommend such a game. The game is *Whist.*"

The fact is that the rules of Whist are simple and few. You can learn them in two minutes. Whist is just about the simplest of all card games to play *at*. What is not so easy is to play *Whist* well, for its extraordinary scope for skillful play lets the expert pull miles ahead of the beginner.

Whist

Players: 4, in partnerships.

Cards: Each receives 13 cards, dealt one at a time. In every suit the cards rank:

(Highest)   **(Lowest)**

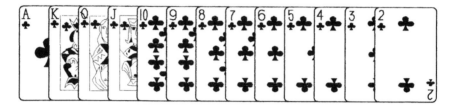

The Deal: The last card of the pack, belonging to the dealer, is exposed to all the players. This card decides the trump suit for that hand.

The Play: The player to the left of the dealer makes the first lead. The hands are played out in tricks. You must *follow suit* to the lead if possible. Otherwise, you may play or lead as you please. However, if a player *revokes* by not following suit when he has in his hand an appropriate card to play, he and his partner have to pay a penalty. The penalty is decided upon before play begins, and may be as severe as two game points for the opponent. The partnership cannot win any trick in which it revokes.

A trick is won by the highest trump in it, or, if it contains no trump, by the highest card of the suit led. The winner of a trick makes the lead for the next trick.

One member of each partnership gathers together all the tricks won by his side. He doesn't throw them together in a single pile but overlaps them crosswise, so that each batch of four cards remains separate from the others.

To Win the Game: Win as many tricks as possible. Points for tricks and honors are accumulated, and the first side to reach a total of seven game points wins.

Scoring: The side that wins the majority of the tricks scores

1 game point for each trick over 6, and, if agreed upon,
2 game points on the occasions when the opponents revoke.

In addition, points are scored for *honors*. The *honors* are the Ace, King, Queen and Jack of trumps.

If 2 honors were dealt to each side, there is no score.
If one side received 3 honors, it scores 2.
For all 4 honors, the score is 4.

Remember that honors are scored by the side to which they are *dealt*, not won in play. Both sides may score in the same deal, one side winning a majority of tricks and the other side holding a majority of honors.

Dummy Whist

Players: 3.

Cards: As in *Whist*.

The Deal: In this adaption of *Whist* for three players, four hands are dealt, as usual, with the extra hand or "dummy" going opposite the dealer.

The Play: The same as in *Whist*, except that the dealer plays the dummy hand as well as his own against the two live opponents. Of course, the dealer must be careful to play each hand at its proper turn.

Scoring: The dealer has a great advantage over his opponents, since he gets to see all 26 cards on his side. The fairest scoring method is to play three, six or nine deals so that each player has the same number of turns to deal. Then the player with the highest score is declared the winner.

Bridge Whist

This game is played in the same way as basic *Whist*, but it has a number of complications.

Players: 4, in partnerships.

Cards: Same as in *Whist*.

Equipment: Score pad and pencil.

Trumps: No trump card is turned. The dealer may name trump, if he wishes, or he may pass. If he does pass, his partner must name the trump. Any of the four suits may be named trump, or the player may call "No trump," meaning that the hand will be played without a trump suit.

Doubles: After the trump—or no trump—is named, either one of the non-dealers may declare "I double." This multiplies the score of the winners by two.

After such a double, either member of the dealer's side may declare "I re-double" or "I double back." The terms may re-double alternately without limit, until one team quits. Then the cards are played.

The Play: After the opening lead by the player to the left of the dealer, the dealer's partner puts her cards face up on the table in vertical rows by suit. The dealer then plays the "dummy" as well as his own hand, just as in *Dummy Whist*.

Scoring: The score is kept on a score pad. The sheet is divided into two halves by a vertical line. All the scores for one team (WE) are entered in the left-hand column, and the scores of the other team (THEY) in the right. The sheet is also divided by a horizontal line, somewhat below the middle. Only odd trick scores are entered below the line, and they are accumulated to determine when a game has been won (total score of 30).

All other scores go above the line. When the play ends, each column is added up to determine the grand total won by each side, for odd tricks, honors, slams, rubbers. For instance, the score sheet may look like this:

	WE	THEY
Honors & Bonuses →	*40* *20* *100*	
Tricks →		
Game 1 →	*30*	*24*
Game 2 →	*120*	
= A Rubber		

Scoring Tricks: The team winning at least six of the 13 tricks has a "book." It will score only tricks in excess of books of six. These score-able tricks are called *odd tricks*. Score them as follows:

If trumps were	♠	♣	♦	♥	No trump
Each odd trick would count	2	4	6	8	10

Each double that was made multiplies the score of the winners by two, each redouble by four.

Scoring Honors: Points are also scored for honors, which are written above the line on your score sheet. These are kept separate from points for tricks, which are written below the line.

The honor count is considerably more complicated than in *Whist*. When the game is played in a trump suit, the five top trumps—Ace, King, Queen, Jack and 10—become honors. You take the odd-trick value and multiply it by the number shown below to get the honor score, which gets written above the line.

Team with 3 honors or *chicane*	**X 2**
(chicane is a hand without a trump)	
4 honors divided between partners	**X 4**
4 honors in one hand	**X 8**
4 honors in one hand, 5th in partner's	**X 9**
5 honors in one hand	**X 10**

When you multiply this out, remember that the score you get is for honors only. It does not affect the scoring of the odd tricks, which you have already written below the line.

In a no-trump game, the honors are the four Aces. Score them as follows:

Team with 3 Aces	**30**
4 Aces, divided	**40**
4 Aces in one hand	**100**

Scoring Bonuses: If one side wins all 13 tricks, it scores a bonus of 40 for *grand slam*. For winning 12 tricks, a *little slam*, there is a bonus of 20. These numbers get written above the line on your score pad.

To Win the Game: The first team to win 30 points in odd tricks wins a game. The team to win a *rubber*—two games—wins a bonus of 100 points, and *the* game.

Nullo Games

In order to win nullo games, you need to *avoid* winning tricks, or avoid taking certin cards in tricks. Most of the games are especially easy for children to learn because they have practically no other rules. Only in *Omnibus Hearts* do we find the added wrinkle that you *do* want to win some cards while you *don't* want to win others.

Four Jacks

Other Name: Polignac

Players: 4, 5, or 6.

Cards: With 4 players, 32 cards as follows:
Ace, King, Queen, Jack, 10, 9, 8, 7—a full deck, but
with all 2s to 6s discarded. All the 32 cards are dealt;
each player receives 8 cards.

With 5 or 6 players, 30 cards—same as above but the
two black 7s are also discarded. Each player receives
6 or 5 cards.

Equipment: A handful of counters—poker chips, matchsticks,
dried beans, etc. Distribute the same number to each
player.

The Play: The player to the left of the dealer leads first. The hands are
played out in tricks. There is no trump suit. Each trick is won by the
highest card played of the suit led.

To Win the Game: Avoid winning any Jacks. But before the opening
lead, any player may announce that he will try to win all the tricks. This
is called *capot*.

Scoring: Payments for holding Jacks and winning capot are made
into a common pool, which is divided equally among all the players
when the game ends. Whenever one player is down to his last counter,
all players take equal numbers of counters from the pool.

If capot is announced and made, every player must pay five
counters. But if the capot player fails to win all the tricks, he alone pays
five counters.

When capot is not announced, the player who takes the Jack of
Spades—called Polignac—must pay two counters into the pool. One
counter must be paid for each of the other three Jacks taken in.

Slobberhannes

This game is played in much the same way as *Four Jacks*, with the difference that what you want to avoid winning are:

first trick
last trick
the Queen of Clubs

Each of these costs one counter, and if you unluckily take all three, you must pay an extra counter—four in all.

9
The Hearts Family

This is the chief group of nullo games. In all of them, the way to win is to avoid winning Hearts.

If you are invited to play *Hearts* with a group that you have never played with before, it's a good idea to ask them to state the rules. Otherwise, you may find yourself playing one game while they play another.

The name of the basic game, *Hearts*, is used loosely for all its offspring, but there are many variations. *Black Maria* and *Black Lady* often denote games that are different from either the *Black Lady* or *Hearts* described here.

Hearts

This is the basic and most simple game of the *Hearts* family, though the most popular is *Black Lady*.

Players: 2 to 6, but almost always 4. Other forms of the game are preferred with more or less than 4.

Cards: Each player receives 13 cards. When you can't divide the cards equally, remove enough deuces from the deck to make the deal come out even. Aces rank highest.

Equipment: A handful of counters—poker chips, matchsticks, toothpicks, dried beans, etc.—the same amount to each player—or pencil and paper.

To Win the Game: Avoid winning any Hearts—or win all 13 of them.

The Play: The player to the left of the dealer makes an opening lead and the cards are played in tricks. A trick is won by the highest card played of the suit led. There is no trump suit, though Hearts are often mistakenly called "trumps." The winner of a trick leads to the next trick.

Scoring with counters: For each Heart that a player wins, he must pay one counter into the pool.

If two or more players took no Hearts, they divide the pool.

But if all players took Hearts, nobody wins the pool. It stays on the table as a *jackpot* and becomes part of the pool for the next deal.

Scoring with pencil and paper: Each Heart taken counts one point against the player. A game can be ended at any agreed-upon time, and the player with the lowest total score is the winner. The usual method is to charge a player 13 if he wins all the Hearts. A good alternative is to deduct 13—(or 26, as agreed) from his score, preserving the principle that a player with a bad hand should have a chance to save himself (or gain) by taking *all* the Hearts.

Heartsette

This game adapts *Hearts* to an odd number of players.

Players: 3 or 5.

Cards: Place a *widow* (a group of cards) on the table—
4 cards if 3 are playing, 2 cards if 5 are playing.

The Deal: Deal out the rest of the cards.

The Play: Play in the same way as *Hearts*, but the widow is turned
face up after the first trick and goes to the winner of that trick. He must
of course pay for any Hearts it contains.

Spot Hearts

This variation features a different scoring method that you can apply to
any member of the Hearts family. The charges for taking Hearts go according to rank:

Ace counts	14
King counts	13
Queen counts	12
Jack counts	11
Others count	face value

Joker Hearts

This is *Hearts*, with a Joker added.

Players: Same.

Cards: **Add a Joker to the pack, discarding the 2 of Clubs to keep the deck at 52 cards.**

The Joker can be beaten only by the Ace, King, Queen or Jack of Hearts. Otherwise, it wins any trick to which it is played.

    If you're playing *Heartsette*, deal an extra card to the widow.

    The Joker counts as one Heart in payment or, in *Spot Hearts* scoring, 20.

Draw Hearts

This is *Hearts* for two players.

Players: 2.

Cards: 13 to each player.

The Deal: Place the rest of the deck face down in the middle of the table, forming the stock.

To Win the Game: Take fewer Hearts.

The Play: The cards are played in tricks. The winner of a trick draws the top card of the stock, and his opponent takes the next. After the stock is exhausted, the hands are played out without drawing.

Auction Hearts

The idea of this game is to let the players bid for the privilege of naming the suit to be avoided.

Each player in turn has one chance to bid, and the highest bidder names the "minus" suit.

Bids are made in numbers of counters that the player is willing to pay into the pool. Settlement is also made with counters, as in basic *Hearts*.

If the pool becomes a jackpot, there is no bidding in the next deal. The same player retains the right to name the minus suit, without further payment, until the jackpot is won. This player also makes the opening lead.

Domino Hearts

Players: 5 or 6.

Cards: Each receives 6 cards.

The Deal: The rest of the pack is put face down in the middle of the table, forming the stock. All tricks must be composed of cards of the same suit—there is no discarding. When a player is unable to follow suit to the lead, he must draw from the stock until he gets a playable card. After the stock is exhausted, he must pass.

When a player's hand is exhausted, he drops out of the deal and the others play on. If he should win a trick with his last card, the player to his left leads for the next trick.

When all but one have dropped out, the last player must add his remaining cards to his own tricks.

Hearts taken are charged at one point each.

To Win the Game: Have the lowest total when another player reaches 31 points.

Black Lady

This is the best-known game of the *Hearts* family. It is what most people refer to when they speak of *Hearts*.

Players: 3 to 7. It is best for 4, without partnerships.

Cards: Deal out the whole pack, giving equal hands to all.
With 4 players it works out correctly.
With 3 players, discard 1 deuce.
With 5 players, discard 2 deuces.
With 6 players, discard 4 deuces.
With 7 players, discard 3 deuces.

Equipment: A handful of counters—poker chips, matchsticks, toothpicks, dried beans, etc.—the same amount to each player or: Pencil and paper for scoring.

The Pass: After looking at his hand, each player passes any three cards he chooses to the player to his left. He must choose which cards he is going to pass and put them on the table before picking up the three cards passed to him by the player to his right.

The Play: The player to the left of the dealer makes the opening lead. The cards are played out in tricks. Aces rank highest. A trick is won by the highest card played of the suit led. The winner of a trick leads to the next trick.

To Win the Game: Avoid taking the Queen of Spades—called Black Lady, Black Maria, Calamity Jane, etc.—and avoid taking Hearts; or else take *all* the Hearts *and* the Queen of Spades, called "shooting the moon."

Scoring: If one player takes all 14 "minus" cards, he can subtract 26 points from his score. Some people play instead that 26 points are added to everyone else's score. Otherwise, one point is charged for each Heart won, and 13 points for the Queen of Spades. A running total score is kept for each player on paper. The first one to reach 100 or more loses the game, and the one with the lowest total at that time wins.

When playing with young children, you may want a shorter game. In this case, set the limit at 50.

An alternative method is to score with counters, settling after each hand. Payments are made into a pool, distributed equally to the players from time to time.

Strategy: See *Omnibus Hearts* (pages 102-103).

Cancellation Hearts

This is a variation for 6 or more players.

Players: **6 or more.**

Cards: **2 packs shuffled together.**

The Deal: Deal the cards as far as they will go evenly. Put the extra cards face down on the table as a widow. This group of cards goes to the winner of the first trick.

The Play: You play the game exactly the same way as *Black Lady*, except:

1. When two identical cards, such as two Aces of Diamonds, are played in the same trick, they cancel each other out, ranking as zero. They cannot win the trick. As a result, if a deuce is led and all the higher cards of the suit played to a trick are paired and therefore cancelled, the deuce would win the trick!

2. When all cards of the suit led are cancelled, the cards stay on the table and go to the next winner of a trick. The same leader leads again.

Scoring: As in *Black Lady*. Counters make for easier scoring than paper and pencil.

Discard Hearts

This is *Black Lady*, except that the three cards are sometimes passed to the left and sometimes to the right. The best plan is to alternate. The pass often allows you to ruin your neighbor. Alternate passing gives her the chance to get back at you.

Omnibus Hearts

Many players regard this as the most interesting game of the Hearts family. It is the same as *Black Lady* with one addition. The Jack of Diamonds, or sometimes the 10, is a "plus" card, counting 10 *for* you if you win it.

As a result, in this game, each suit has its own character: Clubs are neutral, Diamonds contain the plus card, Spades contain the worst minus card, and all the Hearts are minus cards. A player who makes a "take-all" must win all 13 Hearts, the Queen of Spades and the Jack of Diamonds.

Strategy: The most dangerous cards to hold are high Spades—Ace, King, Queen—without enough lower cards to guard them. Pass such high Spades when you are dealt less than three lower Spades. Pass high Hearts if you can afford to, and if they look dangerous, but two *low* Hearts are usually enough to guard them. Any suit outside of Spades is dangerous if you have four or more without any card lower than, say, a six. Even a single very low card—a two or a three—may not be a sufficient guard. Pass one to three cards from the top or middle of such a suit, if you do not have more pressing troubles.

If you do not have any high Spades after the pass, lead Spades at every opportunity. You can never gather Black Maria by a lower Spade lead! You want to try to force her out by Spade leads so that you can save yourself from winning her by discard. If you have her yourself, it is usually best to lead your shortest side suit so as to get rid of it and get a chance to discard Black Maria.

If you are dealt the Jack of Diamonds, pass it if you can afford to. The Jack is musch easier to *catch* than to *save*. It is not often caught by higher Diamonds—and when it is, it is mostly by accident. It usually falls to the winner of the last trick. The hand with which you may hope to catch it has some Aces and Kings, adequately guarded by lower cards, in two or more suits. Of Course, if you hope to catch the Jack, don't pass any higher Diamonds, and don't ever lead Diamonds if you can avoid it. But put a *high* Diamond on any Diamond lead that might be won by the Jack if you were to play low.

Don't attempt a take-all without a very powerful hand. Certain holdings are fatal no matter how strong you are in other suits—low Hearts, for example (not at the end of a long solid suit), and the Jack of Diamonds (without enough Diamond length and strength to save the Jack even if you do not go for take-all). However, if you've got one or two middling-high Hearts, it is not fatal. You may be able to win the tricks simply by leading these Hearts. The players holding higher Hearts may shrink away from taking the tricks.

When your chief ambition is to avoid taking minus cards, which is most of the time, get rid of your high cards early rather than late. Thus, if you have:

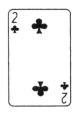

put the Ace on the *first* Club and the Jack on the *second*, saving your 2 to escape having to win the more dangerous third lead. The more often a suit is led, the more likely it becomes that Black Maria or Hearts will be discarded on it.

SECTION 2
10 Minute
Card Games

Introduction

I have long enjoyed playing card games because they have provided me, my family, and friends with wholesome entertainment, camaraderie, and deeper, richer, more meaningful relationships through friendly competition. Hoping, then, to share these benefits with my readers, I have prepared this section of ten-minute card games.

Why titled *Ten-Minute Card Games?* Simply to remind the reader that most card games require only ten minutes or less to play, and that you do not need large blocks of time for a game once you have learned the rules. Probably all basic card games at first required ten minutes or less to play, but some became more complicated and required longer periods of play in response to players' wanting to prolong the game. For example, over a period of time, *Bridge* evolved from *Whist, Black Lady* from the simpler game of *Hearts*, and a host of other cards games from a few basic parent games such as *Seven-Up, Rummy, Straight Poker,* and others.

My first goal in preparing this section was to offer card games that began as and remained ten minute games, as well as those that began as ten minute games but were lengthened somewhat by advanced scoring procedures. In the latter case, I simplified the scoring to return these games to a one-hand, one-game format. However, in each such case I also included the scoring procedure for the higher-score, longer-lasting game for those persons who want to play it.

My second goal was to address both men and women, partly because both play cards, and partly out of a sense of fairness. With this goal in mind, I have used both feminine and masculine pronouns throughout the text.

—William A. Moss

The All Fours Group

Card players have enjoyed games of the All Fours group, including Seven-Up and its many variations, since the late 1600s. Having its origins in England, Seven-Up, along with Whist and Put, was popular in the early 1700s and for years competed with Poker as the favorite gambling game in the United States.

Seven-Up

Players and Deck Used: The game requires two, three, or four persons (when they are playing as partners, two against two) and a full deck of 52 cards. The cards rank as follows:

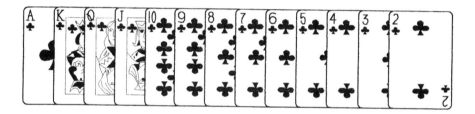

Beginning the Game: The players cut for high card to determine the first deal and partners (when four play). Highest cut becomes the dealer, and high cuts play as partners against low cuts. After the shuffle and cut, the dealer gives six cards to each player, three at a time, in rotation from left to right. After completing the deal, the dealer faces, or turns up, the next card to show the "trump" suit, any card of which will win over any card of another suit. If the card turned up is a Jack, the dealer scores 1 point. If more than two persons are playing, only the dealer and first player can look at their hands until the turned-up card is accepted or rejected as trump. The deal passes to the left at the end of each hand.

The Goals: The goals of the game are: (a) to hold the highest and lowest trumps in play; (b) to turn the Jack for trumps or to capture it in play; and (c) to capture cards in play that count towards game.

Making the Trump: The player seated to the dealer's left has the first right to *stand* or *beg*. If she is satisfied with the trump turned, she "stands" and leads (plays the first card) to the first *trick* (sequence of cards played). If she *begs*, the dealer must either say "Take it" and give her a 1-point *gift* to let the trump stand, or deal three new cards to each player and turn up a new trump. The dealer, however, cannot give her the 1-point gift if it will give her "game" (winning) point. If the dealer chooses to give each player three more cards and turns up a trump that is the same as the first one, the dealer then repeats the process until she turns up a card of a different suit. This process is called *running the deck*. If she turns up the Jack of the rejected trump suit while running the deck, she does not score 1 point for doing so. If a new trump is turned up while running the deck, all players keep their best six cards, discarding the others. However, if the dealer runs the whole deck without turning up a different trump, she collects the cards and redeals.

The Play: The player seated to the dealer's left leads any card. If the card is a trump, the players must follow suit, if possible. If the card is not a trump, the players must follow suit, but, if unable to do so, they may either play a trump or discard. The highest card in the suit led wins, unless the trick is "trumped," in which case the highest trump wins. The winner of each trick leads to the next trick.

Scoring: The players score points as follows:
>   *High*— the highest trump in play. Player to whom dealt gets 1 point.
>   *Low*— the lowest trump in play. Player to whom dealt gets 1 point.
>   *Jack*— Jack of trumps. If in play, scored by the dealer turning it up as trump or by the player taking it in a trick: 1 point.
>   *Game*—won by person holding cards with the highest point count taken during play: 1 point

In counting points for game, 10s count as 10 points; Aces, 4; Kings, 3; Queens, 2; Jacks; 1. If there is a tie for "game" between the dealer and a nondealer, the latter wins; otherwise, no one scores game point. If a player holds the only trump in play, she will win high and low, and, if the card she holds is the trump Jack, she will win high, low, and Jack.

Game: The player taking the greatest number of points in one hand wins the game. Many Seven-Up enthusiasts, however, prefer playing successive hands, usually two to three, until one of the players scores 7 or 10 points, as agreed to at the beginning of the game. In the latter procedure, the first player to score 7 (or 10) points wins the game. For example, if the dealer needs 1 point to "go out" and she turns the Jack of trumps, she wins. If both players take enough points to win the game in the same hand, they score their points in this order: high, low, Jack, and game.

Remedies and Penalties: If a player intentionally or unintentionally exposes a card, she places it face up on the table and plays it when it is legal to do so. If all players agree, they may allow the offender to keep the card in her hand during the play.

A player who revokes, or fails to follow suit when she could have done so, incurs penalties if she does not correct the revoke before the trick is *quitted* (placed face down) and the next lead made. If she does not correct the revoke, she cannot "go out" in that hand, nor can she cumulatively score more than 6 points. Additionally, if the trump Jack is not in play, she forfeits 1 point of her score; if the trump Jack is in play, she forfeits 2 points.

Many players prefer a stiffer penalty for a revoke, such as forfeiture of the game.

Variation: If a player begs in a three-hand game and the dealer decides to give her 1 point instead of running the deck, she must also give 1 point to the other nondealer. If the first player in a three-hand game *stands*, the next player has the right to stand or beg. If both stand, the first player leads to the first trick.

Auction Pitch, or Setback

Auction Pitch is basically the same game as Seven-Up with the following exceptions:

1. Two to seven players usually play *cutthroat*—each for himself. Partnership play is optional.

2. After dealing six cards to each person, three at a time, the trump suit is not decided by the dealer turning it up: instead, the players bid to name the trump suit.

3. The player seated to the left of the dealer opens the bidding. He may pass or bid from 1 to 4 points. If he bids 4 points, which is the maximum bid, he *pitches*, or leads, his trump suit immediately. If he bids less than 4 points, each player in rotation to the left may pass or bid at least 1 point more than the previous bid until a 4-point bid is made or until each player has had one opportunity to bid. Each player bases his bid on the number of points (high, low, Jack, and game) he thinks he can take in play. The high bidder opens the play by pitching the trump of his choice. If he accidently pitches the wrong card, the card pitched remains the trump card. If any player, intentionally or unintentionally, piches a card during the bidding process, he assumes the burden of a 4-point bid.

4. If the high bidder makes his bid, he wins the hand and the game. However, as discussed above in Seven-Up, many players prefer playing until one of them scores 7 or 10 points, as agreed to at the beginning of the game. In this instance, the first person to score 7 (or 10) points wins the game, unless, of course, the pitcher (high bidder) also goes out in the same hand. In the latter case, the pitcher wins.

5. If, in playing the 7- or 10-point game, a pitcher fails to make his bid, he is set back the amount of his bid, and he subtracts that amount from his score. If he is set back more points than he has, he is said to be *in the hole*, and his score is circled or preceded by a minus sign.

6. If a player other than the pitcher revokes, the pitcher cannot be set back, and each nonoffending player scores what he makes. The revoking player, however, is set back the amount of the bid. If the pitcher revokes, he cannot score any points; instead, he is set back the amount of his bid, and the other players score what they make.

Other than the above differences, Auction Pitch and Seven-Up are the same game.

Variations: Many players like to include the jick (same color Jack as trump Jack) and joker in their pitch games. When they do, the Jick and Joker each are worth 1 point, and high cards rank as follows: Ace (high), King, Queen, Jack, Jick, Joker, and 10. The Jick and Joker also count 1 point in determining the winner of game point. If the players use the Jick and Joker, they should adjust the high bid and game score accordingly, usually 6 and 10 points, respectively.

Straight Pitch

Straight pitch differs from Auction Pitch in the following respects:

    1. After the dealer gives each player six cards, three at a time, she turns the top card of the stock to name the trump suit. There is no bidding.

    2. The player sitting to the dealer's left leads to the first trick. The winner of each trick leads to the next trick.

    3. The inclusion of the Jick and Joker in the game is common.

Ranking of Cards in Straight Pitch

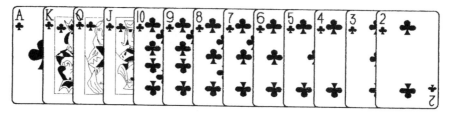

The Poker Group

Poker evolved slowly from an old French game called *Gilet,* which in turn probably had its origins in the Italian game of *Primero.* During the reign of Charles IX (1560-1574), notable for its bloody civil wars between the Catholics and Huguenot Protestants, *Gilet* became the game of *Brelan.* By the time of the French Revolution, the game of *Brelan* developed into *Bouillotte,* which included such devices as the blind, freeze-out, raise, bluff, and table stakes—all of which are common to modern-day Poker.

Bouillotte also gave rise to *Ambigu,* which supplied the draw, and the English game of *Brag,* which was largely a bluffer's game. These three games—*Bouillotte, Ambigu,* and *Brag*—shaped modern-day Poker, along with the adoption of the 52-card deck by 1835 and the introduction of five, instead of three, dealt cards.

Basic Poker

Two to eight persons play Poker with a 52-card deck. The players sometimes limit the number of people allowed to participate according to the game being played and the number of cards needed to fill out the hands. A joker may be added to the deck by mutual consent, and, if the joker is added, it is wild and is used as the holder wishes. The cards rank: 2 (low) to Ace (high). But sometimes at the beginning of a game, the players agree to an Ace's being used as high *or* low, such as in low sequences, or runs.

Seating: Players usually sit where they please, but some prefer to determine the seating arrangement by dealing each person one card face up, letting the person with low sit to the dealer's left, next low to his left, and so forth. Ties are broken by cutting for low card. The players may decide where a newcomer sits by mutual agreement, by the method above, or by some other means of choice.

Chips: By mutual consent, one player assumes the role of banker and takes charge of exchanging chips for money and for settling accounts at the end of the card session. (Matchsticks, beans, etc. may be substituted for chips.) Again by mutual consent, the players decide on the value of white, red, blue, and yellow chips.

Before the Game Begins: Poker players should decide the following at the start of the game: (a) the amount of the ante (preliminary bet made before the deal), as well as who antes (sometimes the dealer only, but usually all players); (b) a bet/raise limit; and (c) a time set to stop the card session. Instead of setting a time to end a session, some players prefer playing *freeze-out*. In freeze-out, all players begin the card session with the same number of chips, and as soon as any player loses his chips, he retires from the session, which continues until one player has won all the chips. Sometimes the players also set a limit to the number of times that a bet may be raised, which oftentimes is three raises, or *bumps*.

Beginning the Game: Players customarily determine the first dealer by having the cards dealt around face up, one at a time, until a Jack falls—the person who receives the first Jack deals. (Some players prefer to draw or cut for high or low card to determine the first dealer.) Before the cards are actually dealt, the dealer and, sometimes, the other players, depending on the game being played, ante chips on the middle of the table to begin the "pot."

The shuffle and cut are as in other card games. However, the person sitting to the dealer's right may decline to cut the deck. If he does decline, the players to his right, in turn, may cut or decline to do so. If all players decline, the deal proceeds. The dealer gives each player his cards, one at a time, in clockwise rotation, beginning with the person to his left. (This applies to *all* Poker games.) The dealer cannot deal the last card; instead, he shuffles this card with the discards to rebuild his dealing stock.

The Stripped Deck: If there are only three or four people playing, they may choose to strip the deck of its 2s, 3s, and, sometimes, 4s. If the players strip the deck and Aces are low, an 8-high straight would consist of: 8, 7, 6, 5, and Ace.

The Goal: The goal of each round of Poker is to hold or draw to the best hand, thereby winning the pot or a portion of it, depending on the game being played. In determining the winner(s) of each pot, the custom among poker players is to "let the cards speak for themselves."

Poker hands rank from high to low as follows:

1. Five of a kind. Five cards of the same rank, or denomination, which is possible only when the joker is included in the deck and/or other wild cards are named.

2. Royal straight flush. An Ace, King, Queen, Jack, and 10 squence, or run, in any suit.

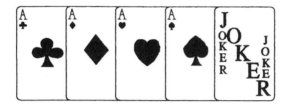

3. Straight flush. A five-card sequence, or run, in any suit ranked by its highest card. For example, a player would call his club sequence of 10, 9, 8, 7, and 6 a straight flush, 10 high. A 10-high straight flush would rank over a 9-high straight flush.

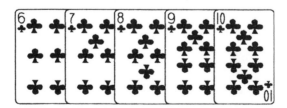

4. Four of a kind, which is ranked by its denomination. For example, four Queens rank over four Jacks.

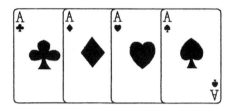

5. Full house. A combination of three cards of one denomination and two cards of another: for example, three Kings and two 10s. The "triplet" (three of a kind) decides rank. For example, three Kings and two 10s rank over three Queens and two Jacks (or three Kings rank over three Queens).

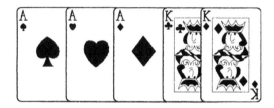

6. Flush. Any five cards in a suit, but not in sequence. A player ranks a flush by the highest card in the flush.

7. Straight. A sequence, or run, of five cards in various suits, which is ranked by its highest card.

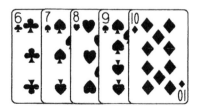

8. Three of a kind, or three cards of the same denomination, which are ranked by their denomination.

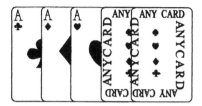

9. Two pairs of any denominations, which are ranked by the highest pair. For example, Jacks and 5s would rank over 10s and 8s.

10. One pair of any denomination with three unmatched cards. A pair is ranked by denomination.

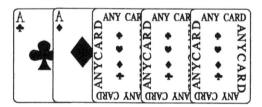

11. High card. A hand with none of the combinations listed above ranked by its highest card. In case of a tie, the player holding a card of the next higher denomination wins.

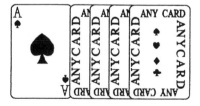

Ties: If the high cards in flushes tie, the next higher cards determine the winner. Ties in straight flushes, full houses, flushes, and straights divide the pot. In dividing such pots, the players usually cut for high card to determine the ownership of odd chips. If players hold four of a kind, a full house (in a seven-card game), two pairs, or one pair tie, their unmatched cards break the tie by rank. If high cards tie, the other cards again break the tie by rank.

Note: In cases where one or two tying hands has a Joker, many players hold that the natural hand, the one without the joker, wins. Other players hold the opposite view, because the odds of drawing a Joker are less than drawing a natural hand. But the latter group also holds that if both tying hands have multiple wild cards, the one with the fewer wild cards wins. *If a poker group wants to break ties involving wild cards by one of the methods just discussed, they should mutually agree to the method at the start of the game to avoid disputes and, perhaps, hard feelings.* Otherwise, tied hands split the pot according to guidelines set forth in the paragraph above.

Table Stakes: While a hand is in progress, a player may, with the consent of the other players, raise the betting limit to *table stakes,* which is the amount of chips he has on the table at the time. No one can raise the amount of the table stakes after looking at any of his cards. If another player does not have enough chips to *call,* or *see,* the table stakes raise, he may call a *sight* of the last bettor's cards for what chips he does have and separate that part of the pot from the rest.

The other players continue their calls and raises; some of these players also may call for a sight and thus fragment the pot further. If the person calling for a sight holds the winning hand during the showdown, he wins only that part of the pot for which he called his sight; the other players decide on the winner of the rest of the pot on the merits of their respective hands.

An accelerated variation of table stakes is the double-up game, wherein each player to the left of the dealer may in turn call for table stakes raises that would stop at a previously agreed-to number of such raises—usually up to six.

Remedies and Penalties: In case of a misdeal, the dealer deals again with the same pack. If a card is exposed in cutting or in reuniting a pack, the dealer must shuffle the deck again and redeal. Other misdeals include; an uncut or improperly reunited deck; a card placed face up in the deck; an incomplete or otherwise imperfect deck. If an extra but unexposed card is accidently given to a player, the dealer can restore it to the top of the deck or continue his deal with it, whichever action is more appropriate.

If a player has a hand of fewer or more than the cards needed for the game, if he has looked at them, and if he has bet on them, his hand is foul. He then must, upon discovery, abandon the hand, forfeiting the chips he has put into the pot and even the pot itself if he won it on that deal. If a player finds that he has too many or too few cards and he has not looked at them, he may request that the dealer remedy the card count by drawing cards from his hand or by dealing additional cards to his hand to leave it at the correct number of cards. However, if more than one hand is irregular in the deal and cannot be easily remedied, the cards must be shuffled, cut, and dealt again.

If a player has looked at any of his cards, he cannot ask for a new deal unless the deck is found to be imperfect. A deal out of turn or with the wrong deck must be stopped before it is completed; otherwise it stands.

If a player bets, calls, and/or raises out of sequence, the turn returns to the appropriate player. However, any chips the offender put in the pot remain there, and when his turn comes around, his bet, call, or raise is regarded as already made. In effect, he can make no further bets or raises until his turn comes around again, if it does. If he owes chips in addition to those put in the pot earlier, he makes up the difference. If he put too many chips in the pot, he forfeits them to the pot.

If a player announces a bet, call, or raise out of turn but does not put the chips in the pot, his announcement is void and the turn to bet, call, or raise reverts to the appropriate player.

If any player puts more chips in the pot than are required by a bet, call, or raise, he forfeits the excess chips to the pot. If he puts too few chips in the pot, he must make up the difference.

Straight, or Bluff, Poker

Straight Poker, the immediate forerunner of all modern-day poker games, at first required four players and a 20-card deck (Aces, Kings, Queens, Jacks, and 10s), with each person being dealt a five-card hand. Although the original game is still a popular two-hand game, it is now more often played by two to eight persons with a 52-card deck.

In Straight Poker, only the dealer antes. After she has done so and the cards are shuffled and cut, she gives each player five cards face down, one at a time, and in clockwise rotation. Beginning with the player at the dealer's left, each person, in turn, may drop from the game, check (put the lowest value of chips in the pot to remain in the game), or make a bet, placing her chips in the middle of the table. Once a bet is made, the other players remaining in the game must either call the bet or drop out of the game. A player calling a bet may also raise it, which requires the other players to call the raise if they want to stay in the game. During this round of betting and raising, a player holding a weak hand might try to bluff the others out of the game by betting and/ or raising excessively, hoping thereby "to buy" the pot. If no one *sees* the bet (meets or equals it), the bettor wins the pot without having to show her cards. If the bet or bet and raises are called, all players still in the game expose their hands face up for the showdown. The best poker hand wins the pot.

Draw Poker

In Draw Poker each player antes, and the dealer gives each person five cards face down, one at a time, and in clockwise rotation. After receiving and examining his cards, each player, beginning with the one at the dealer's left, drops from the game, bets, or checks the bet of the person at his left. After all players pass or after all bets and raises have been called, each player discards his unwanted cards face down, and the dealer gives him replacements.

After the players examine the cards they received on the draw, a second round of betting takes place. Following this second betting interval, the players lay their cards face up on the table for the show-down. The person holding the best hand wins.

Variations of Draw Poker: A player may open the betting without holding a pair. However, many players prefer playing a variation of Draw Poker called *Jacks or Better*, or *Jackpots*. In this variation, a player must hold a pair of Jacks or a hand better than Jacks in order to open the betting. In this variation, if no one can open the betting, everyone antes another chip to the pot and the cards are gathered up, shuffled, cut, and dealt again. If a person opens the betting and is later discovered to not have held the requisite cards to open, he must pay a penalty, which usually is double the size of the final pot.

Another variation of Draw Poker is *Progressive Draw Poker,* wherein a player needs Jacks or better to open the betting. If no one can open with Jacks or better, everyone antes another chip to the pot while the cards are gathered up, shuffled, cut, and dealt again. On the second deal, a player must have Queens or better to open the betting—hence the title Progressive Draw Poker. If no one can open with Queens or better, the third deal requires Kings or better; the fourth deal requires Aces or better; the fifth deal returns to Jacks or better; and so forth. Players like this variation because it builds large pots quickly.

Another popular variation is *Pass and Out*, wherein a player may open the betting holding nothing more than a pair, but in each turn he must either bet or drop out. He cannot "pass," or check, the betting to the next player.

Draw Poker with a Joker: While playing Draw Poker, as well as some other games, some players like to include the Joker, or *bug*, in the deck. The Joker affects the game as follows:

1. The person holding the Joker may use it as any card she wishes with one exception: She cannot use the Joker in a flush to replace a card she already holds. For example, she cannot use it as an Ace with an Ace-high flush and call that flush a double-Ace-high flush or straight flush. Nonetheless, the Joker makes it possible for a player to hold as many as five of a kind, which ranks over all other hands.

2. For showdown purposes, if two hands are equal in all respects, the tied hands split the pot, unless the players agree at the start of the game that a natural hand ranks over one with a Joker or other wild cards.

Deuces Wild

Deuces (twos) Wild is another variation of Draw Poker with a Joker. Deuces affect the game as follows:

    1. Each deuce, or 2, ranks as a Joker and may be used as any card its holder wishes, except the duplicate of a card he already holds in a flush, as explained in Poker with a Joker. The players also may wish to include the Joker in a Deuces Wild game.

    2. For showdown purposes, tied hands split the pot, unless the players agree at the start of the game that the hand with no or the fewest wild cards breaks such ties.

Wild Widow

Wild Widow is a variation of Draw Poker. The two games differ as follows:

    1. The dealer gives the players four cards one at a time face down, turns the next card face up as the Wild Widow in the middle of the table, and then deals one more card face down to each person.

    2. If a player holds a card or cards that match the face-up Wild Widow (the designated wild card), she may call and use them in any way she chooses, as in Deuces Wild. The players also may include the Joker in the deck.

Spit in the Ocean

Spit in the Ocean is another variation of Draw Poker. The two games differ as follows:

    1. The dealer gives each player four cards face down and then turns the next card, which is wild, face up in the middle of the table.

    2. If a player holds a card or cards that match the face-up card, he may call and use them in any way he chooses, as in Deuces Wild.

    3. Each player regards the face-up card as the fifth card of his hand, and he bases his draw on four cards only.

Lowball

Lowball is a variation of Draw Poker, in which the lowest-ranking hand, rather than the highest -ranking, wins the pot. There are no minimum requirements to open the pot, and straights and flushes do not count. In Lowball, Aces are always low; hence a pair of Aces ranks lower than a pair of deuces, and the lowest hand possible is a 5, 4, 3, 2, and Ace, whether it is made up of one or two suits.

During play, a player may check, or pass. If no one bets and the dealer has called for bets twice, a showdown takes place and the lowest hand wins the ante.

Ranking of Cards in Lowball

Lowest Hand of Any Suit or Combination of Suits

Five-Card Stud

Typically, there is no ante in a Stud game, unless one has been agreed to by the players. If one player antes, all ante. After the shuffle and cut, the dealer gives each person one card face down (the hole card), then one card face up, in clockwise rotation. In Five- and Seven-Card Stud, the dealer customarily announces the first bettor in each betting interval by pointing out the high card or best face-up hand. He likewise points out possible hands, such as possible straights, flushes, and so forth.

The players examine their face-down cards, and the person

receiving the highest face-up card must open the betting or drop from the game. In the case of a tie for high card, the person receiving the first high card bets. If this person drops from the game, the person with the next highest card bets, and a betting interval follows.

After the first round of betting is completed, the dealer then gives each player still in the game a second face-up card. With two cards placed face-up, the highest exposed poker combination bets first or drops from the game, as above. Thus, an Ace, King outranks a Queen, Jack, and a pair outranks high cards. After the second round of betting, the dealer gives each active player a third face-up card, which is followed by the person with the best exposed hand opening the betting interval. Finally, the dealer gives each active player a fourth face-up card, for a total of five cards, and again the player with the best exposed hand initiates the betting interval, which is followed by the showdown. The player with the best hand wins the pot.

Remedies and Penalties: If the dealer accidently exposes a card before a betting interval is completed, she buries that card and gives the top card to the player who would have received it if the other card had not been exposed. She completes that round of dealing with the person whose card was accidently exposed and buried.

Mexican Stud

Mexican Stud is a variation of Five-Card Stud. The two games differ as follows:
    1. The dealer deals all five cards face down.
    2. On receiving her second, third, fourth, and fifth cards, each player may decide which of her face-down cards to turn face up. Each player must turn a card face up before each round of betting.

Seven-Card Stud

As in Five-Card Stud, the ante is optional. The dealer begins the game by giving the players two cards face down and a third card face up, one at a time, which is followed by a betting interval as described in Five-

Card Stud. The dealer then gives each player her fourth, fifth, and sixth cards face up in three rounds of dealing. After each round of the deal, the players hold a betting interval. Finally, the dealer gives each person her seventh, and last, card face down, which is followed by a final round of betting and the showdown.

In the showdown, each player selects her best five cards as her poker hand. Only in the case of tied hands would the players use their other two cards; in this event, the higher card(s) would break the tie.

Other than the number of cards and betting intervals, Five- and Seven-Card Stud are the same game.

Baseball

Baseball is the same game as Five- and Seven-Card Stud with the following exceptions:

1. All 9s, whether face up or down, and 3s face down ("in the hole") are wild.

2. If a player receives a face-up 3, he must either "buy the pot" (double its value) or drop out of the game. If he buys the pot, thus staying in the game, all 3s are wild whether face up or face down (in the hole).

3. If a player receives a face-up 4, he receives another face-up card immediately as a bonus card. A 4 dealt face down (in the hole) does not earn a bonus card.

As in other Stud games, the player chooses his best five cards as his Poker hand in the showdown.

High-Low Poker

The concept of High-Low can be applied to most Poker games. When applied, the holder of the high hand and the holder of the low hand split the pot. The holder of the high hand always wins the odd chip.

The lowest-ranking hand is called "the runt hand," and it consists of a hand of different suits whose value is less than a pair. Thus, the lowest runt possible is a 2, 3, 4, 5, and 7 of mixed suits. The highest card determines the rank of a runt.

The Showdown Games Group

Black Jack (Twenty-One)

Number of Players and Deck Used: Any number of persons may play this game (four to eight being best) with a 52-card deck and chips. The cards rank as follow: Each Ace counts as either 1 or 11, depending only on the player's need; each King, Queen, Jack, or 10 counts as 10; each 9 through 2 counts as its pip, or index, value.

Chips and Bet: Before the game actually gets under way, the players agree what number of chips constitutes a minimum and maximum wager, or bet. Each player, except the dealer, must place her bet on the table in front of herself before she receives any cards at the beginning of each round of play. The dealer does not need to make a bet, because she is playing against each of the other players for whatever their individual bets may be.

Beginning the Game: In home games, the players draw or cut cards for first deal. High cut wins. The dealer shuffles, and any player may cut. The dealer then *burns* a card, that is, she turns a card from the top of the deck, makes it visible to all players, and turns it face up on the bottom of the deck, if it is not an Ace. If the card is an Ace, the shuffle, cut, and burn procedure is repeated. Some players will allow the dealer to slip the Ace into the deck and to face and burn another card without repeating the entire shuffle, cut, and burn procedure. Then, in rotation from left to right, the dealer gives each player, including herself, one card face down, and then she deals each player, except herself, a second card face down. She deals her second card face up.

The Goal: The goal of the game is the same for all players: to hold cards whose combined pip value is 21 or the nearest possible number below 21 without exceeding 21. (Pips are the markings on the card that indicate the numerical value of the card. A 10, which has 10 pips, has a numerical value of 10.)

"Taking Hits" and Settling Wagers: If the dealer has dealt herself an Ace and any other card with a pip value of 10, she announces "Black Jack" or "Twenty-One" and collects the wagers of the other players. By agreement before the game starts, the dealer may collect double the original bet. If the dealer does not announce Black Jack, each player looks at her face-down cards and mentally calculates their pip value. If any player holds a Black Jack, she announces it and collects double her bet from the dealer.

After the Black Jacks, if any, have been announced and settlements made, each player in turn, beginning with the one at the dealer's left, looks at the dealer's face-up card to help her decide whether she will *stand pat* or *take a hit* and thereby run the risk of going *bust,* or having cards whose count exceeds 21 points. If she is satisfied with her cards, she will say, "I'll stand pat," thereby letting the dealer know that she does not want any more cards. If she is not satisfied with her cards, she will say, "Hit me, " thereby letting the dealer know that she wants one more card. If she wants more than one hit, she will say, "Hit me, again," for each additional card she wants until she is satisfied or goes bust.

Most players will ask for a hit if the pip value of their cards is 16 or less. If the pip value of their cards is 17, most players will stand pat, unless they have cause to believe that the dealer's cards have a larger combined pip value. One such cause might be that the dealer's face-up card is an 8, 9, 10, or Ace. At this point, most players assess the dealer's demeanor and follow their intuition.

If the player asks for a hit and the total pip value of her cards exceeds 21, she admits that fact and forfeits her bet to the dealer. However, if the total pip value of her cards does not exceed 21 and she does not want to chance another hit, she will stand pat. Thus, each player in rotation will decide to stand pat or take a hit.

When the time comes for the dealer to make a decision to stand pat or take a hit, she turns up her hole, or face-down, card to view. The face-up cards of her opponents and her intuition will prompt her to stand pat or take a hit. Most dealers will stand pat on 17, unless their intuition prompts otherwise. (Some players make it a rule that the dealer must stand pat on 17 and collect or pay accordingly.) If the dealer overdraws or exceeds 21, she pays all players who have not overdrawn their bets. If she stands pat, she pays all players their wagers if the pip value of their cards is greater than the pip value of her cards. She does not pay players holding cards with the same or less pip value than the cards she holds. (All ties are won by the dealer.)

In addition to the procedures above for standing pat, taking hits, and setting bets, the following variation of play may occur: If the dealer deals a player two Aces or another pair whose pip value is 10 each, the player may *split the pair*, advance a second bet equal to the first, and play the Aces or other pair as two separate hands. The dealer then deals a card face down to each card of the pair. When a player splits a pair, she must stand pat, take a hit, or otherwise play out the first hand of the pair before playing the second hand.

After the first round of play is completed, the dealer deals the next round from the unused stock. When the entire stock is exhausted, the dealer gathers all discards and repeats the shuffle, cut, and burn procedure given above. The deal customarily passes to a player who has Black Jack when the dealer has not done so at the same time. When this happens, the dealer completes the play for that hand before passing the deck and deal to the new dealer.

Remedies: If it is discovered that the dealer failed to burn a card, she must on demand shuffle the remainder of the deck and do so. A misdealt card can be accepted or rejected by its recipient.

Variations: While the version of Black Jack above is probably the one played most often, there are other versions with slight variations. One such variation is that the dealer gives each player, including herself, one card face down and the second card face up.

A good rule to follow is to make sure that all players understand which version and variations will be in force before starting a game. This is especially important if you are playing in professional gambling casinos like those found in states with legalized gambling.

Spanish Monte

Spanish Monte, a Latin American gambling game, requires a deck of 40 cards (a 52-card deck stripped of its 8s, 9s, and 10s.) Any number of players may participate.

Beginning the Game: The players draw or cut for low card to determine the first dealer-banker. Ace is lowest. After the shuffle and cut, the dealer, holding the deck face down, draws two cards from the bottom of the deck and turns them face up on the table as the bottom layout. Next, he draws two cards from the top of the deck and turns them face up on the table as the top layout. After the dealer forms these two layouts, each player places his bet(s) on one or both layouts.

The Play and Settling Up: After all bets are made, the dealer turns the deck face up to expose the bottom card, which is the *port*, or *gate*, card. If the suit of the port card matches the suit of either card in the top layout, the dealer pays all bets on that layout. The same holds true if the suit of the port card matches the suit of either card in the bottom layout. If the suit of the port card does not match the suits in either the top or bottom layout, the dealer collects all bets made. Thus, the dealer pays for matches in either or both layouts and collects for no matches.

After the dealer and players settle all bets, the former turns the deck face down and gathers up and discards the four layout cards along with the port card. The dealer then forms two new layouts, as above, and again turns the deck face up to expose a new port card. Thus, the game proceeds until the deck is exhausted.

The Euchre Group

The Euchre group of card games has been closely associated with four different countries. In the United States, the game played is Euchre; in Ireland, Spoil Five; in England, Napoleon; and in France, Écarté. Enthusiasts in each country developed their own variations of the game.

The old Spanish game of *Triumphe*, mentioned in an early sixteenth-century manuscript, probably provided the origin of Euchre. The French modified Triumphe and renamed it French Ruff. With the passage of time and more modification, this game became Écarté, which was introduced by the French into the United States in Louisiana.

An interesting observation about these games is that the King outranks the Ace in both Écarté and some versions of Rams *(Ramsch)*, a German descendant of Euchre. In the older games, the King always headed each suit, and the Ace was the lowest card. It was only after political upheaval that the Ace became the highest-ranking card.

Another theory of Euchre's origin is that the game might have resulted from an effort to play the Irish game of Spoil Five with a Piquet deck. The word *Euchre* is of unknown origin, and it means, as does the word Spoil in Spoil Five, to stop or trick the maker of the trump from taking 3 tricks. An interesting note about this theory is that Spoil Five inherited its highest trump card, the trump 5, from the Irish game of Five Fingers, which, in turn, has its origins in an even older Irish card game called Maw, which was popular during the early 17th century. Since the Piquet deck had no 5, it is believed that the players used the second-ranking trump, the Jack, to head the trump suit, which is, of course, characteristic of Euchre.

Euchre

Euchre is a game for four persons (two against two as partners), three persons, or two persons, the last two being played as cutthroat. The game requires a deck of 32 cards (Ace, King, Queen, Jack, 10, 9, 8, 7), or 28 cards (Ace through 8), or 24 cards (Ace through 9). The Joker is sometimes optionally used.

Cards rank as follows: *in trump suit*— the right bower (Jack of trumps), the left bower (Jack of same color), and then trump Ace, King, Queen, 10, 9, 8, and 7; *in suit of same color*—Ace, King, Queen, 10, 9, 8, 7; *in suits of opposite color*—Ace, King, Queen, Jack, 10, 9, 8, and 7. If the Joker is used, it is the highest-ranking trump, outranking both bowers.

Beginning the Game: In the draw for deal, with Ace being low, low draws play as partners against the high draws. If the Joker is drawn, the player must draw again. After the shuffle and cut, the dealer gives each player five cards (either three and two or two and three), in rotation to the left. The dealer turns the next card face up to propose the trump suit. After each hand, the deal passes to the left.

The dealer must redeal if the deck is imperfect, if there is a card face up in the deck, if she gives the wrong number of cards to any player, if she turns more than one card for trump, or if she does not deal the same number of cards to each player in the same round.

Rank of Cards in Play in Euchre

If Hearts Are Trump

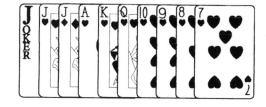

If Hearts Are Trump, Suit of Same Color

If Hearts Are Trump, Suits of Opposite Color

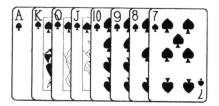

If the Joker is turned for trump, the dealer may, before looking at her hand, declare the suit that the Joker represents to be trump. The players, however, may select such a suit for trump before the game or hand gets under way.

Making the Trump: The player to the dealer's left may say, "I order it up," meaning that she accepts the card turned up and thus proposed as trump by the dealer, or she may pass. If the trump is ordered up, the dealer must immediately discard a card face down from her hand, though she does not take the trump card into her hand before it is her turn to play to the first trick.

If the player to the left of the dealer passes, the dealer's partner may order up the trump by saying, "I assist," or she may pass. If she passes, the next player in rotation has the same option. If all three pass, the dealer may take up the trump or pass. If the dealer passes, she puts face down the card turned as trump. If all four pass, each player in rotation to the left has one chance to name a suit trump, but not the one just rejected, or again pass. The first suit named becomes trump. If all four players pass a second time, the deal is void and passes to the left.

After the trump is taken up, any player may ask the trump maker to name the trump suit, but no one can demand to know its denomination. If the trump is the same color as the face-down proposed trump, this is called *making it next;* if it is the other color, it is called *crossing the suit.*

The person who orders up, takes up, or names the trump may play alone against both opponents. In this case, her partner lays her cards face down on the table and takes no part in the play, but she does share in her partner's victory or defeat. One partner cannot object to the other's going it alone, but the latter must announce her decision to do so when she declares the trump suit. Formerly, a dealer whose partner had assisted was allowed to go it alone; this practice is still observed in some localities.

The Goal: The goal of the trump maker and her partner is to take at least 3 of a possible 5 tricks. The goal of the opponents is to *euchre,* or stop, the trump maker from taking 3 tricks.

The Play: The person to the dealer's left or to the left of the player "going it alone," whatever the case might be, leads any card, and each player in succession plays a card in the same suit, if possible. If not possible, she must either play a trump or discard. It is not necessary to take the trick. If the trick is trumped, the highest trump wins. The winner of each trick leads to the next trick. The winner of each trick must gather it up and quit it, that is, turn it face down. Once quitted, no player may examine the trick until the end of the hand. After 5 tricks have been quitted and tallied for score, the deal passes to the left.

Scoring: If the trump maker and her partner take 3 tricks, they win the hand and the game. If they do not take 3 tricks, they are euchred and they lose the game.

Many Euchre enthusiasts prefer playing a longer game to a score of 5, 7, or 10 points, as agreed to at the beginning of the session. In these games, if the trump maker and her partner take 3 or 4 out of 5 tricks, they score 1 point toward game. If they win all 5 tricks for a *march,* they score 2 points. If the trump maker "goes it alone," she gets 4 points for a march. If the trump maker and her partner fail to get 3 tricks, they are euchred and their opponents score 2 points. Euchre players can use a long-game-scoring procedure with the one-hand, ten-minute game for wagering purposes. In the latter procedure, a scorekeeper keeps a cumulative score until the game ends.

Remedies and Penalties: If a person mistakenly "orders up" or "assists," her side must accept the burden of declaration. If a player names for trump the suit of the rejected proposed trump, her side may not make the trump for that deal.

If a player leads out of turn and everyone plays to the lead, that lead is regarded as valid, and the game continues. However, if the mistake is caught before everyone plays to the erroneous lead, any player may demand that the lead be retracted, left face up on the table, and played at the first legal opportunity. The persons who played to the erroneous lead may restore their cards to their hands without penalty. The opponent who will play last in the next lead of the offending side has the right to name the suit to be led.

If a revoke is made but caught before the trick is quitted, the player may substitute a card. However, if the revoke is not caught until after the trick is quitted, or if the offender or her partner accidently or purposely mixes the cards, the players abandon their hands, and the nonoffenders score 2 points. If the revoke is made against a lone hand, the lone player scores 4 points.

Laps

In this variation of Euchre, partners playing the ten-minute game may use any points scored beyond those needed to win a game for wagering purposes. In the 5-, 7-, or 10-point game, each side may carry over to the next game any points scored beyond those needed to win a game.

Slams

Slams is another variation of Euchre. In the ten-minute game, if the trump maker plays a lone hand and takes 5 tricks for a march, she is credited with winning two games. In the 5-, 7-, or 10-minute game, the side that scores 5 points before the opposition can score is credited with winning two games.

Jambone

Jambone, a lone-hand variation, requires the lone hand to lay her cards down face up on the table and to play them. The player to her left my "call up," or name, the first card to be led by the lone player. (Among some Jambone enthusiasts, the players may take turns calling out all the cards from the Jambone hand.) If the Jambone hand wins 5 tricks in the ten-minute game, she is credited with winning two games and scores 8 points for wagering purposes. If not, regular Euchre scoring proceeds.

Jamboree

This variation of Euchre awards 16 points to the maker of the trump if she holds the five highest trumps. She automatically wins the game without having to play a card. The dealer can get credit for a Jamboree by using the turned-up, or proposed, trump card, if needed.

Cutthroat, or Three-Hand Euchre

When three persons play, two persons play in temporary partnership against the maker of the trump. Scoring is the same as in basic Euchre, but if the temporary partners euchre the maker of the trump, they each score 2 points.

Two-Hand Euchre

When two persons play, they strip the 7s and 8s from the deck. All rules applying to the basic four-hand game of Euchre apply to its two-hand variation.

Six-Hand Euchre

When six persons participate, three play against three, and the partners sit alternately around the table. If a lone hand prevails against three opponents, he scores game. Otherwise, scoring remains the same.

Railroad Euchre

Railroad Euchre, a four-hand variation, differs from the basic game of Euchre as follows:

1. The players use the Joker, which ranks above the right bower. They also mutually select a trump suit in advance in case the Joker is turned up as the proposed trump.

2. The player going it alone may, optionally, discard one card and call for her partner's best card. The partner responds and then lays her hand face down on the table during the play. Conversely, if the dealer's partner decides to go it alone, the dealer may give her partner a card from her hand or the turned-up trump, whichever she deems better.

3. Either opponent may also call for her partner's best card to go it alone against the first lone hand. Euchre of a lone hand by two opponents scores 2 points; euchre of one lone hand by another lone hand scores 4 points. Otherwise, the scoring remains the same.

4. Euchre enthusiasts often combine Laps, Slams, Jambone, and/or Jamboree with Railroad Euchre to form variations in the game.

Buck Euchre

Buck Euchre requires four players to use a 24-card deck, plus the Joker; five players, a 28-card deck, plus the Joker; six players, a 32-card deck, plus the Joker. Apart from these basic requirements, Buck Euchre differs from regular Euchre as follows:

1. Each person plays by and for himself in cutthroat fashion.

2. Before the deal, each player puts 1 chip in the pool, as agreed to at the start of the game.

3. The person ordering up or otherwise making the trump must take 3 tricks or put 1 chip in the pool for each trick he fails to take. Each trick taken is worth 1 chip. If a player takes all 5 tricks, he wins the entire pool.

Call-Ace Euchre

The rules governing the number of players, the kind of deck used, and the deal are the same in Call-Ace Euchre as in Buck Euchre. The differences between the two games are as follow:

1. The Joker is not used.

2. The dealer turns up the trump, leaving three unknown cards in the four-hand game, two in the five-hand game, and one in the six-hand game.

3. The player who orders up or names the trump may call out the best card of any suit, except trumps, and the holder of that card becomes her partner. The partner, however, remains unknown until she plays the card called out. Since all cards are not in play, the best card might be a King, Queen, or Jack. It might be that the trump caller is holding that card herslf, in which case she would not have a partner. The trump caller also might say, "Alone," or call on a suit of which she holds the Ace.

4. If the trump caller and her partner take 3 tricks, they win the hand and the game in a ten-minute game.

If the 5-, 7-, or 10-point game is being played, they each score 1 point; for a march, or 5 tricks, they each score 3 points. If they are euchred, each opponent scores 2 points. A lone hand scores 1 point for 3 tricks. For a march, the lone player scores 1 point for each person playing, including herself, in the game.

SECTION 3
Solitaire Games

A Word About Solitaire Games

What makes the games in this section some of the world's best?

First, every one of them has something about it that is intriguing and challenging—something that makes it especially enjoyable to play.

• You'll find simple counting games that are just right for when you don't want to be overtaxed.

• You'll find complex games that call on every bit of your concentration.

• You'll find games that are irresistible because they have such a great look to them.

• And many are so mesmerizing and compelling that once you start playing them, you can't stop.

Second, all the games are practical. You won't find layouts that you'd have to play on the floor or that require your handling three or four decks of cards.

Third, the ratio between the number of cards you need to lay out and the amount of play in the game is usually a comfortable one. You don't have to lay out two packs of cards only to discover that the game is lost before you even get to make a move! Most of those infuriating games have been eliminated, unless they have a particular fascination of their own—and then you're warned in advance.

All the games in this section are worth trying out—and fun to play. We hope you like them as much as we do, and find a few that become your new favorites.

—Sheila Anne Barry

Before You Begin

We've grouped the one-pack and two-pack solitaire games separately, on the supposition that you probably have only one pack at hand most of the time.

The descriptions at the top of each game will let you know vital information right away—which games are possible to play in a very small area, for example.

They will also tell you which games are easy to win and which are almost impossible—so you know what you're up against.

We've tried to eliminate words that you have to go back and look up, like "reserve" and "tableaux" so you can whip through the instructions and start to play right away.

There are, however, a few terms you need to be familiar with:

Suit—There are four of them: Hearts, Diamonds, Clubs, and Spades.

Suite—A full set of thirteen cards of one suit: Ace to King of Clubs, for example.

To build—To place one card on another to create a sequence—whatever kind is called for. Usually the sequence just goes up or down—the Queen, for example, is placed on the King if the sequence is down, on the Jack if it's up.

Building upward in suit means laying down cards from low to high—from the Ace (or wherever you have to start from)—to the King (or wherever you have to end at)—in one single suit: from the Ace to the King of Hearts, for example.

Building downward in suit means laying down cards from high to low—from the King of Hearts through the ranks to the Ace, for example.

Rank—The card's number. A 10 of Diamonds "ranks" higher than a 9 of Diamonds.

Foundations—The cards that score—the ones you build on. They are usually put up above the layout, as in the most popular solitaire games, *Klondike* and *Canfield*. But sometimes they are place differently—or not placed at all.

The stockpile—The cards that are left in your hand after you have completed the layout.

The wastepile—The collection of discarded cards.

A column—Cards that go vertically in a line.

A row—Cards that go horizontally in a line

Deuces—2s.

Games are arranged alphabetically, but when talking about a prototype game, we've placed the best variations next to it, so that you don't have to leaf back to find the rules for the original game.

Every layout is shown in the book, except when the variations follow a prototype game—or when there's no layout at all, as in *Hit or Miss.*

Solitaire is really the ultimate game—one in which it is very clear that you are competing only against yourself and the run of the cards (sort of like Life?). Win or not, we hope you enjoy playing the games!

One-Pack
GAMES

Accordion

Other Names: Idle Year, Tower of Babel, Methuselah

Space: Small/Moderate.

Level: Difficult.

Play: Start by dealing the cards one at a time face up in a row of four from left to right. Go slowly so that you can keep comparing the cards you deal with their neighbors. Whenever a card matches the card on its left—or third to the left—you move the new card over onto the one it matches. The match may be in suit or rank.

Let's say that the first four cards you turn up are:

The 8 of Spades matches the 8 of Clubs (on its left) and also the 5 of Spades (third to the left). You could move it onto either one. Which one will turn out better? You really can't tell at this point.

Once you move a card over, though, the card on the bottom doesn't have any more significance. The card on top is the one to match.

As soon as you move a card—or a pile—move the later cards over to close up the sequence. That will open up new moves for you, too.

Go on dealing cards, one at a time, stopping after each one to make whatever moves are possible, until you've used up all the cards.

For example, suppose that you deal:

You can move the 2 of Clubs onto the 2 of Hearts. Then close up the row. The 5 of Clubs moves next to the 2s. It's a Club and that's a match! But once you move the 5 over onto the 2 of Clubs, another move opens up: You can move the entire pile over onto the 5 of Spades, which is the third card to the left. So the cards look like this:

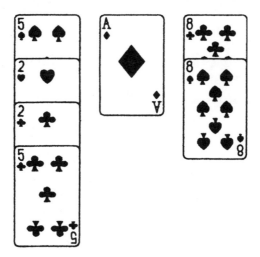

To Win the Game: Get the whole pack into one pile. It's almost impossible. If you end up with five piles, you're doing pretty well.

Aces Up

Other Names: Idiot's Delight, Firing Squad

Space: Smali.

Level: Moderate.

Layout: Deal four cards in a row.

Play: If you have two cards of the same suit, discard the one that is lower in rank. Aces are high.

For example, here you have:

Discard the 5 of Hearts.

When you've made all the moves you can, fill the empty space in the row with any top card from the layout. In this case, where there is only one layer of cards as yet, fill the space from the cards in your hand. Then deal four more cards overlapping the one's you've already set up.

Go through the same process of discarding the lower card of the same suit from the new layer of cards.

And so on until you've gone through the whole pack.

To Win the Game: Discard all the cards—except the Aces, of course.

Auld Lang Syne

Other Name: Patience

Space: Small.

Level: Very Difficult.

Layout: Deal out all four Aces in a row. Underneath each one, deal a card. These cards are the stock from which you are going to build.

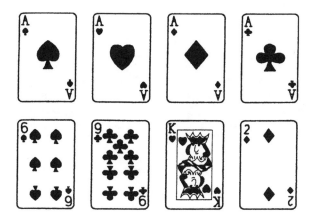

To Win the Game: Build the Aces up to Kings, regardless of suit.

Play: When you've finished the moves you can make with the first set of four cards, deal another row of four right on top of them. Keep going until the stock is exhausted.

Tam O'Shanter

Level: Almost Impossible

Play: Play in exactly the same way as *Auld Lang Syne*, except don't put the Aces up first. Just wait until they show up in the deal.

147

Baker's Dozen

Space: Wide.

Level: Easy.

Layout: Deal 13 columns of four overlapping cards. Aces will go into a foundation row above the layout.

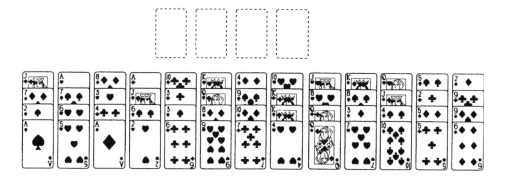

After you lay out the cards, check on the Kings. If a King is in an exposed position, move it underneath the other cards in the column. If a King is lying on another card of the same suit, place it underneath that card.

To Win the Game: Release Aces and build them up to Kings in suit.

Play: Build downward on the cards in the layout, one card at a time, regardless of color or suit. Do not fill any spaces.

Perseverance

Space: Wide.

Level: Moderate.

Play: Play exactly the same way as *Baker's Dozen*, except:
   1. Set Aces in foundation piles from the start.

2. Lay out twelve columns of four overlapping cards each.

3. If a group of cards is in suit and in sequence, starting at the top, you can move the entire sequence as a unit.

4. On the layout, build down in suit only.

5. You have two **redeals**. Gather up the piles in the reverse order of the way you put them down, and then deal them back into twelve columns, as far as they go.

Good Measure

Space: Wide.

Play: Play exactly the same way as *Baker's Dozen*, except:
1. Deal ten columns of five overlapping cards.
2. Start with two Aces in the foundation row.

Baroness

Other Names: Thirteen, Five Piles

Space: Moderate.

Level: Easy/Moderate.

Layout: Deal a row of five cards.

Play: Remove any Kings or any pair of cards that add up to 13. That includes not only:

3 and 10	5 and 8
4 and 9	6 and 7
but also: Ace and Queen and	2 and Jack.

Discard those cards. Then deal the next row of five, on top of the first one, and go through the same process. Only the top cards are available for pairing and discarding.

Deal on, until the pack has been exhausted. The two cards left over at the end can be made into a separate pile. They are also available to be paired and discarded.

To Win the Game: Discard all the cards in pairs that add up to 13.

Redeals: None.

Beleaguered Castle

Other Names: **Laying Siege, Sham Battle**

Space: **Large.**

Level: **Easy.**

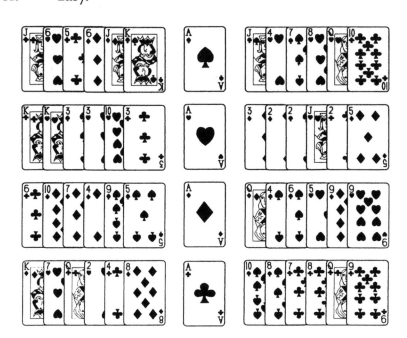

150

Layout: Lay out the cards in two large wings, each made up of four rows of six overlapping cards. In the middle, place a column of Aces—the foundations.

There is a traditional way to lay out the cards: Start with the Aces in a column in the middle. Then deal out a column of four cards along the left-hand side and a column of four cards at the right-hand side. Then alternate in dealing columns, left and right, until the pack is all laid down.

To Win the Game: Build the Aces up to Kings in suit.

Play: The only cards that may be moved onto the foundations are the completely exposed ones on the ends of the wings. The cards on the ends can also be moved onto each other, regardless of suit, going downward in rank. For instance, in the illustration, the 9 of Hearts could go on the 10 of Spades, but not on the 8 of Diamonds.

Should any row in the wing become empty, you can fill it with any exposed card.

Street and Alleys

Play exactly the same way as *Beleaguered Castle*, except:

1. Do not set up the Aces ahead of time—mix them in with the pack.

2. Deal seven cards to the two top rows of the wings on each side.

Citadel

Play exactly the same way as *Beleaguered Castle*, except:

1. Do not set up the Aces ahead of time—mix them in with the pack.

2. During the process of dealing, you may play any cards to the foundations that they are ready to receive. Once an Ace is in place, for example, you may fill in with deuces, and if deuces are there, you could even build 3s or higher.

When a card is placed on a foundation during the dealing, do not replace it in the layout; just leave its space empty.

3. When dealing, once a card is laid down on the wings, it cannot be moved until the dealing is over.

Betrothal

Other Names: Royal Marriage, Coquette, Matrimony

Space: Large.

Level: Easy.

To Win the Game: Get the Queen of Hearts next to the King of Hearts. And while you try to do this, you eliminate some of the spoilsports who come between other "like" couples.

Layout: Start with the Queen of Hearts at your left. Put the King of Hearts at the bottom of the deck. Deal the cards in a row, one by one, next to the Queen, until the whole pack is out on the table.

Play: While you deal, however, you can throw out certain cards—any one or two cards that get between two cards of the same rank or suit.

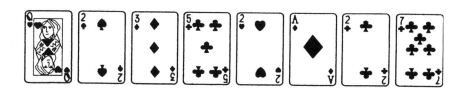

For example, in the illustration above, you can remove the 3 of Diamonds and the 5 of Clubs, because they are between two cards of the same rank, the 2s. You can also remove the Ace of Diamonds because it also lies between two cards of the same rank (2s again).

152

Betsy Ross

Other Names: Musical, Fairest, Quadruple Alliance
Plus Belle, Four Kings

Space: Small.

Level: Moderate.

Layout: Lay out on the table any Ace, 2, 3, and 4. Directly under them lay out any 2, 4, 6, and 8. The four cards on the bottom are foundations. You'll be building on them, but in an odd sort of way.

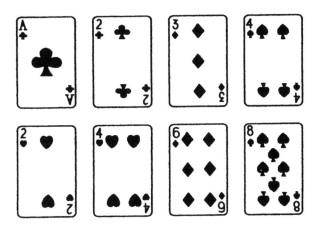

Play: The only purpose of the top row is to remind you of the key numbers you have to build by.

On the 2 you'll build the standard way—by 1s:
2 3 4 5 6 7 8 9 10 J Q K
On the 4 you'll build by 2s:
4 6 8 10 Q A 3 5 7 9 J K
On the 6 you'll build by 3s:
6 9 Q 2 5 8 J A 4 7 10 K
On the 8 you'll build by 4s:
8 Q 3 7 J 2 6 10 A 5 9 K

To Win the Game: Build all the cards into groups of 13 on the foundations.

Redeals: Two.

Bisley

Space: Very wide.

Level: Moderate.

Layout: Remove the Aces from the pack and deal them onto the table as the first four cards in a row of 13. The next nine cards in the pack are then dealt next to them but lower down.

Create three more rows of 13 until all the cards are laid out.

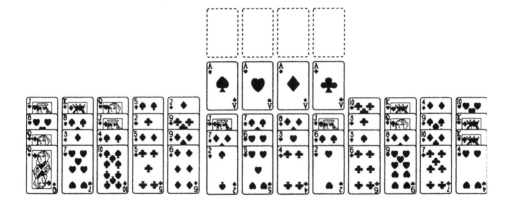

To Win the Game: Build Aces up to Kings in suit and Kings down to Aces.

Play: As they become available, remove the Kings and place them above the Aces. Build on the cards in the layout, upward or downward in suit, playing any cards that you can to the foundations.

Calculation

Other Names: Broken Intervals, The Fairest

Space: Small.

Level: Easy.

Layout: Remove any Ace, 2, 3, and 4 from the pack and set them up in a row. They are your foundations.

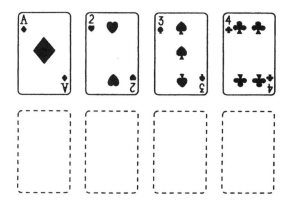

To Win the Game: Build up all the foundations to Kings, each in a different way.

Play: The first card, the Ace, will be built by 1s—the same way you've been building Aces straight along—
            1 2 3 4 5 6 7 8 9 10 J Q K

The second card—the 2—will be built by 2s—
            2 4 6 8 10 Q A 3 5 7 9 J K

The third card—the 3—will be built by 3s—
            3 6 9 Q 2 5 8 J A 4 7 10 K

The fourth card—the 4—will be built by 4s—
            4 8 Q 3 7 J 2 6 10 A 5 9 K

Start by turning over one card at a time, which you can build, regardless of suit, on any foundation that is ready for it. If the card cannot be used on any pile, put it in one of four possible wastepiles underneath the foundations. The top cards of the wastepiles are available to play onto the foundations. The strategy you use to decide where to place an unusable card is crucial. It's okay to keep the cards spread out so you can see what your choices are at any moment.

Canfield

Other Names: Fascination, Thirteen, Demon

Space: Small.

Level: Difficult.

Canfield is one of the most popular solitaire games in the world. A shorter, faster game than *Klondike*, Canfield is played much the same way, but it starts from a different basic layout.

Canfield came by its name in an interesting way. Mr. Canfield owned a gambling house in Saratoga Springs in the 1890s. He used to sell his customers packs of cards at $50 each and then pay them back $5 for every card they were able to score. Estimates are that the average number of cards you could expect to score in a game was five or six, so Mr. Canfield did pretty well.

Layout: Count out 13 cards into one pile and put it in front of you face up and a little to your left. Then put a 14th card to the right of the pile and slightly above it; whatever that card is, it becomes the foundation card of this particular deal. As the other cards of the same rank appear, you'll be placing them too in the foundation row.

To Win the Game: Build the foundation cards into four complete suits of 13 cards each.

Next, you lay out a row of four cards below the foundation card, face up:

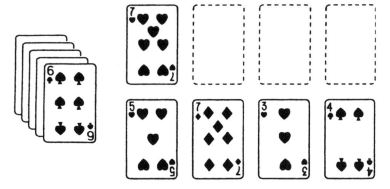

No cards are ever built on the 13-pile. The object is to unload it. For example, in the illustration above, you couldn't put a 5—or any other card—on the 6. Cards from the 13-pile can be played only onto the foundations or into the four-card row when a space opens up.

Play: First check the four-card spread carefully to see whether you can make any moves. Besides playing cards to the foundations, you can build cards onto the four-card spread downward in alternating colors.

For instance, in the illustration above, the 3 of Hearts can go onto the 4 of Spades; the 7 of Diamonds can go up into the foundation row; and the 6 of Spades can come down into the row of four. Once it does, the 5 of Hearts can be played onto it.

You are permitted to move sequences of cards as one unit. For example, the 3 and 4 may be moved together onto the 5 and 6, so your layout would look like this:

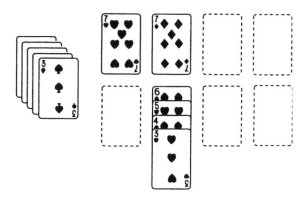

157

Then you can proceed to fill the other open spaces in the four-card row with cards from the 13-pile.

Now start turning up cards from the pack, in batches of three, playing them either to the foundations, to the four-card row or to the wastepile. The top card of the wastepile is always available for play.

As spaces open up in the four-card row, continue to fill them with cards from the 13-card pile. When these are exhausted, you can fill them with cards from your hand or from the wastepile.

Redeal: As many times as you want, or until the game is blocked.

Selective Canfield

Play exactly the same way as *Canfield*, except deal a five-card row instead of four. Choose your foundation yourself from one of these cards.

Rainbow

Play exactly the same way as *Canfield*, except go through the pack one card at a time. You are allowed two **redeals** in some versions of the game—none in others!

Storehouse

Other Names: Provisions, Thirteen Up, Reserve

Space: Small.

Level: Easy.

Play: Play exactly the same way as *Canfield*, except:
    1. Remove the four deuces from the pack and set them up as the foundations.
    2. Build them up in suit to Aces.

Superior Demon

Level: Moderate.

Play: Play exactly the same way as *Canfield*, except:
    1. Spread the 13-card pile so that you can see it and take it into account as you play.
    2. You don't have to fill a space in the layout until you want.
    3. You can shift any part of a sequence to another position—you don't have to move the entire sequence.

Chameleon

Play in exactly the same way as *Canfield*, except:
1. Count out only 12 cards instead of 13 for the 13-card pile.
2. Deal only three cards to the four-card row.
3 The layout looks slightly different, like this:

The Clock

Other Names: Hidden Cards, Four of a Kind, Travellers
                   Sundial, All Fours, Hunt

Space: Moderate.

Level: Difficult.

Layout: Deal the pack into 13 face-down piles of four cards each. Arrange 12 of them in a circle, representing the numbers on a clock dial. Put the 13th pile in the middle of the circle.

It should look like this:

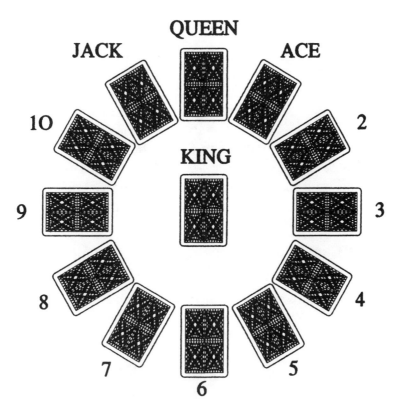

Play: Start by picking up the top card of the middle pile. Suppose it's a 5. Slip it, face up, under the pile of cards that are in the 5 o'clock position. Then pick up the top card of the 5 o'clock pile. Suppose it's a Jack. It would go under the 11 o'clock pile (remember, the King pile is in the middle of the clock—and the Queen is at 12). And you would pick up the top card of the 11 o'clock pile and slip it under whatever pile it belongs in.

When you slip the fourth card of any group into place—and there is no face-down card to turn over—turn over the top card of the next highest card pile.

To Win the Game: Get all the cards turned face up before the fourth King is turned face up.

Double or Quits

Space: Small.

Level: Easy.

Tricky building—and on only one foundation!

Layout: Deal seven cards in a sort of frame shape, as shown below. Then place a card inside the frame. That card is the foundation, and you can build on it from the frame or from the stockpile. If any of the cards in the layout turn out to be Kings, put them on the bottom of the deck and replace them with other cards.

To Win the Game: Build all the cards onto the foundation—except for Kings—doubling the value of the card that has just been placed.

Play: For example, let's say the layout looks like this:

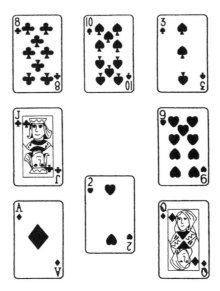

The card you've got to build on is a deuce, so you deal out the cards, one by one, until you come to a 4 of any suit—and place that on the deuce. The cards that you go through before you come to the 4 go on the wastepile.

The next card you need to find is double 4—or an 8. There is one in the frame, so you can use that right away. Spaces in the frame are filled with the top card of the wastepile or, if there is no wastepile, from your hand.

Double 8 is 16. So deduct 13 (the number of cards in a suit) and you get 3: This is the card you need to find next.

So—a sequence goes like this:

2 4 8 3 6 Queen (12) Jack (11) 9 5 10 7 Ace 2

and the sequence repeats.

Redeals: Two

Duchess

Other Name: Glenwood

Space: Small.

Level: Moderate.

Layout: Lay out four fans of three cards each at the top of the table. Leave a space for the foundations, and then deal out a row of four cards.

To Win the Game: Build the four foundation cards into full 13-card suites.

Play: Choose any one of the exposed cards in the fans to be your foundation. For example, in the illustration above, it might make sense to choose the 3 of Diamonds as your foundation, because the 3 of Spades is available to build onto the foundation and so is the 4 of Diamonds.

After you make all possible moves to the foundations, you can start building downward on the row of cards, in alternating colors. You are allowed to move all the cards of one pile onto another pile as a unit, when the cards are in the correct sequence (down by suit).

Go through the stockpile of cards, one by one, building to the foundations or the layout or discarding the unplayable cards to the wastepile.

When spaces open up in the row, fill them from the fans—and when no fans are left, from the wastepile.

Redeals: One.

Eagle Wing

Other Names: Thirteen Down, Wings

Space: Moderate.

Level: Difficult.

Layout: Deal 13 cards and place them face down in a pile in the middle of the table. This pile is known as "the trunk." Then lay out four cards, face up, on one side of the pile, and four cards face up on the other. These are the "wings" of the eagle.

Deal out one more card and place it directly above the pile, so that your layout looks like this:

That last card is a foundation pile. As other 8s appear, they go up in a row alongside it and you build on them as well.

To Win the Game: Build the foundations up to full 13-card suites.

Play: Go through the cards, one by one. If you cannot play a card onto one of the foundation piles, put it in a wastepile. The top of the wastepile is always available for play.

You can also build with the cards in the wings. When a space opens up in the wings, fill it right away with a card from the trunk. The bottom card in the trunk—if you get that far—may be played directly to the foundation without waiting for a place in the wings.

In the building, Aces follow Kings.

Redeals: You are allowed two (three times through the cards).

Fortress

Other Name: Fort

Space: Large.

Level: Difficult.

Layout: Deal out five columns of five cards each on both sides of the playing space. Lay out the entire deck, face up, adding an extra card to the top rows.

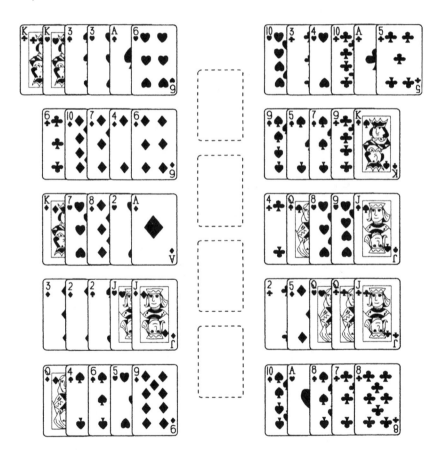

Foundations—Aces, as they become available—are placed in the middle column, as in the illustration.

To Win the Game: Build up the Aces in suit to Kings.

Play: After playing whatever cards you can to the foundations, you can start building in suit on the exposed cards in the layout, one card at a time. You can build up or down on the layout, but not both ways in the same row.

Chessboard

Other Name: Fives

Play: Play in exactly the same way as *Fortress*, except instead of putting Aces in the foundation column, choose whatever card you want after dealing out the layout.

Fourteens

Other Names: Fourteen Puzzle, Fourteen Out, Take Fourteen

Space: Large.

Level: Easy.

Layout: Deal the cards, face up, in 12 columns of four cards each. You'll have four cards left over. Just put them on the first four columns. Arrange the cards so that you can see them all.

Play: Remove pairs of available cards whose totals add up to 14. There will be, of course:

Ace and King	4 and 10
2 and Queen	5 and 9
3 and Jack	6 and 8

Available cards are the ones that are exposed at the bottoms of the columns.

To Win the Game: You win when all the cards have been discarded.

Gaps

Other Name: Spaces

Space: Large.

Level: Difficult.

Layout: Deal all the cards in the pack—in four rows of 13 cards, each face up.

Then remove the Aces. This leaves gaps in the layout. These gaps must be filled by the card that is next higher in rank to the card on the left—and in the same suit. For example, suppose the gap opens up to the right of a 3 of Hearts. It must be filled by a 4 of Hearts.

If the gap opens up in the first space at the left of a row, it may be filled with any deuce.

If the gap opens up after a King, it cannot be filled. Action is blocked. When a King blocks the action in every row, the deal is over.

To Win the Game: Get each row into a sequence of cards from 2 to King, by suit.

Redeals: As many as you want. You need to gather up the cards in a special way for the redeal. Leave in place the deuces that appear at the left end of a row and any cards that follow it in the correct sequence and suit. For example:

Leave these   but not these

Then, gather up all the not-in-place cards, shuffle them, and deal them out as follows:

1. Leave one gap to the right of each sequence.
2. If the only card in place is a 2, leave a gap to the right of it.
3. If there is no 2 in the row, leave a gap at the start of the row, so that a 2 can be moved in.

The Garden

Other Names: Flower Garden, Parterre, Bouquet

Space: Large.

Level: Easy.

Layout: Deal out six columns of six overlapping cards. This is "the garden."

Spread the remaining cards out in front of you. They are "the bouquet." The layout looks like this:

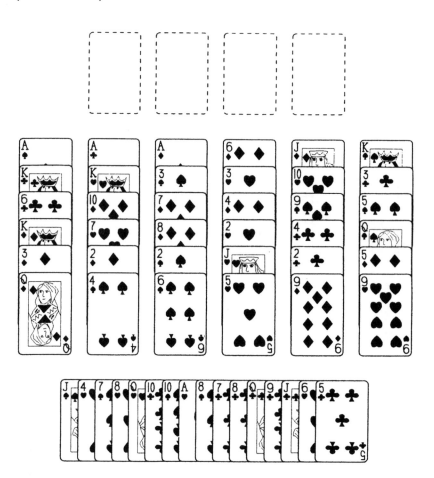

The cards spread out at the bottom are available to play onto the layout, building down one by one regardless of suit.

As the foundations—the Aces—become available, they are placed above the layout.

To Win the Game: Build the Aces up in suit to Kings.

Play: Start building on the exposed cards at the bottom of the columns, one card at a time, and to the foundations. If a complete column is cleared away, the space may be filled by any available card. Every card of the bouquet is available for building at all times.

Golf

Space: Moderate.

Level: Difficult.

Layout: Deal seven rows of five cards each, so that the layout looks like this:

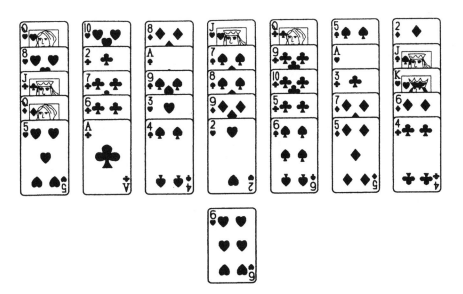

Deal one card below that will start the wastepile.

171

To Win the Game: Get rid of the entire layout by building up and down on the wastepile, regardless of suit.

Play: Only the exposed cards of the layout are available for building. In the example above, the 5 of Hearts can go on the wastepile; the 4 of Spades can go on that, opening the way for the 3 of Hearts. Then you can go in the other direction with the 4 of Clubs, and so on.

You can't build anything on a King. When you put a King on the wastepile, you've ended the sequence. Whenever you end a sequence—by putting down a King or not being able to make another move—you can take a card from the stockpile of 17 cards that never got into the layout. Place the card on the wastepile and resume play. If you use up all the cards in the deck, and still have cards in the layout, you've lost the game.

Grandfather's Clock

Space: Huge.

Level: Easy.

Layout: Remove the following cards from the deck and place them in a circle, as in the following illustration:

2 of Hearts	8 of Diamonds
3 of Spades	9 of Clubs
4 of Diamonds	10 of Hearts
5 of Clubs	Jack of Spades
6 of Hearts	Queen of Diamonds
7 of Spades	King of Clubs

These are the
foundations on
which you are going
to be building a
"real" clock face.

Place the remaining cards in eight columns of five cards each. Overlap
the cards so you can see them all.

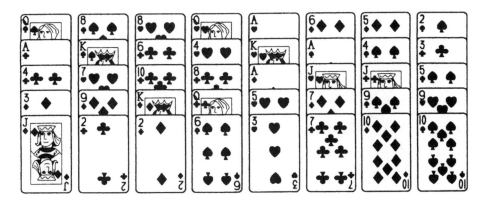

Play: Using the exposed cards in the layout, build the foundations—
the cards on the clock face—up in suit until the cards on the top correspond to the numbers on a real clock face (with Jack as 11 o'clock and
the Queen at 12).

In order to free the cards to do this, build on the cards in the layout—downward, regardless of suit.

Spaces may be filled by any available card.

To Win the Game: Get the clock to have the right number values on its face, as in the illustration below:

Hit or Miss

Other Names: Treize, Talkative, Roll Call, Harvest

Space: Small.

Level: Very Difficult.

Play: Go through the cards one by one, naming each one as you go. The first one would be "Ace," the second "Deuce," the eleventh "Jack," and so on.

When your name and the rank of the card are the same, it's a *hit*, and you get to discard the card.

You are allowed to go through the cards as many times as you want—or until you go through the entire pack twice without a hit.

To Win the Game: Discard every card in the deck.

King Albert

Other Name: Idiot's Delight

Space: Large.

Level: Easy.

Layout: Deal a row of nine cards face up. Then deal a row of eight cards face up on top of them, leaving the first card uncovered. Continue placing rows of cards, each one card less than the row before, leaving the first card uncovered.

You'll have seven cards left when you finish laying out the cards. These are "free" cards, which you can use any way you want—on the layout or the foundations.

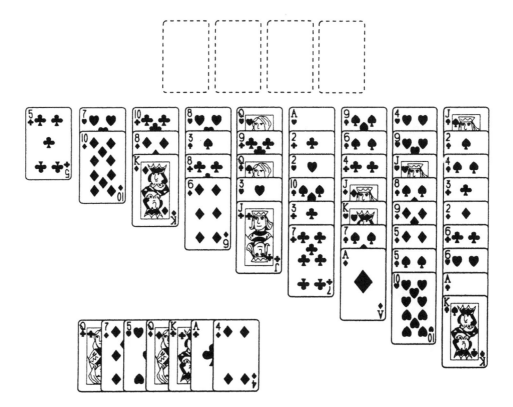

175

To Win the Game: Release the Aces and build them up to Kings in suit.

Play: Once the cards are laid out, play whatever you can to the foundations, which you set up above the layout. Then build on the layout itself—downward in alternating colors.

Only one card at a time may be built on the foundations or the layout.

A space may be filled by any available card.

Klondike

Other Names: Canfield, Fascination, Triangle, Small Triangle, Demon Patience

Space: Moderate.

Level: Difficult.

Layout: Lay out seven cards in a row—face down except for the first card. Then put the eighth card face up on the second card in the row, and complete the row with face-down cards. Place a face-up card on the third pile, and finish off the row in the same way. Continue until you have a face-up card on every pile. Your layout will look like this:

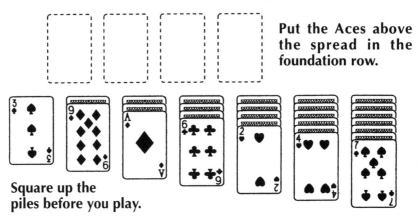

Put the Aces above the spread in the foundation row.

Square up the piles before you play.

Aces are low in this game.

To Win the Game: Build up complete suites from Ace to King.

Play: First, look over the spread carefully. Move any cards that you can to the foundation row—Aces and any cards you can build on them.

You can also build cards on the layout itself. Only the face-up cards are available for this building, and only if they are the exposed cards of the pile. Then you can build downward in alternating colors.

In the example, shown here, you can move the Ace to the foundation row, and then move the black 3 onto the red 4, and the red 2 onto the black 3.

Every time you move a face-up card, you need to turn up the face-down card beneath it. When there are no more face-down cards in a pile, you have a space. Spaces can be filled by any available King.

When you've made all the moves you can, start going through the stockpile one by one, looking for more cards to build onto the foundations and the layout. If you can't place the card, it goes face up onto a wastepile, and the top card of the wastepile is available for play.

Scoring: Five rounds make a game. Add up the number of foundation cards you've come up with in each round for your final score.

Klondike by Threes

This game is exactly the same as *Klondike,* but you go through the stockpile of cards by threes. Because of that, you get redeals. Rules vary about how many redeals you get. Some say two (three trips through the cards), and some say as many as you want.

Redeals: Two (or more).

Agnes

Space: Moderate.

Level: Moderate.

Play: Play exactly the same way as *Klondike*, except:

    1. When you finish the layout, deal the next card above it to make the first foundation. Aces, of course, need to be played between the Kings and 2s.

    2. Below the layout, deal a row of seven cards. These are available to be played onto the layout and the foundations. Play as many of them as you like, and when you have no more moves to make, deal another seven cards on top of them. You'll probably have spaces in that row of seven; be sure not to skip them when you deal the second row. After you deal a third layer of seven cards, you'll have two cards left in your hand. Turn them face up. They are available too.

    3. Spaces in the layout may be filled by any card that is one lower than the foundation card. For example, if the foundation card is a 2, the spaces can be filled only with Aces.

Whitehead

Level: Moderate/Difficult.

Play: Play exactly the same way as *Klondike*, except:

    1. Deal all the cards face up.

    2. Instead of building in alternate colors, build red on red, black on black.

    3. When spaces open up in the layout, fill them with any available card or group of cards.

    4. When moving piles of cards as a unit, you may do it only where the cards are in sequence by suit.

Thumb and Pouch

Level: Easy

Play: Play exactly the same way as *Klondike*, except:
   1. When building, a card can be laid on any card that is one rank higher regardless of color—except one of its own suit.
   2. A space may be filled by any available card or sequence of cards.

La Belle Lucie

Other Names: **The Fan, Clover Leaf, Alexander the Great Midnight Oil, Three Shuffles and a Draw, Fair Lucy**

Space: Large.

Level: Moderate.

This is one of the most delightful solitaire games.

Layout: Lay out the whole deck in sets of three, face up.

One single card will be left over, which becomes a set of its own.
   The only cards that may be moved are the exposed ones on top of the sets. They are built up on the foundations or on the top cards of other sets, by suit, building downward.

To Win the Game: Release the Aces and build them up in suit to Kings.

Play: Once you have the cards laid out, move the Aces that are available onto the foundations. In the example above, the Ace of Hearts is available for one of the foundations; so are the 2 and 3 of Hearts. Then proceed to build on the top cards of the fans, one card at a time. When a fan is entirely eliminated, it is not replaced.

Redeals: Two. To redeal, gather up the fans, shuffle the cards, and set down in groups of three as before. Any leftover cards are sets by themselves.

Special Bonus: In the last redeal, when you're stuck, you get one free move—one card you can pull from underneath one or two others and play in any way you want.

Super Flower Garden

Level: Easy.

Play: Play exactly the same way as *La Belle Lucie*, except building takes place regardless of suit.

Trefoil

Other Name: Les Fleurons

Play: Play exactly the same way as *La Belle Lucie*, except you put the Aces in a foundation row before laying out the fans. You'll then have 16 complete fans.

Shamrocks

Other Name: Three-Card Fan

Level: Easy.

Play: Play exactly the same way as *La Belle Lucie*, except:
   1. If a King is on the top of a set and a card of lower rank in the same suit lies under it, you can put the King under that card.
   2. No fan may contain more than three cards.

Little Spider

Space: Small.

Level: Moderate.

Layout: Lay out four cards face up in a row along the top of your playing space, and four cards in a row beneath them—leaving space for a row in between. That's where the foundations will go—two Aces of one color and two Kings of another—as they become available:

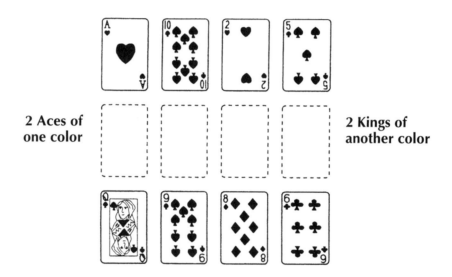

2 Aces of one color

2 Kings of another color

To Win the Game: Build the Aces in suit to Kings and the Kings in suit to Aces.

During the Deal: You can move any card from the top row onto the foundations. But you cannot move a card from the bottom row unless it can be moved straight up into place—into the position directly above its original position. For example, in the illustration on the left on page 183, the 2 of Hearts can go on the Ace of Hearts, but in the illustration on the right, it can't.

Play: When you've made all the moves you can to the foundations, deal another four cards to the top and bottom rows. Make your moves, and then deal again—until all the cards have been laid out.

At this point, the special rules that for "During the deal" no longer apply. You can move any card from the top or bottom rows onto the foundation piles. You can also build top cards from the layout onto each other regardless of suit or color—up or down.

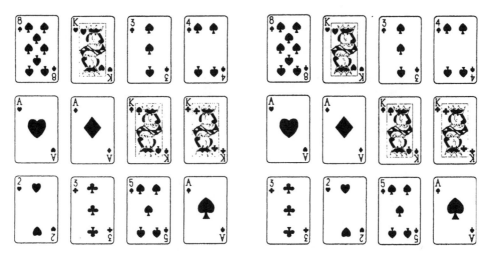

2 of Hearts can go straight up onto the Ace, because the Ace is the same suit.

2 of Hearts cannot go onto the Ace, because it is not directly under the Ace of Hearts.

Spaces in the layout may not be filled. Kings may be placed on Aces.

Monte Carlo

Other Name: Weddings

Space: Moderate.

Level: Moderate.

Layout: Deal five rows of five cards each, so your layout looks like the illustration on the next page.

To Win the Game: Discard the entire deck in pairs of the same rank. You can discard them if they are:

1. Next to each other
2. Above or below each other
3. "Touching" diagonally

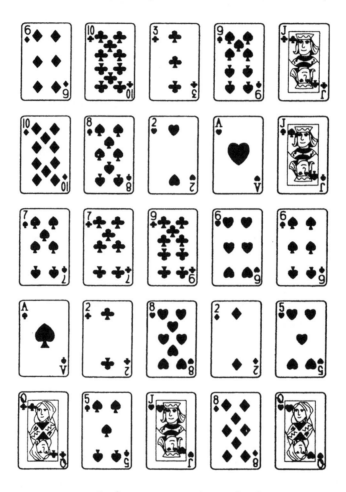

Play: Remove every pair that you can from the layout. When you do, there will be holes. Close up the cards so that all the holes are filled and the cards are in the same order in which you laid them out.

After you make the cards into solid rows again, deal new cards to make up the bottom rows, so that you have five rows of five cards again.

Remove the pairs again in the same way, and when you can't move any more cards, go through the process of closing up the spaces in the layout and filling in at the end with cards from your hand.

Nestor

Other Name: Matrimony

Space: Moderate.

Level: Moderate.

Layout: Deal eight cards face up in a row. Then deal another five rows overlapping them, so that you can see all the rows at one time.

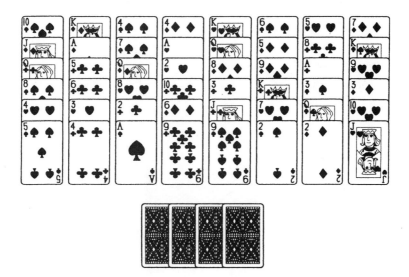

As you deal, make sure you don't have any cards of the same rank in a column. If you're about to deal a deuce onto a column where a deuce already appears, slip the card underneath the pack and deal another card instead.

You'll have four cards left over when you finish dealing. They are the stock.

Play: Remove cards of the same rank by twos from the exposed cards at the ends of the columns. When you can't make any more moves, turn up the first card of the stockpile. If that won't help you, turn up the next, and the next.

To Win the Game: Discard the whole layout by twos.

Osmosis

Other Name: Treasure Trove

Space: Small.

Level: Moderaste.

Layout: Deal four sets of four cards each face down. Then square them off face up and put them in a column at the left side of your playing space. Place the next card in the deck (which becomes the first foundation) to the right of the top card.

Place additional foundation cards (other cards of the same rank), as they become available, in a column under the first.

To Win the Game: Build each foundation card to a full 13 cards in suit but regardless of sequence.

Special Building Rule: No card may be placed in the second, third, or fourth foundation rows unless a card of the same rank has already been placed on the previous foundation card.

Play: Let's see how this works. In the illustration the foundation card is the 5 of Hearts. The first thing to do is to build any other Hearts that are already showing on the table—such as the 10 and the King—and put them alongside the 5, overlapping, so you can see what cards have been played to this foundation.

Then start going through the cards in the stockpile, three at a time, to find additional Hearts and more foundation cards for the other suits.

Let's say you turn up a 5 of Clubs. You place it below the 5 of Hearts.

The next card you turn up is a Queen of Clubs. You cannot place it—because the only cards that have been placed in the Hearts row are the King and the 10. So those are the only Clubs you could put down beside the 5 of Clubs.

The next card you get is the 5 of Diamonds, and you place it under the 5 of Clubs.

And then you get a 10 of Diamonds. You cannot place it next to the 5 of Diamonds—even though there is a 10 of Hearts out on the table, because the 10 of Clubs has not yet been placed.

Redeals: You get to go through the cards until you win the game—or until the game is blocked.

Peek

Play: Play exactly the same way as *Osmosis*, except with the face-down cards turned up and spread so that you can see them all.

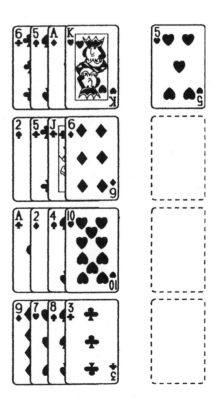

Poker Solitaire

Other Name: Poker Squares

Space: Moderate.

Level: Moderate.

Layout: Deal 25 cards in five rows of five cards each. Each row and each column is a poker hand; so, in any game, you have ten hands with which to build your total score.

To Win the Game: Come up with the highest score.

Play: Rearrange the cards in the layout so that you have the highest-scoring poker hand possible. In some versions of this game, after you move a card once, you cannot move it again.

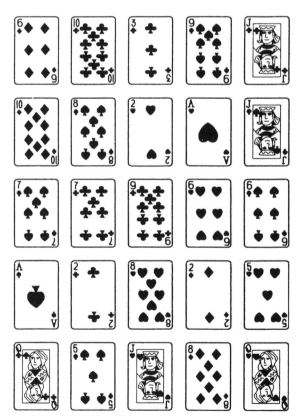

SCORING	American	English
  Royal Flush: Five of the same suit in sequence starting with an Ace	100	30
  Straight Flush: In sequence, five of the same suit	75	30
  Four of a Kind: Four of the same rank	50	16
  Full House: Three of a kind plus two of a kind	25	10
  Flush: Five of the same suit, but not in sequence	20	5

189

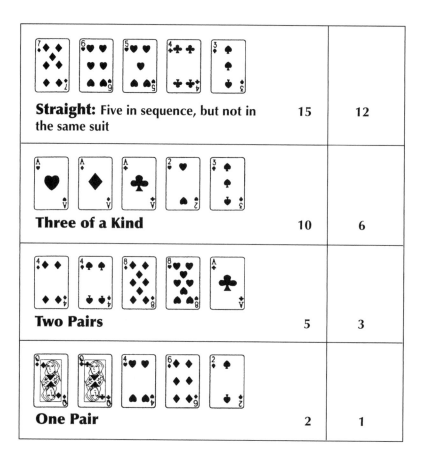

Straight: Five in sequence, but not in the same suit	15	12
Three of a Kind	10	6
Two Pairs	5	3
One Pair	2	1

Pyramid

Other Name: Pile of 28

Space: Moderate.

Level: Difficult.

A sad thing about many solitaire games is that you play a round—or five rounds—and then it's over. You have no special feeling of victory (unless you've played out and won) and no standard with which to compare your score.

    Here's a game that keeps you counting and scoring all the time. You can play it against yourself, against another player, or against "par."

Layout: Lay out the cards in the shape of a pyramid, starting with one card at the top and placing two cards that overlap it, then three overlapping them, and so on, until you have a large triangle with seven cards at its base. Each card has its own numerical value (face value); Kings count as 13, Queens as 12, and Jacks as 11.

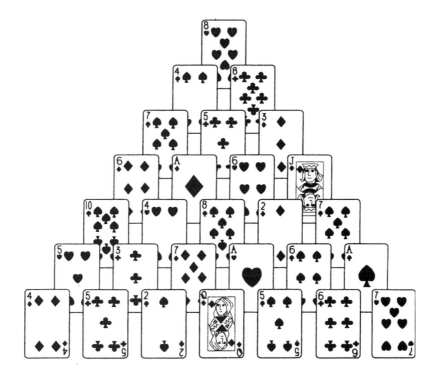

Play: Your job is to remove pairs of cards that add up to 13, with this catch: You cannot remove a card unless it is "exposed"—not covered by any other card.

For example, in the pyramid above, you can remove the 7 and the 6 from the bottom row. This opens up the Ace in the row above, which you can remove with the Queen (worth 12) in the bottom row.

You can remove Kings alone, because they add up to 13 without any help.

Place all the cards you remove in a special "Removed" pile, face up. The top card in this pile can be used again to form another 13-match.

Now you start dealing out the rest of the pack, one by one. If the card you turn up does not form a match with an available card in the pyramid, put it into a wastepile. Don't mix up this pile with your "Removed" pile.

If one of the cards you turn up from your hand is a match with the top card of the "Removed" pile, you can remove both of them.

To Win the Game: You need to remove the entire pyramid plus the cards in your hand.

Redeals: Two.

HOW TO SCORE PYRAMID

A match is six games. Score each game as follows:

50 points—If you get rid of your pyramid in the first deal (once through all the cards in the deck).

50 points minus—If you get rid of the pyramid during the first deal but still have cards in your hand or in the wastepile, score 50 points minus the number of cards in the wastepile.

35 points minus—If you get rid of the pyramid during the second deal, but still have cards in your hand or in the wastepile, score 35 points minus the number of cards in your hand and the wastepile.

20 points minus—If you get rid of the pyramid during the third deal, score 20 points minus the number of cards in your hand or the wastepile.

0 points minus—If you never do succeed in getting rid of your pyramid, deduct one point for each card left in the pyramid as well as each card left in your hand and the wastepile. That's right—a minus score!

"Par" is 0 for six matches. If you do better, you've won!

Quadrille

Other Names: Captive Queens, La Française, Partners

Space: Moderate.

Level: Easy.

Layout: The layout for this game is set up as you play. The design that is to be created appears below:

Play: Start turning up cards from the deck. As soon as the 5s and 6s appear, put them in place and start building on them.

On the 5s you build down: **4 3 2 Ace King.**

On the 6s you build up: **7 8 9 10 Jack.**

The Queens just sit in the middle and look regal.

To Win the Game: Build the 6s up in suit to the Jacks and the 5s down in suit to the Kings.

Redeals: Two.

193

Queen's Audience

Other Name: King's Audience

Space: Moderate.

Level: Easy.

Layout: Make a square of four cards to a side, like this:

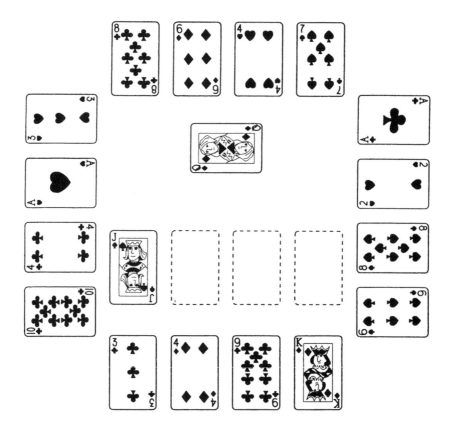

This is the Queen's antechamber. The space inside it is the Queen's Audience. Into the Audience will go the Jacks, as they appear. They are the foundations.

To Win the Game: Build the foundations from Jack to deuce in suit.

Special Buiding Rule: Before a Jack can get into the Queen's Audience, an Ace of the same suit has to go with him. That Ace can come from the walls of the antechamber or from the stockpile. Put the Ace under the Jack.

Kings and Queens get to come into the Audience also, but only in pairs of the same suit. Put the King under the Queen.

Play: Go through the cards one by one, building to the foundations and discarding Queen and King sets into the Audience.

Spaces in the antechamber wall should be filled right away from the top card of the wastepile or the stockpile.

Russian Solitaire

Space: Large.

Level: Very Difficult.

Some people say this is the most difficult solitaire game in the world to win. In any case, it is one of the most intriguing.

Layout: Lay out the cards exactly as you lay them out for *Klondike*, but when you finish, deal the rest of the pack face up on top of the layout, as in the illustration on page 196.

To Win the Game: Free the Aces from the layout and build them up to Kings in suit in a row above the layout.

Play: First, move any Aces that are exposed onto the foundations. Then build downward in suit on the exposed cards of the layout. In order to do this, you will often have to move more than one card at a time—sometimes as many as a whole column of unrelated cards.

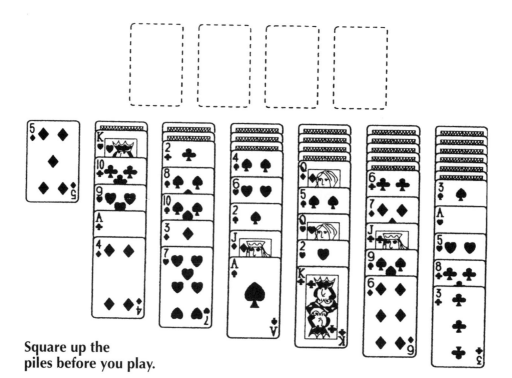

**Square up the
piles before you play.**

In the illustration above, for example:

First, you would move the Ace up to the foundation row, just as in *Klondike*. Then, you would start looking at the other cards that are exposed. The 6 of Diamonds is lying open. You could put the 5 of Diamonds on it, thereby creating a space in the layout. That vacant spot, just as in *Klondike*, can be filled with any King. Suppose you decided to move the King of Hearts. You would have to move the entire column of cards on top of the King to the #1 space. There is only one card underneath the King. Turn it over: it's the King of Diamonds. And it is now the leading card of the second column.

Your next move might be to put the 4 of Diamonds on the 5 of Diamonds. That would open up the Ace of Clubs, which you can put up at the top in the foundation row.

You might then move the 6 of Hearts down onto the 7. Remember that when you move the 6, all the cards on top of it must move too.

Now your layout would look pretty crazy, like the illustration on the next page.

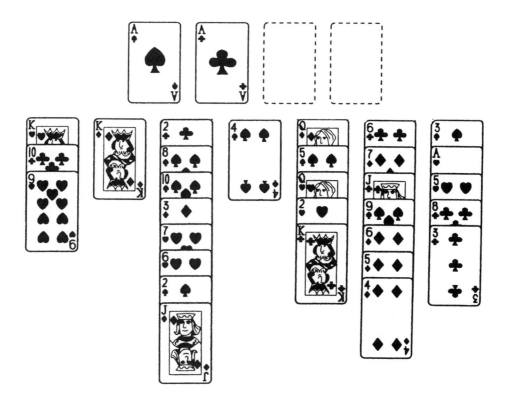

Well, you get the idea.

Play five rounds of this game, adding up the number of points in each for your total score.

Yukon

Level: Moderate.

Play: Play in exactly the same way as *Russian Solitaire*, except building on the bottom cards of the layout is done regardless of suit in alternating colors.

Scorpion

Space: Large.

Level: Moderate.

Layout: Deal a row of seven cards—four face down and three face up. Repeat this same pattern in a second and third row, overlapping the cards each time. Then deal out all the rest of the cards face up on top of this beginning setup. You'll have three cards left over at the end. Put them aside for a few minutes. Your layout will look like this:

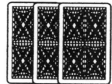

Play: Now you are going to build downward in suit on the exposed cards of the layout. You are not limited to moving one card at a time. You may move any card that meets the requirements of rank and suit— even if it is covered with cards. You just move all the cards with it.

As columns are emptied, you can fill them with Kings—along with the cards that are on top of them. Nothing can be built on an Ace.

When you have exhausted all chances for moves, take the three cards you set aside at the start and place one on each of the bottom cards of the left-hand columns. That picks up the game and can give you a few new moves.

To Win the Game: Build four Kings, right on the layout, with their full suits, like this:

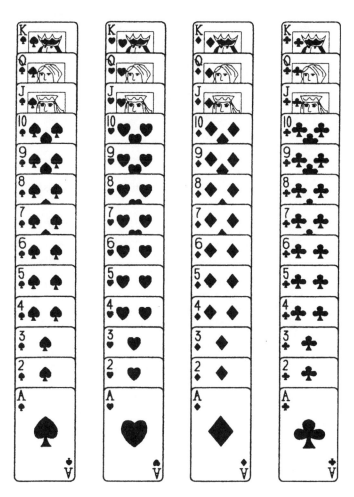

Spiderette

Space: Moderate.

Level: Difficult.

When you're tired and angry at playing *Klondike* and never playing out, you might want to get even with this Cheater's version.

Layout: Lay out the cards the same way you would for *Klondike*, but this time, you're not going to set up any foundation piles.

Square up the piles before you play.

Play: Build downward on the layout, regardless of suits and colors (but try to build in suit where you can). You can move groups of cards when they are in the correct sequence. When a space opens up in the layout, you can fill it with any available card or sequence of cards.

Whenever you run out of moves to make, deal another seven cards on the layout. At the end, put the last three cards on the first three columns.

When you get all 13 cards of one suit in order in one pile, you can discard them.

To Win the Game: Build up and then discard all four complete suits.

Vanishing Cross

Other Names: Corner Card, Corners, Four Seasons, Czarina

Space: Small.

Level: Moderate.

Layout: Place five cards on the table in the shape of a cross. This is the layout. Then place another card in the upper left-hand corner. That is the foundation. The other foundations—the same rank as the corner card—should be placed in the other corners as they become available.

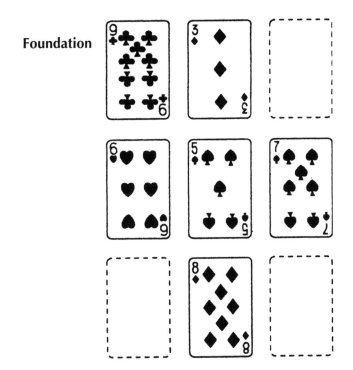

Foundation

201

Play: Build whatever cards you can onto the foundation, upward in suit. Then build whatever cards you can onto others in the cross—downward and regardless of suit. When you've exhausted all the possibilites, start going through the stockpile, one card at a time, playing it to the foundation (going up), to the cards in the cross (going down), or, if unplayable, to a wastepile.

To Win the Game: Build all the corner cards into four suites.

Note: Aces may be placed on Kings.

Two-Pack GAMES

British Square

Space: Moderate.

Level: Easy.

Layout: Deal four rows of four cards each, face up. Four Aces, one of each suit, as they become available, will be placed above the layout as foundations.

To Win the Game: Build the Aces up to Kings in suit—and here's the tricky part—then place another King of the same suit on top of that King and build down in suit to Aces.

Play: Besides building on the foundations, you also build on the layout, up or down in suit. You can build in either direction, but once you decide on a particular direction for any given pile, you have to keep it that way for the entire game.

When you've made all the moves you can make in the layout and to the foundations, start turning over one card at a time to play to the foundations, the layout, or to a wastepile.

You may fill spaces from the top card of the wastepile or from your hand.

Busy Aces

Space: Small.

Level: Easy.

Layout: Deal two rows of six cards each, face up. Aces, as they become available, are foundations and are placed in a row above.

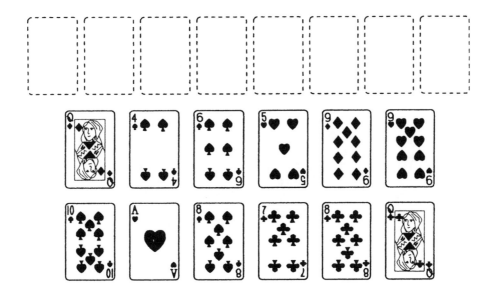

205

Play: Do whatever building you can at the start on the foundations. Then, build on the layout, downward and in suit. After you've made all the moves you can, begin turning over cards one by one, discarding unplayable cards onto a wastepile.

When spaces open up in the layout, fill them from your hand or the wastepile.

To Win the Game: Build all eight Aces up in suit to Kings.

Capricieuse

Space: Moderate.

Level: Easy.

Layout: Select one Ace and one King of each suit, and place them in a single line.

Then deal out the rest of the pack in 12 face-up piles.

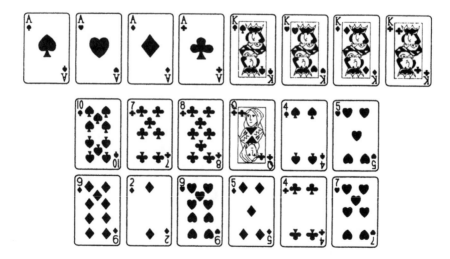

Play: As you deal the cards onto the piles, play any appropriate card from your hand onto the foundations. *Only* cards from your hand can go onto the foundations during the deal—be sure not to move any from the layout.

Don't leave any blanks in the layout as you deal—give a card to each pile. If one card can be played onto the foundation, substitute another card for it in the layout.

When all the cards have been dealt, start building them on each other, in suit.

Kings may not be put on Aces, nor Aces on Kings.

Redeals: Two. When gathering up the cards for a redeal, pick them up in reverse sequence from the way you dealt them.

Congress

Other Name: **President's Cabinet**

Space: **Small.**

Level: **Difficult.**

Layout: Deal a column of four cards to the left and a column of four to the right. Leave enough space between them for the foundations, eight Aces.

To Win the Game: Build the Aces upward in suit to Kings.

Play: First, make whatever moves you can to the foundations. Then, start turning over the cards in your hand one by one, building downward on the layout, regardless of suit, and playing whatever cards you can to the foundations. Fill in spaces from the wastepile or from your hand. Any card on top of a pile is available for building.

207

Cotillion

Other Name: Contradance

Space: Small.

Level: Moderate.

Layout: Select one 5 of every suit and one 6 of every suit. These are the foundations. Set them up like this:

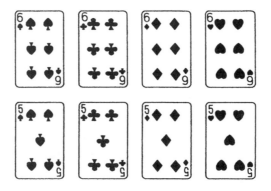

Play: Go through the balance of the cards one by one and play them to the foundations in suit wherever you can.

To Win the Game: Build the 6s up to Queens and the 5s down (through Aces) to Kings.

Redeals: One.

Crescent

Space: Large.

Level: Moderate.

To Win the Game: Build Aces up to Kings in suit and Kings down to Aces in suit

Layout: Select one Ace and one King from each suit and place them in two rows, Kings on top.

Then deal the rest of the cards in a semicircle around them in 16 piles. Put the first five cards face down, the top card face up.

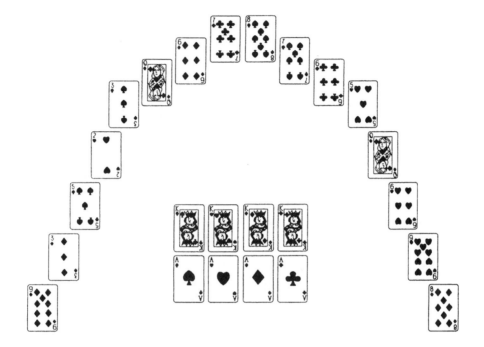

Play: Play whatever cards you can to the foundations. Then you can start building up or down on the layout in suit. When you move the top card of a pile, turn up the card underneath.

When you use up all the cards in a pile and you have an empty space, it cannot be refilled.

Shifting: When you can't make any more moves, take the bottom card from each pile and place it on top of the pile, face up. You need to do this with every pile before you stop to make any moves. You can make this unusual shifting move three times during the game; it's a little like having three redeals.

Reverse: When the top cards of two foundations of the same suit are in sequence, you can transfer one or more cards from one foundation to the other. The original Ace and King may not be transferred.

Open Crescent

Play exactly the same as *Crescent*, but lay out the cards face up and spread them so that you can see them as you play.

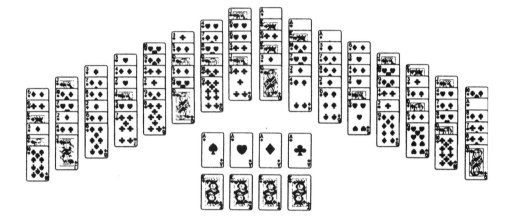

It's a more interesting game when strategy comes into play.

Diplomat

Space: Moderate.

Level: Easy.

Similar to the one-pack *Streets and Alleys*, this game is fairly quick to set up and has lots of action.

Layout: Deal four columns of four overlapping cards, leaving space between them for two columns of side-by-side Aces, which are the foundations as they become available.

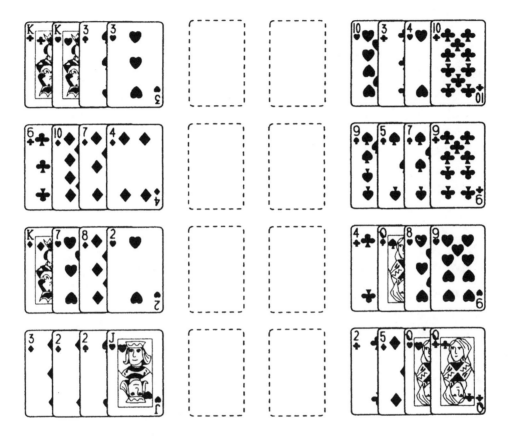

To Win the Game: Build the Aces up in suit to Kings.

Play: After making whatever moves you can to the foundations, you build downward on the exposed cards of the layout, regardless of suit.

When you can't make any more moves, start turning over the cards in your hand, one by one, playing what you can to the layout. Place the unused cards in a wastepile. The top card of the wastepile, the card in your hand, and the exposed cards in the layout are all available to play onto foundations, onto the layout, and to fill any spaces that open up in the layout.

Redeals: One. Just turn over the wastepile.

The Fan

Space: Wide.

Level: Easy/Moderate.

Layout: First, count out 12 cards in one unit. This is the stockpile. Place it face up at the left. Beside it, place an overlapping string of 12 face-up cards. The next card in your hand will be a foundation card. Let's say it's the 10 of Clubs. Leave space next to it for placing the other 10s—seven more of them, as they become available. They will be foundation cards on which you build up from 10s through Aces to 9s.

Underneath this foundation row, deal out four cards from the pack, face up.

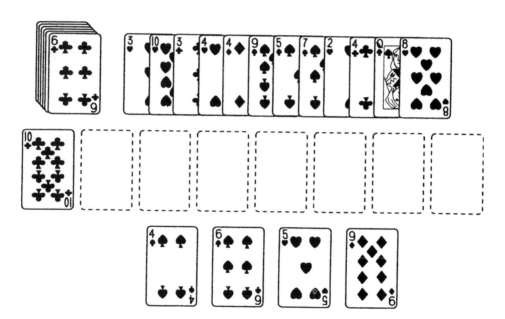

To Win the Game: All foundations are to be built in sequence, regardless of suits, until they contain 13 cards. But whether you build upward or downward is up to you. You can make up your mind after you see how the game is shaping up. You don't have to decide until you're ready to start building, but whatever you decide, it will apply to all the foundations.

Play: Start playing onto the foundations by going through the cards in your hand—one by one. Unplayable cards go into a wastepile.

You can also play onto the foundations with the following cards:
1. the top card of the stockpile
2. the exposed card on the end of the string of overlapping cards
3. the four-card row
4. The top card of the wastepile

If a space opens up in the row of four cards, fill it from the wastepile or the cards in your hand.

Redeals: You get two redeals (that means going through the cards three times).

Forty Thieves

Other Names: Big Forty, Napoleon at St. Helena, Cadran
Roosevelt at San Juan

Space: Large.

Level: Moderate.

Layout: Deal four rows of ten cards each, overlapping, as in the picture. Aces, as thet become available, are moved up above the layout as foundations.

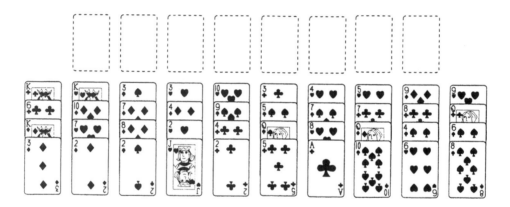

To Win the Game: Build all eight Aces to Kings in suit.

Play: First, build what you can to the foundations. Then build on the layout itself, downward in suit. For example, in the illustration above, the 2 of Diamonds can be placed on the 3 of Diamonds. The Ace of Clubs can be played up to the foundation row. So can the 2. When you have exhausted all the possibilities, start going through the cards one by one, building onto foundations or layout or discarding the unplayable cards into a wastepile. The top card of that wastepile is available too.

   When a space opens up in the layout, you can fill it with any card—one from the layout, the top card from the wastepile, or a card from your hand.

Streets

Space: Large.

Level: Moderate.

Play: Exactly the same as *Forty Thieves*, except build downward on the layout in alternating colors.

Indian

Space: Large.

Level: Easy.

Play: Exactly the same as *Forty Thieves*, except:
    1. For the layout, deal 30 cards in three rows of ten cards each. The first row should be face down.
    2. When building on the layout, cards may go on any suit *except* their own.

Rank and File

Other Names: Dress Parade, Deauville, Emperor

Space: Large.

Level: Moderate.

Play: Exactly the same as *Forty Thieves*, except:
    1. For the layout, deal the first three rows face down.
    2. Build downward on the layout in alternating colors.
    3. When all the cards on the top of a pile are in correct sequence, you're allowed to move them as a unit onto another pile in the layout.

Lucas

Space: Large.

Level: Easy.

Play: Exactly the same as *Forty Thieves*, except:
    1. Set up the Aces in the foundation row before dealing the layout.
    2. For the layout, deal three rows of 13 cards each. This makes for a much easier game.

Maria

Space: Large.

Level: Moderate.

Play: Exactly the same as *Forty Thieves*, except:
    1. For the layout, deal four rows of nine cards each.
    2. Build downward on the layout in alternating colors.

Number Ten

Space: Large.

Level: Moderate.

Play: Exactly the same as *Forty Thieves*, except:
    1. Place the first two rows face down.
    2. Build downward on the layout in alternating colors.
    3. When all the cards on the top of a pile are in correct sequence, you're allowed to move them as a unit onto another pile in the layout.

Frog

Other Names: Toad, Toad-in-the-Hole

Space: Moderate.

Level: Easy/ Moderate.

Layout: Count out 13 cards and place them in one pile face up. Make sure no Aces are within the pile. If there are any, replace them with other cards.

Then place one Ace next to the pack as a foundation. As other Aces appear, they should be placed next to it.

To Win the Game: Build all the Aces up by suit to Kings.

Play: Go through the stockpile, card by card. When cards are unplayable, place them in a row of their own underneath the foundation row—a row of five piles. You can put the cards in any position you choose—all in one pile, if you want.

Fanny

Level: Moderate.

Play: Exactly the same as *Frog*, except:
1. Count out only 12 cards instead of 13 for the face-up pile.
2. Do not set up an Ace to start the foundation row.

Grand Duchess

Other Name: Duchess of Luynes

Space: Small.

Level: Moderate.

Layout: Deal four cards in a row face up and an additional two cards face down to the side. Above them you'll be placing two rows of foundations, Aces (one of each suit) and Kings (one of each suit), as they become available.

To Win the Game: Build the Aces up in suit to Kings and the Kings down in suit to Aces.

Play: Make any possible moves and then deal again—four cards on top of the cards you dealt before and two more cards face down to the side. Make your moves and continue in this fashion, until you've gone through the entire pack.

Then turn up the face-down cards, spreading them out and playing any cards you can to the foundations and making whatever moves are possible.

Redeals: Three (four times through the cards). When you get ready to redeal, pick up the piles in reverse order so that the pile at the right is on the top. Put the face-down pile at the bottom.

The first two redeals are done just as before, spreading out the face-down pile at the end. The last one is different; don't deal any cards face down to the side. Just deal the four cards onto the layout. Don't build up a face-down pile at all.

Parisienne

Play exactly the same as *Grand Duchess*, except lay out the Aces and Kings at the start.

The Harp

Other Name: Klondike (with two packs of cards)

Space: Large.

Level: Easy.

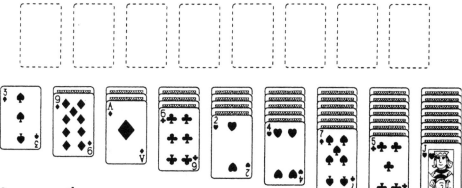

Square up the piles before you play.

Play: Exactly the same as *Klondike*, except:

    1. Use two packs of cards.

    2 Use a nine-card row instead of a seven-card row.

    3. There is no limit to the number of times you can go through the cards, one by one. Do it until you win or until the game is obviously blocked.

    4. When filling a space, you may use an available King, as in *Klondike*, or you may use a group of cards in correct sequence that has a King at the top.

House in the Wood

Other Name: Double Fan

Space: Large.

Level: Easy.

This is a two-pack version of *La Belle Lucie*. But it works out much more often.

Layout: Lay out 34 fans of three cards each, plus one fan of two cards. The top cards of each fan are available for building onto foundations or onto other top cards.

To Win the Game: Free Aces from the fans and build them up in suit to Kings.

Play: After making all initial moves, start building on the exposed cards in the fans—up or down, but always in suit.

    Spaces created by clearing away a fan are not filled.

    Kings may not be put on Aces, nor Aces on Kings.

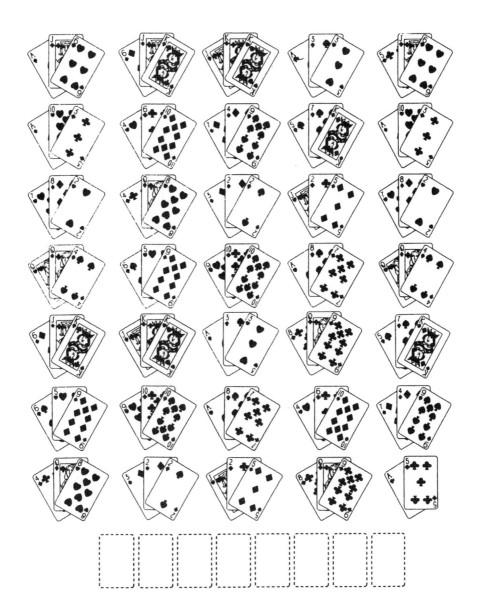

House on the Hill

Play exactly the same as *House in the Wood*, except instead of eight Aces as foundations, lay out one Ace and one King of each suit. Build the Aces up in suit to Kings and the Kings down to Aces.

Intelligence

Space: Moderate.

Level: Moderate/Difficult.

Similar to the one-pack *La Belle Lucie*, but tougher, this is an intriguing game where you need to be bold to get enough cards into play.

Layout: Deal 18 fans of three cards, keeping the rest of the cards in a stockpile. As you deal, if Aces appear, put them right on the foundations and replace each one with the next card.

To Win the Game: Build the eight Aces up in suit to Kings.

Play: Once you've moved all the cards you can to the foundations, you can start building on the exposed cards of the fan, as you would in *La Belle Lucie*, up or down, in suit. You may reverse direction on the same pile.

Each time you completely eliminate a fan, you may replace it with three new cards from your hand. That is the only way to get new cards into play.

Kings may not be put on Aces, nor Aces on Kings.

Redeals: Two. While redealing, you still have the chance to pull Aces out of the fans, replacing them with the next card from your hand.

Matrimony

Space: Moderate.

Level: Difficult.

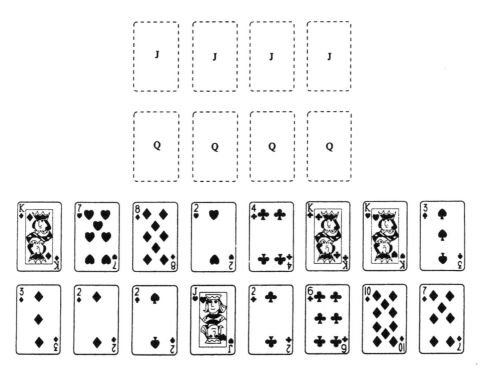

Layout: Lay out two rows of eight cards each. Then, as they become available, place four Queens of each suit and four Jacks of each suit above these rows, as foundations.

To Win the Game: Build the Queens upward in suit through Aces to Jacks, and the Jacks downward in suit through Aces to 10s.

Play: First, move any cards you can from the layout onto the foundations. Then deal 16 cards onto the layout—one on each card—or space (spaces are not filled except by this 16-card deal).

Make whatever moves you can and then, when you get stuck, deal another 16 cards onto the layout. The last deal will be only six cards, but deal it in the same way.

After you have used up all the cards in the deck and made all possible moves, pick up the pile in the lower right-hand corner, turn it face down, and deal the top card face up on its own place. Then continue dealing the pile, on each card in turn, starting at the upper left-hand corner.

Make any moves you can as a result of this play. Then, when you're stuck, pick up the 15th pile, turn it over, and deal that pile, first putting the top card in its own place and going on from there.

Again, make what moves you can. When you're stuck, pick up the next pile to the left and continue the process, until you've gone through all the piles once.

If you get stuck after dealing out pile number one, you've lost the game.

Miss Milligan

Space: Moderate.

Level: Difficult.

To many, this is the ultimate solitaire game.

Layout: Deal out a row of eight cards. Move all Aces up above the row of cards, as they become available. The Aces are foundations.

To Win the Game: Build all eight Aces upward in suit to Kings.

Play: Besides building on the foundations, you also can build within the original row of eight cards—downward in alternating colors.

When you've made all possible moves, deal out another eight cards that overlap the original eight, filling in spaces as you go.

Play off what you can to the foundations, build what you can on the row, and deal another eight cards onto the layout.

Continue this process until you've used up all the cards in your hand. At this point you have the object of "weaving."

Weaving: This is the option of removing one card from the bottom row of the layout temporarily—while you make other moves. When you get that card back into play—either on a foundation or the layout—you are then allowed to remove another card. You can keep doing this until you win the game or you can't find a place for the card.

Special Rules: You are permitted to move two or more cards as a unit—when they are built correctly in rank and sequence and at the end of a column. For example, in the diagram below, you can move the 10 of Diamonds, 9 of Spades, and 8 of Hearts as a unit onto the Jack of Clubs.

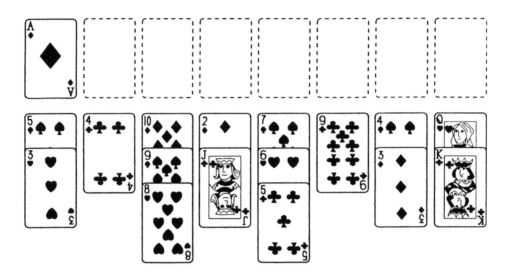

Spaces may be filled with any available King or with a sequence that leads off with a King.

Mount Olympus

Space: Large/Moderate (for alternate layout).

Level: Easy.

Layout: Remove all the Aces and deuces from the pack and set them out in an arch, alternating Aces and deuces, and colors, as in the picture.

All the Aces and deuces are foundations.

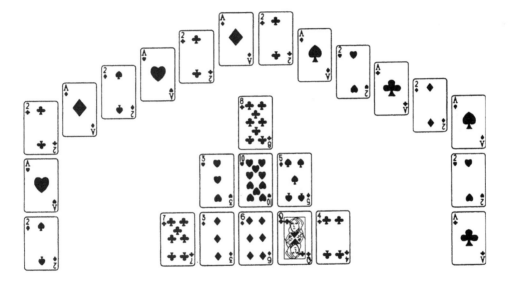

Then place nine cards in a pyramid shape beneath the arch.

To Win the Game: Build the foundations upward in suit by 2s: from Aces to Kings, deuces to Queens.

The Aces build like this: **A 3 5 7 9 J K**
The deuces build like this: **2 4 6 8 10 Q**

Play: You may also build on the cards in the pyramid in the same way—skipping a card as you go. Build them downward in suits.

When cards are in the correct rank and sequence, you can shift an entire pile as a unit.

When a space opens up in the pyramid, fill it at once with a card from the stockpile.

When you have made all possible moves and filled the spaces, deal nine more cards onto the pyramid. Make whatever plays you can onto the foundations, and then deal another nine cards. Continue this process until the stockpile is gone.

Note: If you don't have enough space to create the layout shown on page 227, you can set out the cards like this:

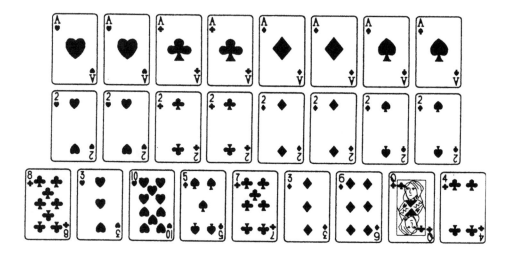

It is also an easier game to play in this format, because it is easier to build on the layout.

Napoleon's Square

Other Name: Quadruple Line

Space: Moderate.

Level: Easy.

To Win the Game: Build all the Aces upward in suit to Kings.

Layout: Deal 12 piles of four cards each, four piles to the left (place them horizontally), four to the right (horizontally), and four across the top of the layout. All eight Aces will be placed in two rows in the middle of the layout as they become available.

Play: First, make all the moves you can. Move Aces to the foundations and then build on the layout itself, downward and in suit. The top card of any pile is available and so are groups of cards that are in sequence and in the same suit.

When a space opens up in the layout, fill it with any available card or group of cards in sequence and the same suit, or from your hand or from the wastepile.

After all initial moves have been made, turn over one card at a time from your hand, discarding unplayable cards to the wastepile. The top card of the wastepile is always available for play.

Odd and Even

Space: Moderate.

Level: Moderate.

Layout: Deal three rows of three cards each. These cards are available for building on foundations.

Play: Start going through the cards in your hand one by one. As soon as an Ace comes up, start a foundation row above the layout. As soon as a two comes up, place it in that row also, as shown in the picture.

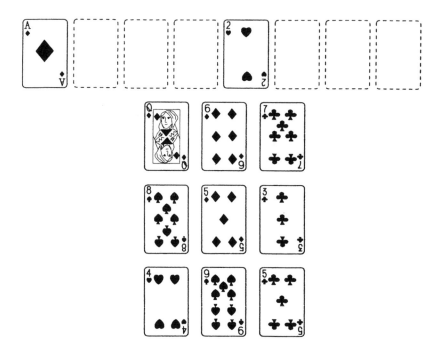

Eventually, you need to place three more Aces and three more deuces in the foundation row. One of each suit should be represented.

If you can't play the card from your hand onto the foundations, put it in a wastepile.

If a space opens up in the group of nine cards, fill it right away from the wastepile, or—if there is none—from your hand.

To Win the Game: Build the foundations upward in suit to full 13-card sequences—but you need to do it by 2s!

The Aces should build like this:

A 3 5 7 9 J K 2 4 6 8 10 Q

The deuces should build like this:

2 4 6 8 10 Q A 3 5 7 9 J K

Redeals: One.

Panama Canal

Other Names: **Precedence, Panama, Order of Precedence**

Space: **Moderate.**

Level: **Easy.**

This is almost as simple as a game can get.

Layout: The layout starts with only one card in place—a King. That card will be followed by seven additional cards—the Queen, Jack, 10, 9, 8, 7, and 6 of any suit—as they become available. These are foundations.

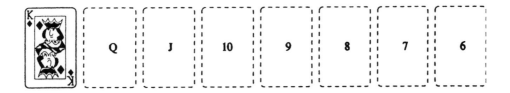

To Win the Game: You need to build each foundation downward and regardless of suit into a sequence of 13 cards.

Play: Start going through the pack, one card at a time. The catch is that you have to place the Queen before you can put down the Jack, and the Jack must be in place before you can place the 10, and so on, down to the 6. You are free, though, to build on the cards that are

231

already in place. For example, you can put a Queen on the King that is already on the table and a Jack on the Queen. Unplayable cards go into a wastepile whose top card is always available.

Circular Sequence: Kings may be built on Aces when the foundation card is something other than an Ace or King.

Redeals: Two.

Queen of Italy

Other Names: Terrace, Signora

Space: Moderate.

Level: Easy.

Layout: Deal 11 cards at the top, overlapping each other, face up. Then deal three cards face up: you get the opportunity to choose from these three which one will be your foundation. You make this choice based on the 11 cards you've already laid out.

After you decide on a foundation card, put it in place below and to the left of the first row. Then, use the two cards you did not select for the foundation to start a nine-card row at the bottom. Deal another seven cards from the stock. This nine-card row is where the action takes place. You may play the cards to the foundations as they become available. You can also build them on each other downward in alternating colors. Only one card at a time may be moved from the layout.

To Win the Game: Build your foundation cards into eight complete 13-card sequences in alternating colors.

Circular Sequence: Kings can be built on Aces, if your foundation card is something other than an Ace or King.

What about those 11 cards at the top? They are out of bounds, playable only onto the foundations, as they become exposed.

Play: Start by making what plays you can to the foundations and within the layout. When you can't make any more moves, go through the cards in your hand one at a time. Play what you can to the foundations and the nine-card row. Put unplayable cards in a wastepile. The top card of the wastepile is always available for play.

Spaces in the nine-card row may be filled from the top card of the wastepile or from the stockpile. Never add any cards to the 11-card overlapping row.

Falling Star

Play exactly the same as *Queen of Italy*, except:
1. The overlapping row represents stars that have to fall for the game to be won.
2. The next card (the 12th) becomes the foundation.

Blondes and Brunettes

Other Name: Wood

Play exactly the same as *Queen of Italy*, except:
1.   Deal only ten cards in the overlapping row instead of 11.
2.   Skip the three-card choice of foundation. The next card becomes the foundation card.
3.   Deal nine cards for the bottom row.

General Patience

Other Name: Thirteen

Play exactly the same as *Queen of Italy*, except:
1. Deal 13 cards instead of 11 for the overlapping row at the top.
2. Build in suit rather than in alternating colors.
3. You do not actually get a redeal, but you are allowed to turn the wastepile over and play until you reach an unusable card. Then the game is over.

Royal Cotillion

Space: Large.

Level: Moderate.

There's something especially intriguing about this game, which is not surprising, considering that it is one of the most popular of the two-pack games.

Layout: First, to your left, deal out three rows of four cards each. To your right, deal out four rows of four cards each. Leave a space between them that is wide enough for two cards which will be the foundation columns. As they become available, move one Ace and one deuce of each suit into this center section.

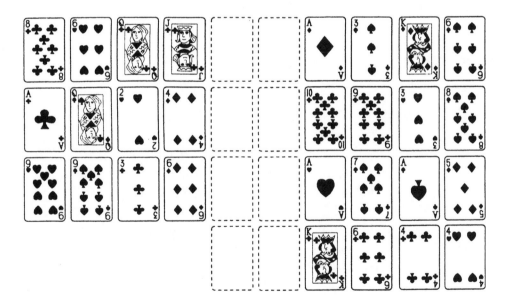

To Win the Game: Build the Aces and deuces in the middle section upward by suit to a full 13-card sequence. The building must be by twos, as follows.

Aces should build:

        A 3 5 7 9 J K 2 4 6 8 10 Q

Deuces should build:

2 4 6 8 10 Q A 3 5 7 9 J K

Play: Go through the cards one by one, building onto the foundations if you can or to the wastepile if you can't.

The cards that are off to your right can all be played onto the foundations, and as soon as spaces open up in this group, you can fill them from the wastepile—or if there is no wastepile, from your hand.

The cards that are off to the left, however, have only one active row—the bottom one. You can't move the cards in the second row until the bottom ones have been moved away. For example, in the illustration, only the 9 of Hearts, the 9 of Spades, the 3 of Clubs, and the 6 of Diamonds would be available to play onto the foundations. Spaces in the left-hand group are never filled in.

Gavotte

Other Names: Odd and Even

Space: Large.

Level: Easy.

Play: Play exactly the same as *Royal Cotillion*, except:
1. Lay out four rows of four cards on the left as well as on the right.
2. Either the left-hand group or the right-hand group can be the one that moves and is filled in. Take your choice, but whichever way you decide, you need to keep it that way for the whole game.
3. Foundations can be whatever cards you choose—3 and 7, Queen and Jack—whatever.

Royal Rendezvous

Other Names: None

Space: Moderate.

Level: Easy.

There's enough variety in this game to make it fun, even if there are few surprises!

Layout: First, lay out all eight Aces in two rows, one on top of the other. Each row should have one Ace of each suit. Then lay out one deuce of each suit—two on each side of the bottom row, as in the picture. Underneath this row, deal out two rows of eight cards each. They can be played onto the foundations.

To Win the Game: Build up all eight Aces and four deuces in suit as follows:

1. The top row of Aces gets built up in suit to Queens.
2. The bottom row of Aces gets built up by twos to Kings, like this:
   A 3 5 7 9 J K
3. The deuces get built up by twos to Queens, like this:
   2 4 6 8 10 Q
4. Four Kings get put at the top of the layout—but not until after their counterparts have already appeared in the lowest foundation row.

Play: Go through the cards, one by one, and build them onto the foundations if you can. If not, discard them to a wastepile. If a space opens up in the bottom two rows, you must fill it with the top card of the wastepile, or, if there isn't any, with the card from your hand.

St. Helena

Other Names: **Napoleon's Favorite, Washington's Favorite, Privileged Four**

Space: **Moderate.**

Level: **Easy/Moderate.**

With its odd and changing rules, this game has a peculiar fascination. Maybe that's why Napoleon is said to have played it while in exile. Others say that's unlikely because the game hadn't even been invented then. There's an enormous amount of laying out of cards, but in the end, it's worth it.

Layout: Start by removing one Ace and one King of each suit from the cards and setting them up in 2 rows, Kings on top. These are your foundations.

Then deal out the rest of the pack in 12 piles clockwise: four on top, two on the right side, four on the bottom of the foundations, and two on the left side, as in the illustration.

Keep on dealing, one card on each of the 12 piles, until you've laid out all the cards.

To Win the Game: Build the Aces up in suit to Kings and the Kings down in suit to Aces.

Play: Only the cards on the tops of the piles can be moved. First, build them onto the foundations; then build them on each other, one card at a time, either up or down, regardless of suit or color. You can reverse direction on the same pile.

When building, only a Queen can go on a King (or vice versa) and only a deuce can go on an Ace.

When you run out of moves, the deal is over.

Special: In the first deal, you are limited in placing cards on the foundations.

    1.   Only the cards at the sides of the layout can go on any foundation.

    2.   The cards at the top may be played only to the Kings line.

    3.   The cards at the bottom may go only on the Aces line. In redeals (you get two), any card of the right suit and rank can go on any foundation. You're not limited in this odd way.

Redeals: Two. To redeal, gather the piles counter-clockwise, starting in the upper left-hand corner. Then deal the cards, starting at the left-hand corner, as far as they go.

Louis

Other Names: St. Louis, Newport

Level: Moderate.

Play: Exactly the same as *St. Helena*, except:

    1. After you deal the first 12 cards of the piles, play everything you can onto the foundations; then fill the spaces from the stockpile. After that, deal the rest of the cards.

    2. All cards in the layout can be played to the foundations without any restrictions—in all deals.

    3. Building on the layout piles must be in suit.

Box Kite

Play exactly the same as *St. Helena*, except:

    1.   There is only one deal, with no restrictions on it.

    2.   Aces can be built on Kings and Kings on Aces.

    3.   When the top cards of two foundations of the same suit are in sequence, one or more cards may be transferred onto the other foundation. The original Ace and King may not be transferred, however.

Sly Fox

Other Name: Twenty

Space: Moderate.

Level: Easy.

Fate or free will? It's free will in this game of choices!

Layout: Set out four Aces—one of each suit—vertically at the left, and four Kings—one of each suit—vertically at the right. Then deal out four rows of five cards between them. The Aces and Kings are foundations on which you are going to build.

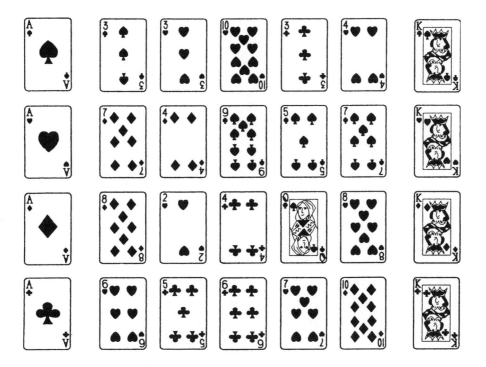

To Win the Game: The Aces need to get built up to Kings, and the Kings down to Aces, by suit.

Play: Build on the foundations using the cards in the middle of the layout. As each space opens up, fill it with a card from your hand.

When you can't make any more plays, start going through the cards, one by one. If you can play a card onto a foundation, do so. But if you can't, place it on one of the 20 cards that lie between the foundations. You have your choice of which one. As you place it there, count it (do not count the ones that you put on the foundations, though).

When you have placed 20 cards on the 20 cards that lie between the foundations, stop going through the cards. Now you can make any new plays that have become possible in the layout.

Each time play comes to a standstill, start going through the cards again. But this time, don't fill the spaces with cards from your hand. And as before, after you place 20 more "unplayable" cards onto the layout, stop and make the moves to the foundations that have become possible.

Note: There is no limitation on the number of cards that you may play to any card in the layout. You could play all 20 on one card, if you wanted to. Or, you can be sly, like a fox!

Colorado

Space: Large.

Level: Easy.

Some say this is *Sly Fox* in sheep's clothing. It is very similar to that game.

Layout: Deal two ten-card rows of cards. Above them, you'll set up a foundation row of four Aces and four Kings, as they become available.

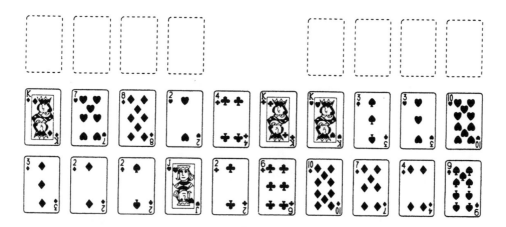

To Win the Game: Build the Aces up to Kings and the Kings down to Aces in suit.

Play: First, play whatever you can to the foundations. As spaces open up in the layout, fill them at once with cards from the stockpile.

When you've made every move you can, start playing one card at a time from your hand. If the card can't go on the foundation, you can put it on top of any card in the layout.

No card can be moved off the layout except to place on a foundation.

Spider

Space: Large.

Level: Difficult.

This game has been called "the king of all solitaires."

Layout: Deal out 54 cards in ten piles as follows: six cards in the first four piles, five in the last six piles. Only the top cards should be face up. These piles are the foundations and the layout at the same time, and all the action takes place on them.

To Win the Game: Build eight sequences in downward order from Kings to Aces right on the layout. Once a sequence is built, it is discarded. So to win the game is to have nothing on the table.

Play: After you lay out the cards, make all the moves you can, building down, regardless of suit. Note, however, that even though you're *permitted* to build regardless of suit, you limit yourself when you do it. You are permitted to move a group of cards as a unit only when they are in suit and in correct rank—so while you would never be able to win the game by making only moves that were in suit, it is certainly better to build in suit, if you have the choice.

When you move an entire pile, leaving a blank space, you may move any available card or group of cards into it. Keep in mind, though, that a King cannot move, except into a blank space. It cannot be placed on an Ace.

When you can't make any more moves, deal ten more cards, one on each pile. And again, make whatever moves you can. Follow this procedure for the entire game, dealing another ten cards whenever you're stuck.

All spaces must be filled before you are allowed to deal another ten cards onto the layout.

After you have put together a complete sequence, you don't have to discard it right away. You may be able to use it to help build other sequences.

The Sultan of Turkey

Other Names: The Sultan, The Harem, Emperor of Germany

Space: Moderate.

Level: Easy.

Layout: Remove the eight Kings and one Ace of Hearts from the pack and place them as shown in the illustration. Add four cards from the pack on both sides of the Kings. You can use these cards to build onto the foundations.

All the Kings—and the Ace—are foundations, except for the King of Hearts that is in the middle of the square. Don't build on it.

To Win the Game: Build all the Kings (except the middle King of Hearts) up to Queens, in suit—and build the Ace of Hearts to a Queen, also.

Of course, in order to build up the Kings, you're going to need to add an Ace before starting on the deuces.

Play: Go through the cards one by one and start adding to the foundations. Any cards you can't use go into a wastepile.

As soon as a space opens up in the layout, fill it at once, either from the wastepile or from your hand.

Redeals: Two. Shuffle well before going through the cards a second and third time.

The most delightful aspect of this game is the way it looks when you win. Try it.

Tournament

Space: Large.

Level: Easy/Moderate.

Layout: First, deal two columns of four cards each, one to your left, one to your right. These are the "kibitzers." If no Aces or Kings appear among them, put the cards back and deal again.

Next, deal six columns of four overlapping cards each. They are called the "dormitzers."

Then, as they become available, place one Ace and one King of each suit—the foundations—between the kibitzers, as in the illustration on the next page.

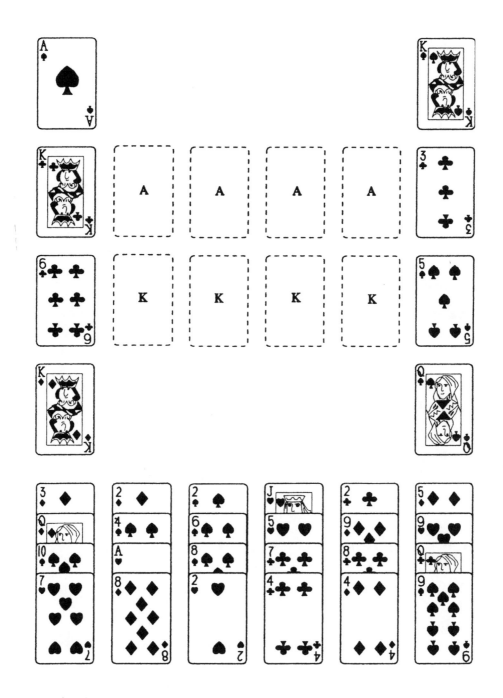

To Win the Game: Build Aces up to Kings and Kings down to Aces in suit.

All the kibitzers and the exposed cards of the dormitzers are available for playing onto the foundations.

A space in the dormitzers must be filled right away with four cards from the stockpile. A space in the kibitzers may be filled by any available (exposed) card from the dormitzers, but you can do it whenever you want.

Play: Make whatever moves you can from the kibitzers and the dormitzers to the foundations. When there are no more moves to be made, deal another four cards to each of the six piles of the dormitzers. If you have less than 24 cards to deal, that's all right—just put them down as far as they will go.

Reversal: When the top cards of two foundations of the same suit are in sequence, one card may be transferred onto the other.

Redeals: Two. To redeal, pick up just the dormitzers, with the last pile on top.

Weavers

Other Name: Leoni's Own

Space: Moderate.

Level: Moderate.

Layout: Select from the pack one Ace and one King of each suit. Place them in two rows, Kings on top. These are the foundations.

Now, below them, deal out two rows of six face-up cards each. As you deal them out, count to yourself, "Ace, 2, 3, 4, 5, 6, 7, 8, 9, 10, Jack, Queen, King" (the King space is off to the right, as in the illustration). If the card you name appears as you name it, that card is an Exile. Put it aside at your left, face down. Deal another card in its place, repeating the same card name. In that way, deal out the entire pack of cards.

248

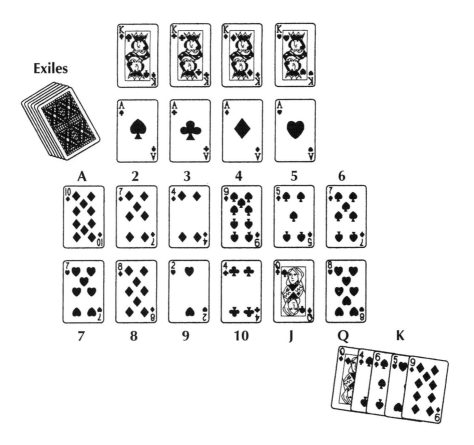

Play: When all the cards are laid out, build what you can to the foundations. All the top cards of the piles are available, plus all the cards in the Kings pile. Spread the Kings pile, so that you can view all the cards at the same time.

Then uncover one card from the cards at your left—the Exiles. If the Exile card can be played onto a foundation, you must play it. If it cannot, place it at the bottom of the pile that corresponds to its number. If it is a 3, for example, slip it under the 3s pile. Then take the top card from the 3s pile—let's say it's a Queen—and slip it under the Queens pile. Continue in this way until you can place something on a foundation. If you turn up a King, however, all play stops.

Slip the King on the bottom of the Kings pile, and turn up the next Exile card.

249

Reversal: When the Ace foundation and the King foundation of the same suit are in sequence, you are permitted to shift all the cards from one foundation onto the other. Let's say, for instance, that you have built the Ace foundation up to the 6 and the King foundation down to the 7. According to this rule, you could move the 6, 5, 4, 3, and the 2 onto the King foundation. You are not allowed, though, to move the original Ace or King.

Redeals: Two. To redeal, gather the cards up beginning with the Kings pile and go backwards through the cards to the Ace pile, so that Kings are on top, Aces on the bottom.

Windmill

Other Names: Propeller

Space: Moderate.

Level: Moderate.

There's plenty of action in this hypnotic game, and some strategy is useful.

Layout: Put an Ace in the middle of the design, and then deal two more cards in each direction in the shape of a windmill.

Play: Go through the cards in your hand, one by one. As Kings become available, put them in the angles of the windmill, as shown in the illustration by the dotted lines. They are the foundations. You will build down on them, regardless of suit. The central Ace is also a foundation. You will build up on it regardless of suit. Put unplayable cards in a wastepile.

To Win the Game: Build the Kings down to Aces, regardless of suit, and build up the Ace in a continuous sequence (also regardless of suit) until it contains 52 cards—four times through the Ace-to-King sequence.

You can use the cards in the windmill shape for foundation building. When a space opens up in the windmill, fill it from the wastepile or, if there is no wastepile, from the cards in your hand.

It is legal to steal the top card from a King foundation to use for the Ace foundation on these conditions: that you use only one card at a time, and that the next card to go on the Ace foundation must come from a regular source.

What the Terms Mean

Around the corner: Refers to the ranking of the cards. Ace can be high and low.

Ante up: To put counters into the pool, so that they may be won during the game.

Base cards: In solitaire, refers to scoring cards, usually but not always Aces, which are built up to complete a set, usually a full 13-card suit.

Bidding: Stating what you are willing to pay or predicting the number of tricks you hope to win.

Book: The basic number of tricks bid. In *Whist*, the first six tricks won. In *Authors*, four cards of the same rank.

Capot: Trying to win all the tricks.

Chicane: A hand without a trump card in it.

Deuce: A 2 of any suit.

Follow suit: Put down a card that matches the suit of the lead.

Gin: To lay down your whole melded hand, face up, ending the play.

Honor card: Ace, King, Queen, Jack of trumps, and sometimes the 10.

Knock: To lay down all melds and declare the face value of unmelded cards.

Lead: The first play that establishes the suit to follow.

Marriage: A meld of King and Queen in the same suit.

Meld: To match up three or four cards of a kind or in sequence. Can be held in hand or put down on the table. A matched set.

Nullo games: Games in which you must avoid taking certain cards.

Picture cards: Jack, Queen or King.

Revoke: Not following suit when you could have and were supposed to.

Spot cards: Any card from 2 to 10.

Suits: There are four: Hearts, Diamonds, Clubs and Spades.

Sweep: In *Casino*, capturing all the cards on the table in one play.

Trick: A sequence of cards in which each person plays a card according to certain rules.

Trump suit: A named suit that can overtake others, chosen in a specific way for each game.

Upcard: The top card of the stock, turned over beside the stockpile, which starts the discard pile.

Widow: An extra hand or number of cards that may be substituted for a player's own hand or held until a certain point in the game. Also, extra cards taken with the first tricks in *Hearts*.

Wild cards: Cards that prior to the game may be given any value you choose.

Index

256

Giant Book of
CARD
TRICKS
By BOB LONGE

Sterling Publishing Company, Inc.
New York

10 9 8 7 6 5 4 3 2 1

Published In 1998 by Sterling Publishing Company, Inc.
387 Park Avenue South, New York, N.Y. 10016

Material in this collection was adapted from
Great Card Tricks
World's Best Card Tricks, and
World's Greatest Card Tricks
© Bob Longe

Distributed in Canada by Sterling Publishing
c/o Canadian Manda Group
One Atlantic Avenue, Suite 105
Toronto, Ontario, Canada M6K 3E7

Distributed in Great Britain and Europe by Chris Lloyd
463 Ashley Road, Parkstone, Poole,
Dorset, BH14 0AX, United Kingdom

Distibuted in Australia by Capricorn Link (Australia) Pty Ltd.
P.O. Box 6651, Baulkham Hills, Business Centre,
NSW 2153, Australia

Sterling ISBN 0-8069-2077-7

CONTENTS

The Great
CARD TRICKS

INTRODUCTION

The purpose of this book is to teach you great card tricks and tell you exactly how to perform them. This includes step-by-step instruction and tips on presentation.

The ability to perform good card tricks is not unlike the gift of playing a musical instrument well. As with a musical instrument, you can enjoy the solitary practise, and you can share your skill with others.

Are there other rewards? Certainly. The admiration of spectators, for instance. Who doesn't enjoy being the center of attention? But even better is the sharing. You, the card expert, enliven every occasion and contribute to everyone's enjoyment.

When performing card tricks, however, some magicians miss the main point. The object is not merely to fool spectators, nor to impress with a variety of flourishes. The object is to *entertain*. And magic is the central theme. The tools are many: good tricks, practised skill, interesting patter, humor, and—above all—a sharing of the fun.

The idea is to entertain an audience, as well as yourself.

You'll feel enormously pleased with yourself as you develop greater skill with your tricks, and well you should. Just don't forget to share the joy.

Getting Started
THE MOVES

Every trick, whether it calls for prestidigitation or not, requires considerable skill. What skill? The skill of *presenting a trick properly*. I have seen performers with amazing technical ability who never amaze, nor do they entertain or amuse. Worst of all, they never perform *magic*. They do astonish with their flourishes, in the same way a juggler astonishes. We want to astonish, all right, but we also want to do magic, to create an atmosphere of mystery and romance. It takes skill.

It is not enough merely to "know" a trick. Even the simplest trick requires the four Ps: *preparation*, thorough *practise*, convincing *patter*, and smooth *presentation*.

Preparation: Read over the trick, going through every aspect with a deck of cards. Run through it a few times to make sure you understand the basic principle. Now *think* about it. No two persons are going to do a trick exactly the same way. See if you can develop a unique angle or a simplification that will particularly suit you.

There is nothing absolutely binding about anyone's instructions, including mine. Understand, however, that in this book the method given is tried and true; the trick has been done hundreds of times to good effect using the exact method described.

Practise: Work out every move precisely. You must be *smooth*.

Patter: Here is where mystery, romance, and magic come in. Spectators *want* to be amazed; give them an excuse, a reason. Make strength of weakness. Why must they count the cards? You want to be scrupulously fair. Why are you removing a card from the top? It's your lucky card, and the spectator must tap the deck with it. It doesn't matter how preposterous the story is. Often as not, the more ridiculous the story, the more entertaining the trick.

Do *not* narrate, "Now I deal three cards, and now I place them over here." No spectator likes being treated like an idiot. Obviously, you must sometimes explain what you are doing and why you are doing it, but do not make this your standard procedure.

Develop the kind of patter appropriate to your personality. If you are bombastic, develop lively, high-tension patter. If you are reserved, present reasoned experiments. Don't try to be something you aren't. In other words, don't don the magician's cape, becoming the all-knowing, the all-powerful. Just be yourself. Knowing a few cards tricks does not make you superior. And if you are, in fact, superior, try to keep this fact concealed. In other words, try not to be obnoxious. Many magicians neglect this step.

Presentation: Take care of the first three Ps, and you won't have to worry about the fourth P, *presentation.* There are two rules: Never do a trick twice, and quit while you're ahead.

Some tricks are designed to be repeated—the mystery is enhanced with repetition—but most should be done only once. A repetition could lead to discovery.

Occasionally spectators will insist that you do a trick again. Perhaps they will say, "You're afraid we'll catch on." This is quite true, of course. But you respond, "Not at all. A repetition would bore you. It would certainly bore me. I have many other wonders to show you."

When asked to perform, you will be tempted to do at least a dozen tricks. Three or four are plenty. If your audience begs for more, you can always accommodate them.

I explain the tricks in considerable detail, perhaps more than you need or want. One reason is that I have always resented it when a card-book author left out important details. Another reason is that it is not enough for you to know just the basic trick; it's important that you learn *exactly* what I do. Often enough, the real secret of a successful trick is something which may, to the casual reader, seem insignificant: a word, a gesture, pacing, whatever.

I recommend, then, that you try each trick in much the same way as it is presented here. Inevitably, you will come to perform it your own way.

You have heard of "self-working" tricks. There is no such thing. *All* tricks—from those requiring several sleights to those requiring none—must be worked skillfully by the performer.

TIPS

You are about to learn lessons I paid for with failure, chagrin, and self-recrimination.

1. When a card is selected, have it shown to other spectators. Yes, it's true—sometimes a spectator will lie.

2. No matter how ardently you are importuned, do not reveal how a trick is done. This applies to even the simplest trick. When you give a trick away, you spoil it for the spectators, and you ruin your reputation as "Mr. Magic." The spectators can no longer enjoy the mystery and the romance, and instead of a magician, you have become someone who bought a book the spectators did not buy. You will be delighted to follow this advice once you have explained a trick and have heard a spectator say, "Oh, is that all?"

Spectators *want* to believe in magic. Years ago, I violated this principle. A lady I knew fairly well told me that she had seen a marvellous trick the night before. A friend of the family had placed an empty beer bottle on the kitchen table, had wrapped it in paper, and had then squashed the paper. The bottle had disappeared!

I reluctantly gave in to her entreaties to explain the trick. "He was sitting at the table, right? The paper he wrapped the bottle in had to be stiff enough to hold the shape. As he talked, he brought the wrapped bottle over the edge of the table and let the bottle drop in his lap."

"But that isn't what he did," my friend insisted.

"No problem," I said. "Then it was magic."

Since then, I have *never* explained a trick.

3. *Never* let a spectator do a trick. If pressed, tell the spectator he can perform when you are done. If he insists, you *are* done. Give him the deck and walk away.

Sometimes I explain, "I don't think I could survive seeing for the five-hundredth time someone dealing out three rows of cards with seven cards in each row."

Quite often, disappointment marks the face of the aspiring performer. "Oh, do you know that one?" he asks ruefully.

4. A card is selected, and you find it. No matter how many different ways you find the card, you are still doing only one trick. You can do this several times, and it might be entertaining. But throw in some variety. Very few of the tricks in this book begin with "Take a card," so you have a nice variety to choose from. Mix up your tricks. The more diversity you display, the more entertained the spectators will be, and the more impressed they will be with your ability.

5. If you are fascinated with performing card tricks, you will undoubtedly consult many other books of legerdemain. Just remember this: It's not enough that a trick may be easy to do; it must also be *worth* doing.

THE PEEK

Magicians use *The Peek* to sneak a look at a card without being observed. There are many methods, most of them requiring some sleight of hand.

The Peek is often called *The Glimpse.* I prefer the former term— it sounds sneakier.

The methods I present here are actually *Peek* substitutes, but that does not matter. You need to know the name of a particular card in the deck—the top, the bottom, or the second from the bottom—but you do not wish to unduly arouse the suspicions of your audience.

Suppose you wish to learn the name of the top card. Choose from these four methods.

1. Peek at the bottom card while toying with the deck and chatting with the spectators. Give the cards an overhand shuffle, (pages 28 & 29) drawing off the last few cards individually so that the bottom card ends up on top.

2. Look at it ahead of time.

3. Fan through the deck, saying, "I want to get a mental picture of all the cards," or (even more preposterously),"I want to make sure all the cards are here." Note the top card.

4. Fan through the cards, saying, "I want to remove my bad luck card. Otherwise this might not work." Fan through once, noting the top card. Then find the queen of spades, or some other "bad luck card," and toss it aside. This method is particularly effective.

There are many other methods of sighting a card. If you investigate card-trick literature, you will come across at least a half-dozen.

THE GLIDE

Used properly—which is to say, sparingly—this is one of the most useful moves in card magic. You show the bottom card of the deck and, presumably, place it on the table. Only it is not the same card. You actually deal out the second card from the bottom.

The maneuver, of course, should never be used as a trick by itself. Even the dullest spectator will have an inkling as to what actually happened.

ILLUSTRATION 1:
Hold the deck in your left hand,
at the sides, and from above.

ILLUSTRATION 2:
Lift the cards and show the
bottom card to the spectators.

The deck is held in the left hand at the sides from above (Illustration 1). The cards are lifted, showing the bottom card to the spectators (Illustration 2). Note that the hand is gripping nearer the back of the deck than the front, and that the second and third fingers extend over the side of the deck past the first joint. The reason will become apparent.

The deck is tilted down again, and the second and third fingers bend under and draw the bottom card back one-half inch or so. Illustration 3 shows the view from underneath. The second card from the bottom is now drawn out with the second and third fingers of the right hand. When the card is drawn out about an inch, the right thumb takes it at the top so that the card is gripped beneath by the second and third fingers and at the top by the thumb. The card is placed face down on the table.

ILLUSTRATION 3:
Draw the bottom card back one-half inch.
This view is from underneath.

CONTROLLING A CARD

It's vital that you be able to control a selected card, usually bringing it to the top. Here are eight different ways to accomplish this.

Double-Cut

This is a complete cut of the deck. Suppose you wish to bring a card to the top. Spread the deck for the return of a selected card. The spectator sticks the card into the deck. As you close up the deck, slightly lift the cards above the chosen card with the fingers of your right hand. This will enable you to secure a break with your little finger above the chosen card (Illustration 4). (If the card is to be brought to the bottom, secure a break *below* the selected card.)

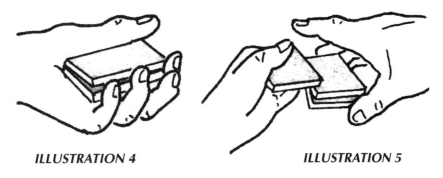

ILLUSTRATION 4   *ILLUSTRATION 5*

Holding the deck from above in your right hand, transfer the break to your right thumb. With your left hand, take some of the cards from the bottom and place them on top (Illustration 5). Take the remainder of the cards below the break and place them on top. (It is perhaps more deceptive if you move three small packets from below the break instead of two).

This is, by far, the most common way in which magicians control a card to the top or bottom.

As you will see, this is also a sleight which has many other uses in certain tricks.

Delayed Shuffle

You do *not* get a little-finger break when the selected card is returned. Instead, in the process of closing up the deck, you move the cards above the selected card *forward* about half an inch. With your left thumb, push the chosen card to the right. Continuing the process of closing up the deck, move forward the remaining cards in your left hand (Illustration 6). You now have an in-jogged card above the chosen card.

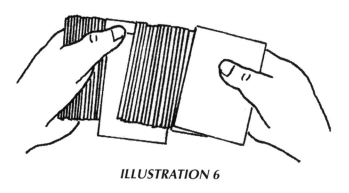

ILLUSTRATION 6

Immediately drop your left hand with the deck to your side and chat for a moment with the spectators. When you're ready, bring your left hand up in the overhand shuffle position. Your right hand takes the deck, and your right thumb *pushes up* on the protruding card, obtaining a break. Small packets are shuffled into your left hand until the break is reached. All the cards below the break are dropped on top. The chosen card is now on top. (See *Controlling a Group of Cards*, page 32, for a complete explanation of the overhand shuffle using an injogged card. Note particularly Illustrations 17 and 18).

Simple Overhand Shuffle

Have the spectator place his card on top. False-shuffle the cards and give them a false cut. This works as well as anything else. (See *False Cuts*, page 25, and *Shuffles*, page 29).

Don't Pass It Up

I thought I'd invented this method of bringing a card to the top, but I discovered that Martin Gardner had beaten me to it by a considerable number of years.

A card is selected. As you ask the spectator to show it around, hold the deck in the dealing position in your left hand. Your right hand also holds the cards, gripping them from above with your fingers at the outer end and your thumb at the inner end. With your left fingers, pull the bottom card down about a quarter inch. Your right thumb secures a break between this card and the rest of the deck (Illustration 7). The maneuver is completely covered by your right hand.

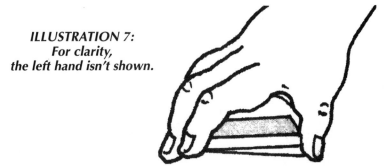

ILLUSTRATION 7:
For clarity,
the left hand isn't shown.

You're about to perform the first part of a legitimate one-finger cut in preparation for a very tricky move indeed. Bring your left hand behind the deck and, from below with your left forefinger, revolve about half the cards so that they fall into your hand at the front of the deck (Illustration 8). At this point you're holding half the deck in your left hand, which is in front of your right hand. Extend the cards in your left hand, indicating that the chosen card should be replaced on top. In your right hand is the original lower portion of the deck, at the bottom of which you are holding one card separated with your right thumb.

After the spectator places his card on top of the pile in your left hand, bring the cards in your right hand, ever so briefly, over

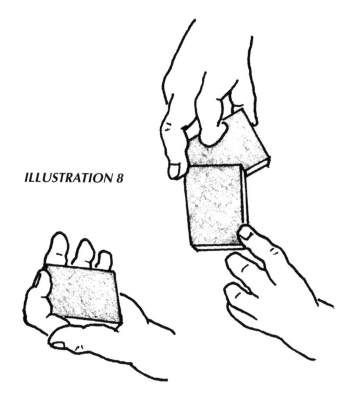

ILLUSTRATION 8

those in your left hand. Let the bottom card of the packet in your right hand drop on top of the packet in your left hand. As you begin the forward motion of your right hand, say something like, "You had complete freedom of choice, right?" At the beginning of the question, drop the card on top of the packet in your left hand. As you complete the question, continue moving your right hand forward with its packet. Raise your right first finger from the packet and point your finger at the spectator. The whole procedure should appear to be one movement, as you apparently are merely emphasizing your statement by moving the packet forward and pointing a finger at the spectator.

Thumb off the top card of those in your left hand onto the top of those in your right. Place the rest of the cards in your left hand on top of all.

Apparently, you very fairly placed the spectator's card in the middle; actually, it's on top.

20

Easy Way

Get a little-finger break above the selected card. With your right hand, cut a small pile from the top of the deck. Place the pile face down on the table. Cut off another small pile and place it on top of the pile on the table. Repeat, taking off all the cards above your little-finger break. Finally, place the remaining cards on top of the pile. The chosen card is now on top. It's even more effective if you place the piles on a spectator's outstretched hand.

Easy Control

Ian Land and I independently arrived at a similar card control. Let's call mine *Easy Control* and his *Even Easier Control*. My method is not a complete cut of the deck, so it is useful only for bringing a chosen card to the top or within a few cards from the top.

You are holding a break above the chosen card with your left little finger. Fan through about half of the cards *that are above the break,* saying, "We know your card is in here somewhere." With your right fingers on the right side, flip this group face up onto the deck. Rapidly fan through these face-up cards, saying, "Could be here." Stop fanning when you get to the first face-down card.

Close up the fanned cards so that they slide into your right hand. Hold this group separate as you continue fanning down to the break held by your left little finger. With the tips of the right fingers flip over the cards you just fanned out so that they are now face up on the balance of the deck.

Here's the situation: In your right hand is a group of face-up cards. On top of the balance of the deck is another group of face-up cards, which you have just flipped over.

As soon as these cards land face-up, rapidly fan through them, adding them below the cards in your right hand. Say, "Could be here." Stop fanning when you get to the first face-down card (the chosen card).

Again, loosely close up the fanned cards. Hold them slightly to one side as you flip the remaining cards face up with your left thumb. Add these to the bottom (or rear) of those in your right hand as you fan through them, saying, "Could be here." Stop about two-thirds of the way through, saying "Who knows?" Close up the entire bunch and turn the deck face down. The chosen card is now on top.

During this last fanning, make sure you do not reveal the lowermost card, which is the one chosen.

Even Easier Control

Ian Land's method is similar to mine, but his is a complete cut of the deck. Since the bottom card is revealed during the move, you can't use it to bring a card to the bottom. You *can* use it, however, to bring a card within a small number of cards from the bottom. And it can be used to bring a card to the top or within a small number of cards from the top. I think you'll like the simplicity of this method.

Again, you're holding a break above the chosen card with your left little finger. Turn over the top card of the deck, saying, "Your card is not on top." Replace the card face down.

ILLUSTRATION 9

With the palm-down right hand, grasp all the cards above the break at the left side. Pivot them in an arc to the right, as though opening a book from the back (Illustration 9). "It's not here in the middle."

Move your right hand with its cards a bit to the right. With your left thumb, flip over the cards that are in your left hand, saying, "And not on the bottom."

Place the face-up cards that are in your right hand on top of the face-up cards that are in your left hand. Turn the deck over. The chosen card is now on top.

Key-Card Control

In some instances, using a key card for control works best. For example, you might want to bring the chosen card to within a fairly high number of cards from the top. This control would do perfectly, as I'll explain.

Before the spectator chooses a card, sneak a peek at the bottom card of the deck. This is your key card. You can do this as you separate the deck in two, preparing to do a riffle shuffle. Easier yet, look at the bottom card as you tap the side of the deck on the table, apparently evening up the cards. Then, when you shuffle, keep the card on the bottom.

So you know the bottom card of the deck. Fan out the deck, and a spectator selects a card. Close up the deck. From the top of the deck, lift off a small packet of cards and drop it onto the table. Lift off another small packet and drop it on top of the first one. After dropping several packets like this, say to the spectator, "Put your card here whenever you want." After you drop one of your packets, he places his card on top. You put the rest of the deck on top of it. Even up the cards and pick them up. The key card which you peeked at is now above the chosen card.

Start fanning through the cards, faces towards yourself. Mutter something such as, "This is going to be really hard." Fan off several cards. Cut them to the rear of the deck. Fan off several more. Again, cut them to the rear. You're establishing a pattern so that it won't seem so odd when you finally cut the chosen card into position.

Let's say you simply want the card available on top of the deck. Continue fanning groups of cards and placing them at the rear until you see that you'll soon arrive at the key card. Cut the cards so that the key card becomes the top card of the deck. Just below it, of course, is the chosen card. Turn the deck face down.

"I can't seem to find your card." Turn over the top card of the deck (the key card). "This isn't it, is it?" No. Turn the card over and stick it into the middle of the deck. Turn the deck face up. "How about this one?" No. Take the bottom card and stick it into the middle of the deck. Turn the deck face down. The chosen card is at your disposal on top of the deck.

Suppose, for purposes of a specific trick, you want the chosen card to be tenth from the top. Again you start by fanning off small groups and cutting them to the rear of the deck. When you get to the chosen card, you start counting to yourself. You count the chosen card as "One." Count the next card as "Two." Cut the cards so that the card at "Ten" becomes the top card. The chosen card is now tenth from the top.

Clearly you can use the same method to arrange to spell the chosen card from the top, dealing off one card for each letter in the spelling.

FALSE CUTS

After a card is returned and brought to the top, it's not a bad idea to further convince spectators that the card is lost by giving the pack a false cut or false shuffle.

False cuts are also very useful when you have a set-up deck and you want to convince the spectators that the cards are mixed.

Casual Cut

Most versions of this false cut involve a sweeping movement which reveals that *something* peculiar has taken place. Hold the cards in the basic dealing position in your left hand, but with the cards tilted clockwise at about a 45° angle. Approach from the rear with your palm-down right hand. With your right thumb and fingers, grasp approximately the *bottom* half of the deck at the sides. Pull this portion towards you. As soon as the packet clears, lower your left hand a few inches. This creates a compelling illusion that the packet came from the top of the deck. Bring the packet *over* the cards in your left hand and slap it onto the table.

Your right hand, from above, now takes the packet from your left hand. Slap this packet on top of the packet on the table. As you do this, grasp the combined packets and pick them up. Return the complete deck to your left hand.

Multiple-Pile Cut

Set the deck on the table at position "A." Cut off a small portion ("B") and set it somewhat away and to the right of "A." Cut another small pile off "A" and set it to the right of "B;" this is pile "C." Continue with piles "D," "E," "F." Place "B" on "C," place "BC" on "D," and so on to "F." Pick up the combined pile. As an afterthought, notice "A." Place the cards in your hand on "A" and pick all up. The cards are back as they were at the beginning.

Gall Cut

This cut, attributed to Jay Ose, takes a bit of nerve.

With your left thumb riffle down about a third of the deck. Lift off this pile and place it on the table. As you place this pile down, with your left thumb riffle down about half of the remaining cards. Lift these off and place them to the right of the first pile.

Your right hand takes the remaining pile and slaps it down to the right of the other two piles. With your right hand, place the first pile on the second. Pick up the combined pile and place it on the third. The deck is back in its original order.

The One-Finger Cut

This is unique among false cuts, in that the phony one looks more genuine than the real one.

First, the *real* cut. The deck is held from above in the right hand near the right edge, second finger at the front, thumb at the back, and first finger either curled or slightly bent. The left hand, fingers up, approaches the deck from the rear (Illustration 10).

The first finger of the left hand does the work. With the tip, it pivots the top half of the deck, revolving the cards around the second finger of the right hand (Illustration 11). The left hand moves directly in front of the of the right hand so that the top half of the deck drops into the left hand (Illustration 12).

To complete the legitimate cut, the right hand places its half on top of the cards in the left hand.

Here is the *false* cut. After you pivot the top half into the left hand, bring the cards in the right hand directly over the top of the portion in the left hand and set them on the table. The right hand returns, takes the pile from the left hand, which has remained stationary, and places the pile on top of the cards on the table.

There are two keys: bringing the pile in your right hand *directly over* the cards in your left hand as you set the pile on the table, and keeping your left hand stationary when you return with your right hand to get the other half. The cut takes just a few seconds and is totally deceptive.

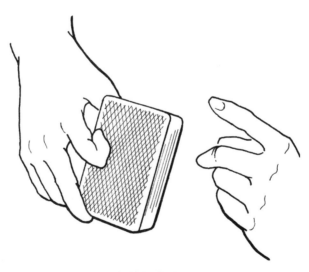

ILLUSTRATION 10:
The first step of a "true" cut.

27

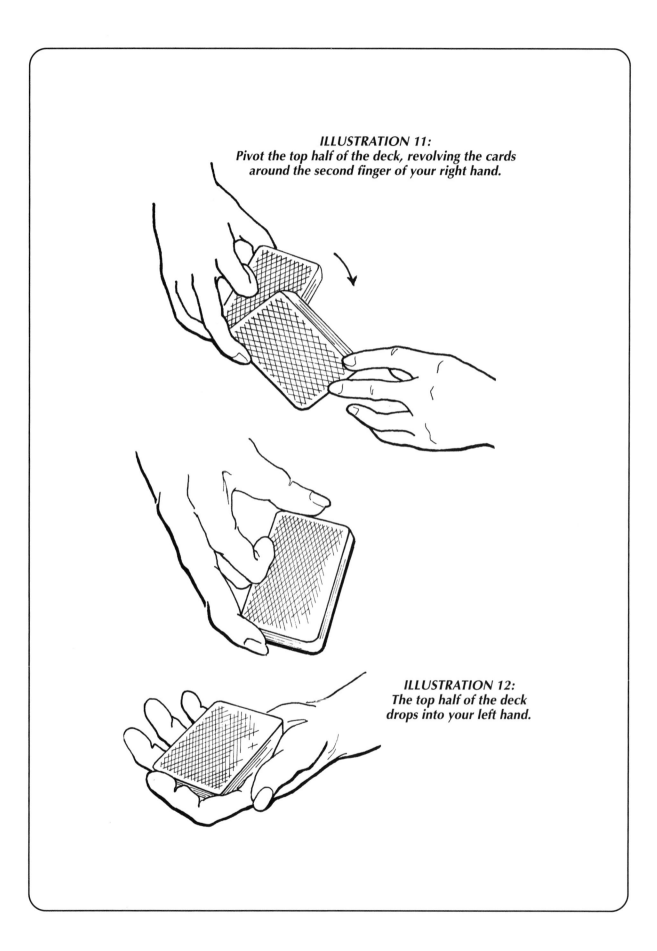

ILLUSTRATION 11:
Pivot the top half of the deck, revolving the cards around the second finger of your right hand.

ILLUSTRATION 12:
The top half of the deck drops into your left hand.

SHUFFLES

To perform some of the tricks in this book, you must know how to do two kinds of shuffle, the Hindu shuffle and the overhand shuffle. Neither is difficult, but mastering the *false* overhand shuffle will take some practice.

Hindu Shuffle

With the Hindu shuffle, you can do a variety of sleights. Here we are just concerned with the mechanics of the shuffle, as well as a very easy force.

Start with the deck in the dealing position in your left hand. With your palm-down right hand, grasp the cards at the near narrow end. Bring the deck towards you with your right hand, allowing your left fingers to draw off a small packet from the top (Illustration 13). This packet falls into your left hand. Draw off another packet, letting it fall onto the one in your left hand. Continue until only a small packet remains in your right hand. Drop this on top of the others.

Now the force: You have your force card on the bottom of the deck. With your first move, you not only withdraw a packet from the top, but you also cling to a small packet on the bottom with

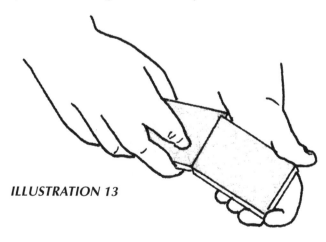

ILLUSTRATION 13

29

your left thumb and left fingers. The packet from the top falls on top of this packet. Complete the shuffle in the usual way. Apparently you've performed a regular Hindu shuffle; actually, the bottom several cards remain exactly as they were. This means, of course, that the force card is still on the bottom. Perform this maneuver a few times.

Ask a spectator to tell you when to stop as you shuffle the cards. Perform the regular Hindu shuffle, taking quite small packets with each move. When the spectator tells you to stop, avert your head and tilt up the packet in your right hand, showing the spectator the bottom card. Then place this packet on top of the cards in your left hand.

Overhand Shuffle

Normal Shuffle

Hold the deck in your left hand as shown in Illustration 14. With your right hand, pick up from the bottom of the deck all but a small packet (Illustration 15). Bring your right hand down (Illustration 16) and let a small packet drop from the top of these cards onto the top of the cards in your left hand.

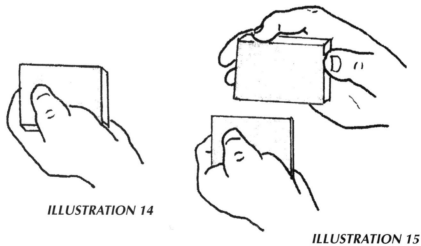

ILLUSTRATION 14

ILLUSTRATION 15

Your left thumb lifts a little, allowing passage. The release of these cards from the top of those in your right hand is effected by very slightly relaxing the pressure of your thumb and fingers at the ends.

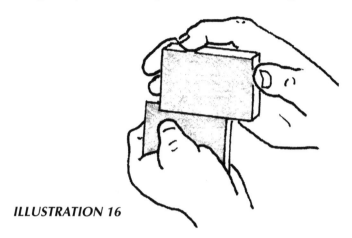

ILLUSTRATION 16

As the packet is lifted again by your right hand, your left thumb, which was drawn back, returns to the back of the cards being accepted by your left hand. (This is particularly important in the various false shuffles, as you will see.)

Continue dropping packets in the same manner until all the cards are in your left hand.

Bringing the Top Card to the Bottom
In the first move of an overhand shuffle, draw off a single card with your left thumb. Shuffle the rest on top of it. The top card is now on the bottom.

Bringing the Bottom Card to the Top
Start the overhand shuffle. When all that remains in your right hand is a very small packet, draw off cards singly with your left thumb until all have been shuffled off. The bottom card is now on top. (In the same way, you can bring several cards to the top, simply making sure that you draw off the last several cards one at a time.)

Controlling a Group of Cards

The key to all false shuffling is performing casually. Don't stare at your hands. Chat as you do your dirty work.

The idea is to keep a packet on top in order. Again start by picking up from the bottom of the deck all but a small packet. (This small packet will eventually be returned to the top.) As your right hand returns, it's slightly closer to your body. A packet is not released; instead, your left thumb draws off one card. Because your right hand is slightly closer to your body, the card is automatically jogged inward approximately half an inch (Illustration 17). (This move is known as the *injog.*)

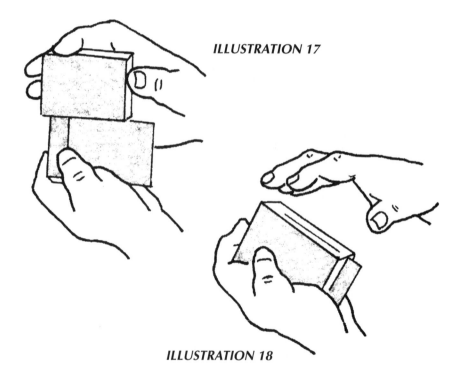

ILLUSTRATION 17

ILLUSTRATION 18

Your right hand moves slightly forward; now the cards released into the left hand in small packets will be even with the rest of the deck. At the conclusion of this phase, the deck should look like Illustration 18.

In phase two, as your right hand takes the deck, your thumb pushes up on the protruding card, obtaining a break (Illustration 19). In the overhand shuffle, small packets are dropped into your left hand until the break is reached. All the cards below the break are dropped on top. Thus, the original top packet is back on top.

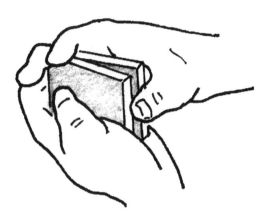

ILLUSTRATION 19:
For clarity, the break is exaggerated.

FORCES

Usually, the magician forces a card as an essential part of a trick. Every force, however, can be presented as mind reading. The judicious choice of some of these can enhance a mental routine. When using a force as mind reading, explain that you don't want to influence a spectator psychologically, so the card to be thought of should be chosen completely by chance; then proceed with the force.

Standard Force

The standard force isn't perfect for even the most advanced card expert, but it's well worth learning. No method appears more natural. What's more, if you fail to force a particular card, you simply proceed with a trick where a force isn't required. Any time you do a trick where a card is chosen, try to force a card. The more you practise, the better you'll get. Eventually, you'll be able to force nine times out of ten.

My method is standard, except perhaps for setting up the force card. Clearly, whenever you force a card, you must peek at a card and then get it in position for the force.

To use my method of preparing for the force, you must know how to do the Hindu shuffle (page 29). Take the deck in the Hindu shuffle position, both hands slightly tilted clockwise. Draw off a small packet in the first move of the Hindu shuffle. As you do so, you are holding most of the deck in your right hand. Turn your right hand even more clockwise until you can see the bottom card (Illustration 20). This is your force card. Now tilt your right hand back to the normal position. Continue drawing off small packets to about half the deck, and then toss the rest of the deck on top, letting the cards fall on top of your inserted little finger, which holds a small break (See Illustration 4, page 17).

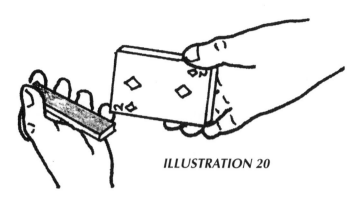

ILLUSTRATION 20

The little finger is now holding a break at the middle of the deck below the card you sighted. Immediately begin to fan the cards into your right hand, pushing with your left thumb on top and pulling with your right fingers underneath. Approach a spectator, saying, "I'd like you to select a card." As he reaches, arrange to have your sighted card fall under his fingertips. How? Coordinate the speed of your fanning and the extension of the deck towards the spectator. Also, you expose the surface of the sighted card a little more as the spectator's hand nears the deck (Illustration 21).

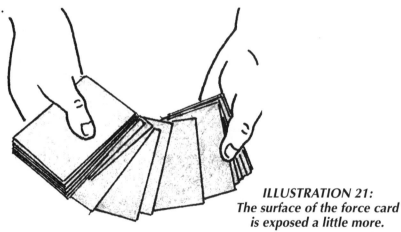

ILLUSTRATION 21:
The surface of the force card
is exposed a little more.

If all this seems a bit vague, it is because forcing is more of an art than it is an exact science. There's only one way you'll really get the knack: practising on spectators.

Two Tricks with the Force
Quick Trick
When you successfully force a card, say to the spectator, "Now show the ten of clubs around, but don't let me see it." You'll be quite gratified by the delayed reaction.

Blackstone's Stunt
Harry Blackstone (the elder) used to force a card and, just as the spectator was withdrawing it from the deck, he'd say, "Take any card but the five of spades." When the spectator showed that he indeed had taken the five of spades, Blackstone would express chagrin, and proceed to force it on him again.

Riffle Force
Sneak a peek at the bottom card. Shuffle it to the top in an overhand shuffle. Perform another overhand shuffle, lifting about half the deck with the first move. Draw off one card with your left thumb, injogging the card. Shuffle off the rest. (See *Controlling a Group of Cards*, page 32.) Place the deck in the dealing position in your left hand. Retaining the deck in your left hand, grip the cards from above with your right hand, fingers at the outer end, thumb at the inner end. As you do so, with the right thumb lift the injogged card. Now you're holding a break above the force card with your right thumb.

Riffle down the left side of the deck a few times with your left thumb. Say to a spectator, "I'd like you to tell me when to stop as I riffle the deck." Slowly riffle down the side of the deck with your left thumb. The spectator will probalby tell you to stop somewhere around the middle. If the spectator waits until you're well past the middle, quickly riffle down the remainder of the deck. Start the riffle again, saying, "Tell me to stop anytime." When you're told to stop, tilt the deck slightly forward as you lift off all the cards above the break. Move these cards forward and then to one side. Offer

the pile in your left hand, saying, "Take a look at your card, please."
Or, if the trick calls for it, say "Take your card, please, and show it
around."

Simon Says

The first person I saw using this force was Simon Lovell; hence the
title.

The top card of the deck is your force card. Hold the deck in
the dealing position in your left hand. Fold your left first finger
under the deck; this will facilitate the following move. Riffle down
the left side of the deck with your left thumb, saying to a spectator,
"Tell me when to stop." Stop immediately at the exact point he
indicates. Your left thumb now is bending down all the cards below the break. (Illustration 22).

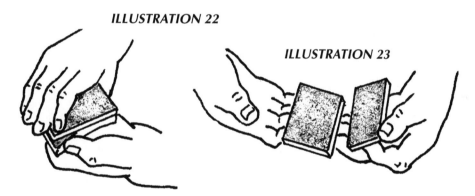

ILLUSTRATION 22

ILLUSTRATION 23

Hold your right hand palm up next to your left hand. Tilt your
left hand clockwise, until the cards above your left thumb fall face
up on the extended fingers of your right hand. The right edge of
the pile in your right hand should rest along the first joint of your
right fingers (Illustration 23). The second and third fingers of your
left hand flip the pile over so that it falls face down in your right
hand. Immediately extend your right hand towards the spectator.
Say, "Please look at your card." He looks at the original top card
of the deck.

One-Cut Force

You must know the top card. See *The Peek* (page 14). As you hold the deck, have a spectator cut off a portion of cards and turn them face up on the rest of the deck.

Immediately turn the deck over and spread the cards out on the table (Illustration 24).

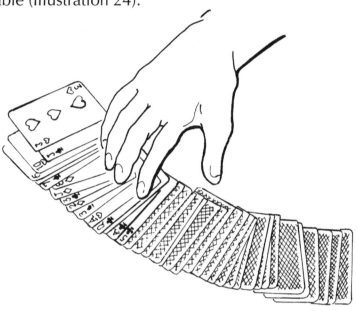

ILLUSTRATION 24:
One means of forcing the top card in a deck.
As you hold the deck, have a spectator cut off a portion of the cards,
and then have him place them face up on the rest of the deck.
Turn the deck over and spread the cards out on the table.

Push through the face-up cards to the first face-down card. Point to it, saying, "Please take a look at the card." It is, of course, the original top card which you sighted.

There is a temptation to say, "Look at the card you cut to." I think it's a mistake to be that specific. I don't want the spectator to be thinking, "Hmm. *Is* that the card I cut to?"

The Face-Up Force

This is a quick, deceptive force, which I occasionally use to discover a chosen card. You must know the top card. Have a spectator take a card from the deck, turn it face up, and place it on top. He then cuts a pile from the top and sets it on the table. You turn the remaining cards in your hand face up and place them beside the cutoff portion. Take the cutoff portion (with the face-up card on top), turn it face up, and place it on top of the other pile.

Pick up the deck and turn it face down. Hand it to the spectator and ask him to look through to the face-up card and look at the randomly selected card below it.

You may prefer to fan through yourself, chatting about freedom of choice in cutting the cards. Separate the cards below the face-up card and offer the next card (originally the top card, of course) for him to look at.

Actually, all that has happened is that a face-up card was placed upon the force card and the cards were cut. The handling, however, obscures this and convinces the spectator that he has freely chosen the card. Practise this one a bit before trying it in public; smoothness is the key.

Double-Turnover Force

Again you must know the top card. See *The Peek* (page 14). As you hold the deck, ask a spectator to cut off a small packet and turn it face up on the deck. Then have him cut off a larger packet and turn it face up on the deck. Fan through the face up cards to the first face-down card. Extend the face down pile to the spectator, asking him to look at his card. It is the original top card.

Crisscross Force

You must know the top card of the deck. Set the deck on the table. Ask a spectator to cut off a pile and place it on the table. Pick up the bottom portion and place it crosswise on the cut-off portion.

Chat with the spectator for a moment so that he has a chance to forget about the true position of the two piles. (This is known as "time misdirection.") Point to the top card of the lower pile, saying, "Take a look at your card, please." As before, it's the original top card of the deck.

DROP SLEIGHT

This is a wonderful utility move in which one card is secretly exchanged for another. Separate a card at the bottom of the deck, holding a break above it with your right thumb, and then perform the first part of a legitimate one-finger cut: From behind the deck, with your upraised left first finger, revolve about half of the cards from the top of the deck so that they fall into your left hand.

Now for the sleight itself. With your left thumb, push off the top card of those in your left hand. With the left edge of the packet in your right hand, flip this card over so that it turns face up on the lower portion of the deck (Illustration 25). At the conclusion of the move, your right hand, with its packet, swings naturally over the cards in your left hand. Display the card, saying, for instance, "Here we have the six of hearts."

Continue with patter suited to the trick you're doing as you flip the card face down in the same way as you flipped it face up. This time, as your right hand comes over the deck, drop the card separated by your thumb. It falls on top of the lower packet as your right hand continues its sweeping move to the left for an inch or so. This small movement to the left covers the sleight, making it completely invisible.

The original top card of the deck has now been exchanged for the original bottom card of the deck. This maneuver is useful in a number of tricks, as you will see.

Usually, after the sleight is performed, your hands are separated, and the top card of the packet in your left hand is thumbed face down onto the table.

ILLUSTRATION 25

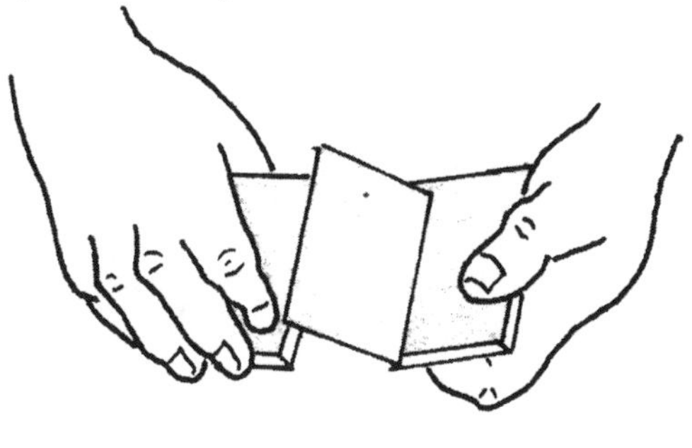

41

DOUBLE-LIFT

The double-lift is used in many tricks. A proficient card handler should definitely know how to do one. There are at least a dozen different ways of performing a good double-lift. The three below work extremely well.

Snap Double-Lift

I was told that this was one of John Scarne's favorite methods. I don't know whether he invented it.

Apparently a card is casually snapped face up and flipped back on top of the deck. Actually, it's two cards.

First, you should practise the display of a *single* card by snapping it face up. Incidentally, if you want to make the double-lift believable, always display a card in the same way as you do when performing the sleight.

Hold the deck high in your left hand (Illustration 26). Your right hand lifts off the top card, holding it as shown in Illustration 27. Squeeze the card so that it bevels downwards, as shown in Illustration 28.

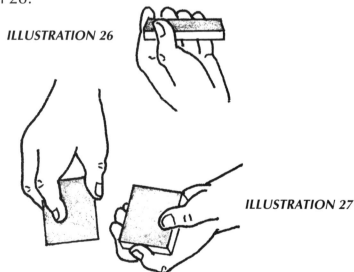

ILLUSTRATION 26

ILLUSTRATION 27

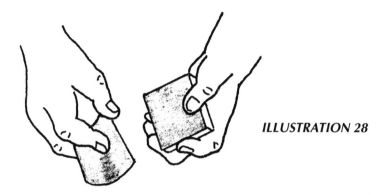

ILLUSTRATION 28

The idea now is to press down slightly with the first finger and continue bending the card, until by straightening the second finger slightly you snap the card loose from that digit and hold the card between your thumb and first finger (Illustration 29). At the same time as you snap the card, turn your hand clockwise so that the card is clearly displayed. The entire move is done in an instant.

The card is returned to the deck by laying its side on the tips of your left hand fingers, and flipping it over with your right hand first finger (Illustration 30).

ILLUSTRATION 29

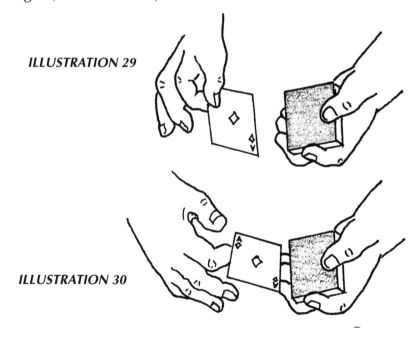

ILLUSTRATION 30

Practise the entire maneuver until you can do it smoothly and naturally.

For the double-lift, you duplicate precisely the actions in the single lift. Holding the deck high in your hand, casually riffle the left side of the deck near the rear with your right thumb (Illustration 31). In doing this, separate the top two cards from the rest of the deck and hold the break with your *left* thumb (Illustration 32).

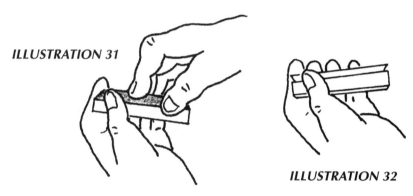

ILLUSTRATION 31

ILLUSTRATION 32

Take the two cards with your right hand *exactly as you took the single card.* Snap the two cards face up. Name the card. Roll the two back on top. Do all this in precisely the same way as you did the single card.

There's a knack. At first, the cards may separate slightly, but if you treat the two *precisely* as you would a single card, they won't. Alternate snapping over a single card and a double card. Within half an hour, you should have the move mastered.

Efficient Double-Lift

I developed this double-lift some time ago. Since then, I've seen other magicians use double-lifts that are similar, if not identical. I believe that the details make this one of the best: It looks natural, it requires no preparatory move, and the return to the deck is extremely simple.

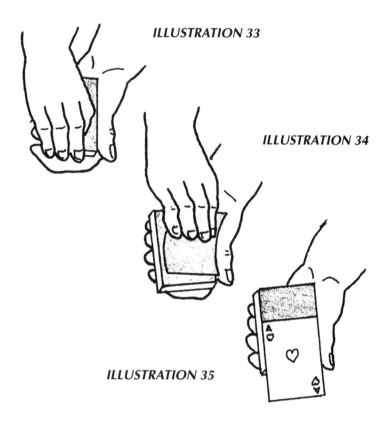

ILLUSTRATION 33

ILLUSTRATION 34

ILLUSTRATION 35

Hold the deck in your left hand, thumb along the left side. With your right hand, grip the deck from above, thumb at the rear, first finger folded on top, and the remaining fingers at the outer end (Illustration 33).

Bevel the cards back slightly. With your right thumb, lift two cards about a quarter inch. The backward bevel helps with this. Slide your fingers back along the surface of the double card so that you're gripping it at the back end between fingers and thumb (Illustration 34). Immediately snap the double card over end for end, moving your right hand forward as you do so. Set the card down so that it projects about an inch-and-a-half beyond the front of the deck (Illustration 35).

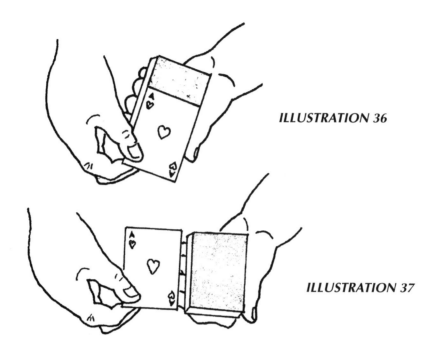

ILLUSTRATION 36

ILLUSTRATION 37

After pausing a few moments, with your palm-up right hand grasp the double card at the right outer side, fingers below and thumb on top (Illustration 36). Lift it off the deck and bring it to the right side of the deck (Illustration 37). With your right fingers beneath, flip the double card face down on top of the deck.

Note: It may be difficult at first to separate two cards from the deck with your right thumb. A good way to practise is to perform the double-lift, then deal the top card down. Perform another double -lift; deal the top card down. Continue on through the deck. Eventually, you'll have no trouble at all.

Original Double-Lift

The double-lift I learned as a kid is quite easy and will still do the job for a great many tricks.

As with *Efficient Double-Lift* (page 44), hold the deck in your left hand with your thumb along the side. Grip the deck with your right hand, as in the previous double-lift (Illustration 33, page 45). As you chat with the spectators, separate two cards at the rear of the deck with your right thumb. Push these two cards forward about a quarter-inch.

With your right hand, grasp the two cards at the outer end, fingers beneath and thumb on top. This is precisely the same grip shown in Illustration 36 (page 46), except that, in this instance, the card taken with your right hand is face down. Turn the two cards over end-for-end, and set them down so that they project about an inch beyond the front of the deck.

When ready, grasp the cards at the outer end again, turn them end-for-end, and return them, face down, to the top of the deck.

The Great CARD TRICKS

PREDICTION

Presto Prediction

This trick appeared almost forty years ago in a booklet I published. The trick was recently credited to someone else. I don't invent so many good tricks that I can afford to let that pass: I invented it, and besides, my version is better.

Few tricks have a climax as startling as this one. The principle is just about impossible to detect, but what really makes the trick work is the patter, the romance. I have always felt that a weakness can be turned into a strength if you only give the problem enough thought. In this instance, the spectators are dealing cards, selecting, counting down. In other words, this has all the earmarks of a "mathematical" trick, a no-brainer, a trick anyone could do. Indeed it is. But the patter makes it all seem logical, if not absolutely necessary. So at the climax of the trick, be sure to try the suggested patter.

Hand the deck to a spectator for shuffling, saying, "Now I am going to attempt to predict the future. The odds are fifty-two to one against my doing this, but I think it's going to work this time. You see, I've missed the last sixty-three times, so I'm way overdue."

Take the deck back, holding it with your fingertips, so that all can see that you are doing nothing tricky. "Watch carefully. I want you to see that I do not change the position of a single card. I'm going to fan through the deck and remove a prediction card."

Demonstrate by fanning through the cards, faces towards you, noting the value of the top card. Close up the cards. Let us suppose that the top card is an eight.

"Watch carefully now!" With the cards facing you, again fan through them, starting at the bottom. Since you noted an eight on top, count to eight from the bottom and note the card at that position. Let us say it is the five of diamonds. Continue fanning until you come to the corresponding card in color and value—in this instance, the five of hearts. Meticulously lift the five of hearts from the deck and place it face down on the table, stating, "This is my prediction card." While doing all this, handle the cards openly to emphasize that you are doing *nothing tricky* with the deck.

Hand the deck to a second spectator. "Please turn the deck face up and deal the cards one at a time into a pile." Once he deals past the card you noted, casually say, "You can stop whenever you want." When he does stop, tell him he may deal a few more, take a few back, whatever he wishes.

Take the undealt cards from the spectator and place them face down. Turn the dealt cards face down. The position now is as follows: The top card of the undealt pile indicates the number down in the dealt pile at which the match for your prediction card lies. In our example, the top card of one pile is an eight, and the eighth card down in the other pile is the five of diamonds, which corresponds to your prediction card, the five of hearts.

Point out the two face-down piles to a third spectator. "Perhaps you have seen demonstrations where the performer asks you to choose a pile and then he takes whatever pile he wants. In this case, I want you to pick up a pile. That will be the pile that you will actually use."

Sound convincing? Of course. But, as you will see, it doesn't matter which pile he picks up. Suppose he takes the pile with the eight on top. You say, "What we are going to do is turn over the top card of your pile—not yet—and count down that number in this pile." Pick up the other pile and continue, "An ace has a value of one, a jack eleven, a queen twelve, and a king thirteen."

This statement is particularly effective when the card is *not* one of these, for it creates the impression that you have no idea what the card is.

The third spectator turns over the top card of his pile; you slowly count off the cards from your pile, setting aside the card arrived at. In your example, the spectator turned over an eight, so you count off eight cards, setting aside the eighth one, the five of diamonds.

Suppose that when you offer the choice of piles the third spectator picks up the pile containing the card that matches your prediction card. Simply say, "Now I will turn over the top card of my pile, and we will count down that number in the pile you have chosen." Be sure to mention the business about the value of ace, jack, queen, and king. Let the spectator count off the cards, and you take the final card of the count and place it face down on the table.

You now have two face-down cards on the table: your prediction card and the card "chosen" by the spectators. Gather up the rest of the deck, leaving the two face-down cards.

What you say now triples the trick's effectiveness. "Let's review. First the deck was thoroughly shuffled. Without changing the position of a single card, I removed the prediction card. Then you (the second spectator) dealt off as many cards as you wanted, stopped whenever you wanted. Finally, you (the third spectator) chose a pile, and we actually used the pile you chose. In other words, we tried to arrive at the choice of a card completely by chance. Why did we go through all this? Because if I offered you the choice of a card, you might think I had some way of forcing my selection on you. Instead, we have guaranteed that a card was chosen at random."

Set aside the deck. Take the two cards at the outer edge. "If I have correctly predicted the future, these two cards should match each other in color—and in value." Face the two cards simultaneously. When you gather the cards up after enjoying their astonishment, it's fun to add, "I feel sorry for the next fifty-one people I do this for."

Note: Occasionally, when fanning through the cards for your prediction card, you will see that it is among those that will be counted off. Obviously, the trick will not work. Shake your head, close up the cards and hand them to a spectator, saying, "Please shuffle them again. I can't seem to picture a card; the vibrations just aren't right. Perhaps another shuffle will help."

Colorful Prediction

With this trick, by using an unprepared deck, you apparently correctly estimate the number of red and black cards in two piles.

For this one, you need a complete deck of fifty-two cards. Let a spectator shuffle the deck. Take it back and begin dealing into a face-down pile. After you have dealt fifteen or more, invite the spectator to tell you to stop whenever he wishes.

As you deal, count the cards. Try to keep your lips from moving. When he says stop, give him the dealt pile. Ask him his favorite color, red or black. Suppose he says red, and further suppose that his pile contains twenty-three cards. You say, "Bad luck. I have three more red cards than you have black."

Repeat the assertion. Now deal your cards face up, counting the red cards aloud as you go. The spectator deals his cards face up, counting the blacks. Sure enough, you have three more reds than he has blacks.

Why?

To understand, take a deck of cards, shuffle it, and deal it into two piles of twenty-six cards each. Suppose you have nineteen black cards in one pile. You must also have seven red cards in that pile. This means that the other pile must contain nineteen red cards and seven black cards. So, no matter how you shuffle, when you have two piles of twenty-six cards, you will always have the same number of black cards in one pile as you have red cards in the other.

This will be clearer if we take an extreme example or two. If you have twenty-six black cards in one pile, you will have twenty-six red cards in the other. You could say, "I have the same number of reds in my pile as you have blacks in yours."

It would work the same if you had twenty-five red cards and one black in your pile. The spectator would have twenty-five blacks and one red. And you, naturally would have the same number of red cards as he has blacks.

If you tried to pass that off as a trick, however, very few spectators would be deceived, particularly if you do repeats. Therefore, you disguise the principle by working with unequal piles and perfoming a simple calculation.

When you performed the trick as above, the spectator had twenty-three cards. That's three less than twenty-six. You, therefore, have three more than twenty-six. This means that you have three more red cards than he has black. For that matter, you have three more black cards than he has red.

Back to the trick. The spectator is astonished at your clairvoyance, but you have only just begun. Have the spectator shuffle his packet of twenty-three, and you shuffle your packet. You may even exchange packets and shuffle. Then you take your original packet and begin dealing onto his, asking him again to tell you when to stop. Once more you keep track of the number.

He had twenty-three, so you begin counting with twenty-four. When he tells you to stop, you again know the number of cards he has in his pile.

"Which do you want this time, red or black?" Suppose he chooses black, and that he now has thirty cards in his pile.

"Good selection. You now hold four more blacks than I have reds."

In other words, he has four more cards than twenty-six.

You may repeat the trick a number of times, remembering to deal from the larger packet to the smaller. In our example, the piles would be shuffled again, and you would make sure to deal from the pile of thirty onto the other, which, of course, contains twenty-two.

The trick, like many good ones, is a combination of a hidden principle and verbal chicanery. You can throw spectators off further by stating your prediction in different ways.

There are four ways you could state the preceding prediction:

1. You now hold four more blacks than I have reds.
2. You now have four more reds than I have blacks.
3. I now have four fewer blacks than you have reds.
4. I now have four fewer reds than you have blacks.

Three-Card Surprise

When I invented this trick, I discovered that it is doubly astonishing. It is absolutely baffling and entertaining to spectators. And it is astonishing to me that it should be so well received. I consider it among the best tricks I perform.

The original version of this trick must be as old as card tricks. Long ago I came across a good version. Unfortunately, two decks were required (an automatic turn-off for me), and the move required at the end seemed contrived, unnecessary, and unsatisfactory. Recently I solved the problem of the ending, and in the process came up with what amounts to a new trick—with one deck.

Because the effect is similar to that of *Presto Prediction*, you should probably not do these two in the same set. The effect is that you correctly predict three cards chosen by a spectator or spectators.

Have the deck shuffled. Take the cards back and fan through them, faces towards you, saying, "We are going to take turns selecting cards. First I'll select one, and then you'll select one."

As you spread the cards, note the top card. Remove a card from the deck of the same value and color. If the top card is the six of diamonds, for instance, you remove the six of hearts. Without showing it to the spectators, place it face down on the table. Spread the rest of the cards face down on the table, inviting a spectator to choose one and place it face up on your card. It is important that you make no mention of telling the future or matching cards; you two are simply taking turns selecting cards.

Tell the spectator, "A very good choice. Now I'll select another one." Fan through the cards as before, and remove the card that is the same color and value as the one which he just placed face up. As you do so, mutter about now this must be the world's most tedious card experiment. Place the card face down to the right of your first choice. Set the deck down and say, "You will choose each card in a different way. This time, I would like you to cut a pile off the deck."

When he cuts the cards, take the one he cut to and place it face up on top of your second choice. Make sure you replace the cutoff pile on top so that the card you originally sighted remains on top.

Compliment the spectator on his selection and fan through the cards once more, muttering about how boring this experiment is. This time remove a card of the same color and value as the spectator's second selection and place the card face down to the right of the other two.

"Now we'll try yet another way of selecting a card," you say. Retaining the deck in your hand, tell the spectator, "Cut off a small packet, turn it face up, and place it on top of the deck." After he does so, say, "Now cut off a larger packet, turn it face up, and place it on top of the deck." This is *Double-Turnover Force* (page 39).

Explain, "Now we'll go to the card you cut to." Fan through the face-up cards and take out the first face-down card. It, of course, is the original top card, the one you sighted at the beginning of the trick. Place the card face up on top of your third face-down card.

It is important that you more or less follow the patter I have given. You don't want to put the spectators on guard by mentioning things like prediction or coincidence or any of the usual baloney.

Set the rest of the deck aside, saying, "I know exactly what you're thinking. Are there extra cards on the table? Did he slip in an extra card or two?"

Place the third set of two, the one on your right, on top of the middle set. Then place the set on the left on top of all. Now the top card matches the bottom card, and the other two pairs match each other face-to-face. I have inserted a little sneakiness into the routine here. "I can assure you that there are exactly six cards here."

Pick up the packet of six and hold it in the dealing position in the left hand. Take off the top card in your right hand with your right thumb, counting out, "One." Take off the second card in the same way, dealing it on top of the first in your right hand. You count, "Two."

Continue through the fifth card, counting aloud for each one. For the sixth card, you pause ever so slightly, saying, "And six." And place the sixth card on the bottom.

Instantly, take off the top two cards and drop them on the table. Next to them drop the next two cards. And next to them drop the last set of two. While doing this, say, "Six cards. Three sets of two."

The business of counting the cards and dropping them on the table in pairs has taken some time to explain. But the execution must be done snappily.

After a brief pause, turn over the face-down card in each pair, showing that the pairs match up in color and value. At this point it is frivolous to say anything; the climax speaks for itself. You will be delighted to hear such comments as, "But how could you know that I would pick that?"

TRANSPOSITION

Tick Tock Trick

To my delight, this trick of mine appeared in the September, 1949 issue of *Conjurors' Magazine.* This trick is always received well, and it is a nice change of pace from more conventional effects.

You deal twelve cards in a face-up circle, each card indicating an hour on the clock. Start with one o'clock and deal around to twelve o'clock, calling off each number (or time) as you deal. The card at twelve o'clock should be pushed a little above the circle so that spectators will have no trouble telling what card lies at what time. The queen of spades is placed in the middle and is dubbed "the card of mystery." A spectator mentally selects one of the cards and remembers the time at which it lies.

Turn your back and tell the spectator to quietly count from the deck a number of cards equal to the hour at which his selected card lies. If his card lies at five o'clock, he counts off five cards. These cards are placed in the spectator's pocket, or are otherwise concealed.

Now gather up the cards, apparently casually. Chat with the spectators as you do so. Pick up "the card of mystery" first and place it face up in your left hand. Pick up the rest of the cards in reverse order, starting with the card at twelve o'clock. The last one placed face up in your left hand is the card at one o'clock. Put these cards face down on top of the deck.

Now would be a good time to perform the *One-Finger Cut,* on page 26.

Have the spectator take the cards he has concealed and place them on top of the deck while you look away. You must now get rid of the top card. Riffle the end of the deck a few times, and then say, "No, I didn't do anything." Take off the top card and show it.

"See? It's not *your* card, and it's not the card of mystery." Place the card in the middle of the deck. To throw a little dust in their eyes, take the bottom card also, show it, and place it in the middle of the deck.

Deal the cards face down into a circle, starting with one o'clock. The thirteenth card is placed in the middle, and you refer to it as "the card of mystery."

Ask the spectator what time he selected. The card at that time is turned over; it is "the card of mystery." And the card in the center? Ask the spectator to name his card. Turn over the center card, saying, "Ah, your card is the new card of mystery."

Easy Aces

Every card trickster knows at least one four-ace trick, and most know several. Card performers love to do false shuffles, multiple palms, and top changes as they magically collect the aces into one pile. This version magically collects the aces into one pile, and requires no sleights.

When you hear how this one is done, you may decide that it's a little too gutsy for you. "Aw, shucks! Everyone will see how it's done." *No one* will see how it's done. The dirty work is done before anyone expects it, and with excellent misdirection.

Take the four aces from the pack, show them, and place them in a face-down row on the table. On top of each ace deal three cards face down. Set aside the rest of the deck. Place the piles one on top of the other, forming one pile.

"Obviously," you explain, "every fourth card is an ace." Fan the cards before the spectators, showing that this is true. As you fan through, say, "Three cards and an ace, three cards and an ace, three cards and an ace, and three cards and an ace." Even up the cards slowly and meticulously, demonstrating that you are performing no sleights.

From the top of the packet, deal four cards in a row on the table, saying, "Here we have one, two, three, ace." Casually take the top card of the packet in your hand. "So what's this card?" you ask, tapping the ace with the card in your hand.

The spectator will probably say that it is an ace. Regardless, you say, "Turn it over, please."

As he does so, *casually place the card in your hand on the bottom of the packet.* All attention, of course, is on the card being turned over.

Turn the ace face down. Deal a row of cards on top of the cards you just dealt, saying, "One, two, three, ace." Finish dealing the rest of the packet in the same manner, repeating, "One, two, three, ace."

The spectators are convinced that the four aces are in the fourth pile. Actually, the bottom card of the fourth pile is an ace, and the rest of the pile consists of ordinary cards. The bottom one of the third pile is an ordinary card, while the other three in that pile are aces.

Pick up piles one and two, and drop them on the deck. Take the ace from the bottom of the original fourth pile and place it face up in front of that pile. Take the ordinary card from the bottom of the original third pile and place it face up in front of that pile.

"One pile of aces," you say, "and one pile of ordinary cards." Then, suiting action to words, you add, "All we have to do is exchange the markers, snap the fingers, and the cards magically change places."

Turn over the three ordinary cards first, saying, "Now *these* are the ordinary cards." Turn over the aces, as you say, "And *these* are the aces."

Tricky Transpo

This trick is the easiest transposition trick ever—it is also a baffler. A word of warning, however. The participating spectators are required to remember both a card and a number. Do not perform this one as a part of youir regular routine; save it for times when you have bright, cooperative spectators.

Ask for the assistance of two spectators. Give the deck to the first spectator and then turn your back. Give these directions to the first spectator: "Please shuffle the cards. Now think of an even number, preferably one under twenty. Quietly count off that number of cards. When you are done, hand the deck to my other assistant."

Direct the second spectator as follows: "Will you shuffle the deck, please? Now think of an odd number, preferably one under twenty. Quietly count off that number of cards."

When the second spectator is done, continue: "Please set the rest of the deck aside; we won't be using it anymore. Now put both piles together, and I would like one of you to shuffle the new pile. Now, without changing the position of any card, I want both of you to see what card lies at the number you thought of. I would like each of you to remember your card and the number you thought of."

Turn back to the spectators and take the pile of cards. Place them behind your back, saying, "I am going to attempt to transpose the two selected cards."

When you put the cards behind your back, take the bottom card in your right hand and, starting with the top card, *quietly* deal the rest of the cards on top of it, reversing their order. While doing this, make small talk about the tremendous miracle you are attempting to perform. Bring the cards forward. Ask the first spectator for his even number. He tells you and, without changing the position of any cards (taking them one *under* the other), count down to that number. Ask the second spectator to name his card. Show that his card now lies at that number.

Replace the card in the exact same spot in the pile, and replace the cards on top so that they are in precisely the same order. Ask the second spectator what his nuber was. Count down to that number in the same way as you did previously. Before showing the card at that number, ask the first spectator to name his card. Show that it is now at that number.

The trick is a little complex, but I love it. I'm still not dead sure why it works, so every time I perform it, I am at least as astonished as the spectators.

One in Four

This trick is quite similar to the previous trick in its basic principle. But its *effect* is quite different. Roy Walton combined tricks by Al Baker and Dai Vernon; my only contribution is to add a slightly different handling.

Remove from the deck the four, three, two and ace of any suit. (Let's assume that you're using diamonds). First find the four and place it face up on the table. On top of this place the face-up three, followed by the two and the ace.

Ask Jeanine to choose a card and show it around. When she returns it to the deck, bring it to the top. (See *Controlling a Card*, page 17).

Hold the deck in the dealing position in your left hand. Pick up the four face-up cards from the table and drop them face up on top of the deck. Spread them out, along with another card or two. Say, "Here we have the ace, two, three, and four of diamonds." As you close up the four diamonds with your palm-up right hand, get a break with your left little finger below the fifth card. Immediately, turn your right hand palm down and lift off the packet of five cards, fingers at the other end, thumb at the inner end. The top, face-up card of the packet is the ace of diamonds, followed by the other three diamonds in order. On the bottom of the packet is the face-down chosen card.

"It's important that you remember the order of the cards," you say. "First, we have the ace." You now turn over the ace lengthwise and add it to the bottom of the packet. Here's precisely how: Move the packet in your right hand over the deck and hold down the ace with your left thumb as you move the rest of the packet to the right, drawing off the ace. The ace should extend over the right side of the deck about half its width (Illustration 38). From below, lift the packet in your right hand so that its left edge flips the ace over sideways. *Leave your left thumb in place, so that the ace falls on it.* Bring your right hand over the face-down ace, so that the ace is added to the bottom of the packet.

66

ILLUSTRATION 38

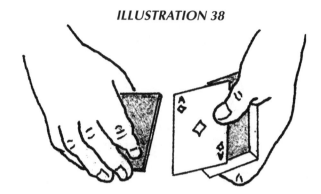

Call attention to the two of diamonds, saying, "And here we have the two." In the same way as you did the ace, turn the two of diamonds face down and add it to the bottom of the packet.

In exactly the same way, show the three and then the four. Drop the packet on top of the deck.

On top of the deck is the chosen card, followed by the ace, two, three, and four of diamonds.

Say to Jeanine, "I'd like you to choose one of the four cards—ace, two, three, or four. In fact, think of one, and then change your mind. I want you to have complete freedom of choice." She chooses one of the cards.

Suppose the ace is chosen. Deal the top card face down onto the table, saying, "All right, there's the ace. Now let's see how the two behaves." Without showing the top card, place it second from the top. Tap the top card and then turn it over. Apparently the two has returned to the top. Place the two *face up* next to the card on the table.

"Let's check the three." Place the top card second from the top. Tap the top card and turn it over. The three has returned. Deal it face up next to the two.

"And the four?" Again, place the top card second from the top. Tap the top card and turn it over, showing that the four has returned. Deal it face up to the right of the three.

Gesture towards the table. "So we have ace, two, three, four of diamonds. And you chose the ace. What's the name of your card?" The spectator names it. Turn over the face-down card. Success!

Suppose the spectator chooses two, three, or four. In each instance, the chosen number is simply dealt face down onto the table; each of the others is placed second from the top, brought back to the top, turned face up and dealt face up onto the table.

Let's suppose Jeanine chooses three, for instance. "Fine," you say. "Let's see how the ace behaves." Place the top card second from the top. Tap the top card, showing that the ace has returned. Place the ace on the table face up.

Place the top card second from the top, saying, "Let's see what the two does." Tap the top card. Sure enough, the two has returned to the top. Deal it face up to the right of the ace. Deal the next card face down to the right of the other two cards, saying, "Here's your three."

Once more place the top card second from the top, saying, "Let's see what the four does." Tap the top card; the four has returned to the top. Deal it face up to the right of the other three cards.

In all instances, you finally ask the name of the chosen card and then turn it face up.

Travelling Hearts

In concept, *Travelling Hearts* is similar to the preceeding trick.

The original of this trick, which was shown to me by Bob Stencel, required a bottom deal. I changed the trick to suit my abilities.

Look through the deck so that the spectators can't see the faces. Cut the ace of spades to the top. Then toss out these hearts, in any order, face up onto the table: ace, two, three, four, five, six.

Set down the deck and put the cards in order, the ace being at the face of the face-up packet and the six at the bottom. As you do so, say, "Try to remember what these cards are. For whatever reason, some people don't pay attention: all they can think of is the ace of spades. *Please* . . . these are hearts!"

As you speak, pick up the deck and hold it in your left hand in the dealing position. With your right hand, pick up the packet of hearts and place it face up on top of the deck. You'll now add a card to the packet, exactly as described in the previous trick. Spread out the hearts, displaying them. As you do so, casually spread out a few additional cards. As you close up the cards with your palm-up right hand, get a slight break with your left little finger under the seventh card. Turn your right hand palm down and lift off all seven cards with your right hand, fingers at the outer end, thumb at the inner end. Set the rest of the deck aside.

You're now holding the six hearts face up, with the ace of spades face down on the bottom. Take the packet in your left hand.

Say, "Try to remember these cards . . . *and* their order." Take the ace of hearts in your right hand, saying its name. Turn the card face down and place it face down on the bottom of the packet. With your right hand, turn the packet over, showing the ace on the bottom. Repeat, "Ace of hearts."

Perform the exact same procedure with the two of hearts. For the rest, you simply announce the name of the card, turn it over and place it on the bottom. The last card you place on the bottom is, of course, the six of hearts. Casually drop the packet on top of the deck.

The top six cards of the deck are, from the top: ace of spades, ace of hearts, two of hearts, three of hearts, four of hearts, and five of hearts.

Deal the top six cards into a row on the table. As you place the cards down, say, "Ace, two, three, four, five, six."

Pause. "Now watch this. We exchange the ace and the two." Change the places of the first two cards. Snap your fingers. Turn over the first card in the row. "The ace of hearts returns. Let's try the two."

Leaving the ace face up, do the same exchange with the second and third cards. Snap your fingers. "The two is back. Let's try the three."

Leave the two face up.

Perform the same maneuver with the third card, the fourth card and the fifth card. At this point, you have face up on the table the ace, two, three, four and five of hearts, along with the face-down ace of spades.

"So we have one card left. And, of course, we all know what it is." Pause. "Well, what is it?"

Most of the time, the answer will be, "The six of hearts."

Shake your head. Turn the ace of spades over. "Just as I say, some people just don't pay attention."

Once in a while, a spectator will guess the ace of spades.

"Right you are!" you say. "At least *some* people pay attention."

Joker Helps

Before I explain this Jack Avis transposition trick, I'll teach you a sleight called *Mexican Turnover*. It's a quite useful method for exchanging two cards.

Place a card face down on the table. Take another card face down in your right hand, holding it at the lower right corner with your thumb on top and your first two fingers beneath (Illustration 39). The third and fourth fingers of your right hand are curled into your palm. Presumably, you'll turn over the card on the table with the card in your hand.

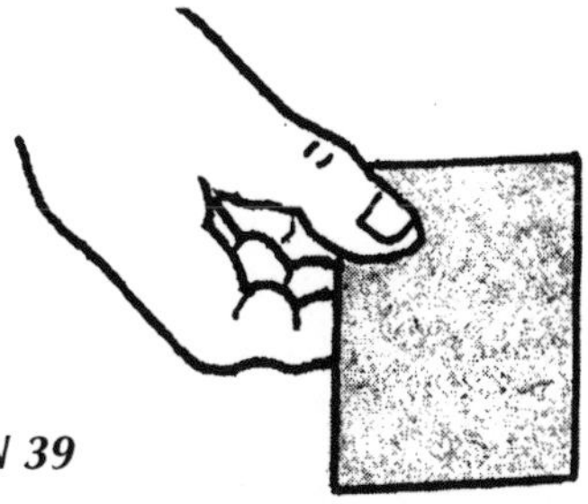

ILLUSTRATION 39

Place your left first finger on the lower left corner of the card on the table, tilting the opposite side up slightly. Slide the card in your hand under the right side of the table card, so that the bottom card extends a little less than an inch above the upper card (Illustration 40). Tilt both hands counter clockwise slightly.

ILLUSTRATION 40

As you do so, your right thumb and second finger grip the *upper* card. This card is lifted several inches at about a 45°. In that same motion, your right first finger flips the lower card face up—sideways. (Naturally, as you perform the flipping action, your left hand moves to the left, releasing the hold of its first finger on the card which was originally; on the table.) The sleight should be performed at medium speed: *don't rush it!*

You might practise by alternately performing a legitimate turnover and *Mexican Turnover.*

Now, the trick. Lay three cards out on the table, left to right: an ace, a joker, and a three. Emphasize the position of the ace and the three. Pick up the face-up joker and apparently turn the three face down. Actually, perform *Mexican Turnover.* Make sure that no one sees that the face-down three is in your right hand as you continue moving the card to the left and drop it face down on the face-up ace.

Pick up the two cards and hold them in the dealer's grip in your left hand. The three is face down on top; the ace is face up on the bottom. Turn over your left hand and push the cards through your hand with your left thumb (Illustration 41). Take them at the outer end with your right hand. Now the ace is on top face down and the three is on the bottom face up. Turn your left hand palm up and replace the two cards there. Fan the two cards, revealing the three (Illustration 42).

ILLUSTRATION 41

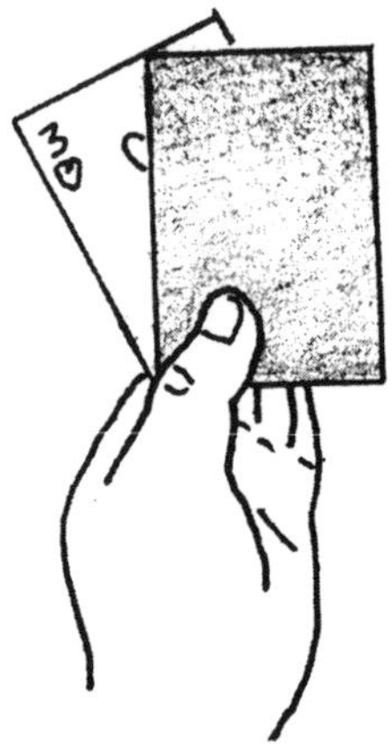

ILLUSTRATION 42

Set aside the face-up three. Now exchange the face-down ace with the face-down joker on the table, using *Mexican Turnover.* The ace and the three have changed places. Casually toss the joker face up onto the table.

Join the Knavery

Fan through the deck, faces towards yourself. Make no attempt at concealment as you cut the queen of diamonds to the top. Place the queen of spades on top of that. So, the second card from the top of the deck is the queen of diamonds; the top card is the queen of spades. Toss the two black jacks and the queen of hearts face up onto the table.

As you do the above, say, "I'd like to tell you a tale of two loving sisters, who happened to be queens, and another queen, who happened to be an evil witch."

You now do half of a legitimate one-finger cut, described in detail at the beginning of *Don't Pass It Up*, page 19. Your left first finger is pointed upwards behind the deck. In this instance, however, you revolve about *two-thirds* of the cards from the top of the deck so that they fall into your left hand. Place the part remaining in your right hand on the table to your left. "Here we have the castle in which one of the red queens lived." Touch the queen of hearts, which is face up on the table. "This queen, in fact. One day, two evil knaves came to the castle and kidnapped the queen and took her into the forest. Once there, they blindfolded her." Say to Oliver, a willing spectator, "To show that, please put her face down between the two evil knaves." He makes a sandwich of the three cards, the queen of hearts being face down between the two face-up jacks.

" 'What are you going to do to me?' asked the queen.

" 'When evening comes, we'll leave you to be eaten by wild beasts.'

" 'But besides you two, there are no wild beasts in this forest.'

" 'Then when evening comes, we'll kill you.'

" 'That's more like it,' said the queen, who was something of a perfectionist.

"And who was responsible for the kidnapping? This wicked witch, who also happened to be a queen—the queen of spades."

With the packet in your hand, now perform *Drop Sleight*, exactly as described on page 41. During the previous patter, you do the necessary preparation of letting the bottom card drop slightly and holding a break with your right thumb between this card and the rest of the packet. Then you proceed with half of a one-finger cut, and the actual sleight. As you say, "—the queen of spades," turn the top card of the left-hand packet over, using the left edge of the cards in your right hand. It is, of course, the queen of spades. Continue your patter as you complete the sleight, replacing the queen of spades with an indifferent card.

"She didn't have a castle, so she had the red queen kidnapped and took over her castle."

Place the cards in your right hand on the table, slightly to the right. With your right hand take off the top card of those in your left hand and plce it on top of the pile on the left. Apparently this card is the queen of spades.

As you proceed with the patter, place the cards in your left hand on top of those you just set on the table. Pick up the entire packet and hold it in your left hand.

The situation: On top of the packet you're holding is the queen of spades. Below it is the queen of diamonds.

"How wicked was she? Why, she'd talk with her mouth full of food. She'd cry when she didn't get her own way. And, worst of all, she'd torture her subjects by singing off-key until they begged for mercy.

"Now, with all this talk, I'll bet some of you can't remember which red queen we have in the forest. Is it the diamond queen or her sister, the heart queen?"

Pick up the three cards on the table and hold them fanned in your right hand. Meanwhile, push off the top card of the packet slightly and draw it back, getting a left little-finger break beneath it. Close up the three-card fan onto the packet, adding the additional card to the bottom of the group. Immediately lift off all four cards with your palm-down right hand, fingers at the outer end and thumb at the inner end.

"Can you remember which one was kidnapped? Was it the heart queen or the diamond queen?" Whatever the answer, with your left thumb draw the top face-up jack onto the packet. Thumb it face up onto the table. With your left thumb, draw the face-down queen of hearts onto the packet, letting it hang over the right side of the packet about half its width. Flip it over with the left side of the double card in your right hand, again letting it hang over about half its width.

"Ah, it's the queen of hearts—*not* her wonderful sister, the queen of diamonds."

With the right side of the double card, flip the queen of hearts face down, even with the top of the packet. With the same motion, drop the double card on top. Immediately fan off the top two cards, take them in your right hand, and place them on the jack on the table. The three should be spread out, forming a fan.

The queen of spades is now face down between the two face-up jacks, and the queen of hearts is on top of the packet in your hand. The second card from the top is the queen of diamonds. Do a double-lift, showing the queen of diamonds. Ask, "How many of you thought it was really the queen of diamonds?" Turn the double card face down. "Wrong, wrong, wrong!" Hold the packet from above in your right hand. Draw off the top card (the presumed queen of diamonds) with your *left* hand. "The diamond queen left her castle . . ." Move your right hand up and down slightly, indicating that the packet there is the castle in question. Place the card which is in your left hand on top of the packet on your left. ". . . and went to the wicked queen to beg for her sister's life."

Place the packet which is in your right hand down to your right.

" 'Please spare my sister's life!' she begged.

" 'Nuts to you with shells on,' said the evil queen.

" 'Then you'll be sorry,' said the diamond queen.

" 'Why should I be sorry? I'm an evil witch and I have evil witch powers.'

"And the diamond queen said, 'But I'm a good witch, and I have good witch powers—which are way stronger than evil witch powers. And now, I'll sing a magic spell (sing) When you wish upon a star, Makes no . . . Wait a minute . . . wrong movie. I've got it . . . (sing) Bibbety, bobbety, bibbety, bobbety, bibbety, bobbety boo.' And with that, both castles shook a little."

Casually show that both hands are empty. Reach out and simultaneously give each pile a little riffle.

"Instantly . . . the diamond queen was back in her castle." Turn over the top card of the pile on the right, leaving it face up on top. "And . . ." Turn over the top card of the other pile. ". . . the heart queen was back in her castle." Pause. During the following, spread the two jacks aside and turn over the queen of spades: "And the evil queen was alone in the forest with the two nasty knaves!" Before the audience has a chance to react, immediately say, "Soooo . . . they all lived happily ever after."

Quite Quaint Queens

This trick requires very little work but accomplishes an extraordinary result. This gem is the brainchild of Alan Brown.

Since you already have most of the cards you need on the table from the previous trick, you can continue the story by doing this trick. You may, however, prefer to perform this trick by itself.

Take out the jacks from the deck. Place the two red jacks, face up and fanned out, upon the table to the left; place the two black jacks, face up and fanned out, upon the table to the right. Remove the queen of spades and queen of hearts from the deck and place them near you, face up upon the table.

"The black jacks," you say, "are evil knaves. They work for this evil queen." Tap the queen of spades.

"The red jacks, however, are nice guys. They work for this very good queen." Tap the queen of hearts."

One day, the evil queen had the good queen kidnapped by her evil knaves." Place the queen of hearts face up between the two face-up black jacks, so that the lady becomes the middle card of the three-card fan. "They took her into the forest and blindfolded her." Ask Arnold to turn the queen of hearts face down, indicating that the queen's blindfolded. So the three-card fan now consists of the face-down queen of hearts surrounded by the two face-up black jacks.

Pick up the queen of spades. "While this was going on, the evil queen held the good guys prisoner with her crossbow." Place the queen of spades *face up* between the two red jacks, so that the three cards form a fan on the table.

"Why did the evil queen do this? Because she wanted this castle for herself." As you say "this castle," hold out the deck, showing that it represents the castle. "So the evil queen of spades went inside the castle with the two nice guys, the red jacks." (This is to implant the precise position in the minds of the spectators).

Hold the deck in the dealing position in your left hand. Pick up the fan of the red jacks and the queen of spades. Retaining their order (jacks on the outside), turn the three face down, and place them on top of the deck. As you close up the face-down trio, get a break with your right thumb below the top card. Double-undercut the deck, bringing the top card to the bottom. (See *Double-Cut, page 17*). "There go the red jacks and the evil queen of spades."

Gesture towards the remaining trio on the table. "The evil knaves were really stupid, and they forgot why they'd kidnapped the good queen of hearts. So they returned to the castle."

With your right hand, reach over to pick up the top black jack. As you do so, push off the top card of the deck slightly with your left thumb. Draw the card back on top of the deck, getting a tiny break beneath it with the tip of your left little finger. Place the black jack *face up* on top of the deck. "One evil knave entered the castle." Pick up the queen of hearts and place it face down on top of the deck. "When the good queen of hearts got into the castle, she slammed the door, and ran away."

You now have the queen of hearts on top, and the card below it is a black jack. Below the third card from the top, you have a little-finger break. Double-undercut the deck, bringing the top three cards to the bottom.

All the dirty work is done.

"The other evil knave finally managed to get the door open . . ." Pick up the other back jack and place it face up on top. " . . . and he immediately began searching for the queen of hearts." Give the cards a legitimate cut in the middle. Then cut off an additional small packet (ten cards or so) and complete the cut.

Snap the ends of the cards. "Now let's see what happened." Fan through the cards to the face-up black jacks and the face-down card between them. "The evil knaves finally found the queen in the dark. So they dragged her out of the castle and took her into the forest." Remove the three cards together from the deck and place the three on the table. Close up the deck.

"But they made one little mistake. They had the wrong queen." Turn the middle card of the three over, showing that it's the queen of spades.

"And what about the queen of hearts?" Turn the deck face up and fan through so that all can see. "Let's find those nice guys, the red jacks. There they are. And right between them, we have the good queen of hearts . . . just as it should be."

ESTIMATION

Easy Estimation

Tricks don't get much better than this one. Apparently you can gauge the precise number of cards a spectator cuts.

Have the deck shuffled and set down. Tell a spectator to cut off a packet of cards, not too large. Then you cut off a packet, making sure it contains several more cards than the spectator's pile. Turn your back, saying, "We'll each count our cards. Then I'll tell you exactly how many you have."

With your back turned to the spectator, count your cards as he counts his. Suppose you have twenty-two. Can you make a trick out of telling the spectator that you have twenty-two cards? It doesn't seem likely, does it? Yet that is, in effect, exactly what you do.

When you turn back to the spectator, say, "I have the same number you have, three left over, and enough more to make your pile total nineteen." Repeat the statement to make sure it sinks in.

"Now let's count our cards together." As he counts his cards into a pile, you simultaneously count yours into a separate pile. The cards should be counted deliberately, and you should count out loud.

Let us suppose he had thirteen cards. You stop dealing at the same time as he does. "Thirteen," you say. "The same number you have. And I said, three left over." Deal three cards from your pile to one side, counting aloud. "Three left over. And I said that I had enough left over to make your pile total nineteen." Point to his pile. "You have thirteen." *Count now on his pile.* "Fourteen, fifteen, sixteen, seventeen, eighteen, nineteen." You were exactly right.

So far as I know, this is the only trick based *solely* on the use of words. As I indicated, what you *really* said to the spectator was, "I counted my cards, and it turned out I had twenty-two."

Let's try another form: "I have the same number you have and enought more to make a total of twenty-two." Wouln't fool many people, would it?

Try this: "I have twenty-two cards, but I decided to subtract three from it giving me nineteen."

Still not tricky enough? Here's the actual form again: "I have the same number you have, three left over, and enough more to make your pile total nineteen."

You could also say, "I have the same number you have, two left over, and enough more to make your pile total twenty."

What you do, of course, is subtract a small number—two, three, or four—from your total number of cards. In the example, you counted twenty-two cards. Supposing that, instead of three, you decide that four should be the number left over. You subtract four from twenty-two, giving you eighteen. You now have two critical numbers, and you say, "I have the same number you have, four left over, and enough more to make your pile total eighteen." Note that these statements will work when you have a pile containing several more cards that the spectator's.

The trick can be repeated with no danger of spectators discovering the secret. To throw them off the track, use different numbers—two, three, four—for the number of cards left over.

Let's make sure you have it. The spectator cuts off a packet. Make sure it's no more than twenty cards. Cut off a pile containing several more cards than his. Turn away, telling the spectator to count his cards while you count yours. Suppose you have twenty-five. You will choose a small number—two, three, or four—to subtract from it. Let's say you choose two. You subtract two from twenty-five, giving you twenty-three. When you turn back, you state, "I have the same number you have, two left over, and enough more to make your pile total twenty-three." Then complete the trick as described above.

There are two things that throw the spectators off: the few extra cards that you count off, and the completion of the count, not on your pile, *but on the spectator's pile.*

Digital Estimation

Here's one I made up many, many years ago. I have had considerable fun with it ever since. It's a pretty good follow-up to *Easy Estimation.*

You need a complete fifty-two-card deck. Two spectators each cut off a pile and are asked to hold the packets flat in their palms. You say, "I am going to estimate the number of cards each of you is holding and break the result down to its lowest digit. Then I will find a card to verify my estimation."

The effectiveness of this trick depends on your ability to playact. As you do the following, pause from time to time and study the piles the spectators are holding, creating the impression that you are performing a difficult feat of judgment.

What you actually do is run the remaining cards from hand to hand, faces toward you, apparently seeking an appropriate estimation card, but actually counting them. You will find you can do the counting rapidly and easily if you run the cards in groups of three. Don't forget to pause in your counting here and there to gauge the spectator's piles.

When you get the total, reduce it to a digit. Suppose the total is twenty-three; add the two and three together, giving you five. With a total of twenty-nine, add the two and nine, giving you eleven; then you add one and one, giving you a final digit of two.

Subtract your digit from either seven or sixteen, whichever gives you a single digit. Continuing to fan through the cards, find a card of that value and place it face down on the table.

For example, if you count twenty-three cards, add the digits together, giving you five. Subtract five from seven, giving you two. Find a two among your cards and place it face down on the table.

Another example: You count twenty-five cards. Add the two digits and you get seven. You are to subtract from either seven or sixteen. Since subtracting it from seven would give you zero, you subtract it from sixteen, giving you nine. Find a nine among your cards and place it face down on the table.

82

Now tell the spectators this: "I would like you each to count your cards carefully, and then mentally break your total down to one digit. For example, if you have fifteen cards, you would add the one and five together, giving you six."

When the spectators are done, have them each give their digit. Add these two together and break them down to a single figure. Turn over your estimation card and take a bow.

Why does it work? Let's start with a fifty-two card deck. The digits five and two add up to seven. And no matter how you divide the fifty-two-card deck, the various piles when added together and broken down to a digit will produce seven.

So, when you count your pile, presumably looking for a card to signify your estimation, you can get the right answer by reducing your total to a digit and subtracting from seven, or from any two numbers that add up to seven, like sixteen, twenty-five, thirty-four, forty-three, or fifty-two, so long as you reduce your total to a single digit.

The trick can be repeated as above, but I prefer this: "To make it even more difficult, I will try to estimate the number of cards held by *three* spectators. Again, I will break down the total and select an estimation card."

Have three spectators cut off small packets and hold them flat on their palms. Scrutinize the packets. Then fan through the remaining cards, finding your estimation card by counting and subtracting from seven or sixteen, as before. The spectators count their piles, reduce the number in each pile to a digit, add the totals, and reduce that result to a digit. Naturally, your estimation is correct. Performing this twice works out about right. No use pushing your luck.

Note: Occasionally you cannot find the appropriate estimation card in your group of cards. Sometimes you can make do by removing two cards which add up to the appropriate number. Once in a blue moon, you might have to take out three cards. If it gets worse, just *tell* them the number before they count. Most of the time, however, you'll find one estimation card.

The Perfect Pile

Long ago, while working on the same principle used in *Digital Estimation*, I came up with the idea of making an estimation using a pile of cards. I removed from the deck a pile of cards to verify my estimation, not letting the spectators see the exact number, which was eight. Then I had two specators divide the rest of the deck. Both counted their piles, reduced their number to a digit, added the digits together, and reduced the result to a digit. Naturally, the result was eight. Since the spectators had forty-four cards to divide (fifty-two minus eight), and four plus four is eight, they always ended up with eight.

So, the estimation always worked out. But the trick could not be repeated, at least not by the performer. But it certainly could be repeated by a spectator. If the spectator did exactly what the performer had done, he would duplicate the trick. So, over the years, I did not perform the trick very often. I have always liked the principle, however, and recently figured out a version that is a bit more mysterious and that will bear repeating.

Hand the deck to a spectator. "I would like you to shuffle those cards, and then cut off a pile and hand the rest of the deck to me."

After he does so, say, "I am going to try to make an exact estimation. But to make it more difficult for me, I want you to deal some cards into a separate pile, which we will not use. You can deal no cards, a few cards, or several cards."

Notice you use the word "deal" instead of "count." You don't want the spectator to think in terms of counting the cards. The reason? While feigning indifference, you *are* counting the cards he deals aside.

So the spectator deals the card, cards, or no cards into a pile, and you have surreptitiously noted the number. The situation now is this: Some cards have been set aside, the spectator has a pile, and you have the rest of the deck.

Next comes some major-league baloney. Appraising the spectator's pile, you say, "This is most difficult. Not only must I estimate the number of cards, but also reduce that number to a digit."

Remove some cards from your pile, keeping the number secret from the spectators. You may hide them under your hand or stick them under a magazine—whatever. Hand the rest of your pile to a second spectator. Explain, "I have made my estimation and have placed a number of cards under my hand to confirm my choice."

As in *Digital Estimation*, have each spectator count his pile and reduce the number to a digit. Then the digits are added together and reduced to a single number.

Have one of the spectators count your estimation pile. It is the same number as the digit arrived at by the spectators. This is a good one to do at least one more time.

How do you know how many cards to take for your estimation pile? You can work it out for yourself if you're of a mind, but basically it depends on how many cards the spectator deals off and discards. You have two numbers to remember: sixteen and twenty-five. If the spectator deals off an even number, *you* use an even number—sixteen. If the spectator deals off an odd number, *you* use an odd number—twenty-five. Note that in both instances, you use a number whose digits add up to seven. In both cases, you subtract the number the spectator dealt off, and divide by two. This give you the estimation number.

For example: The spectator deals off four cards. Since four is an even number, you will subtract it from sixteen. Four from sixteen is twelve. Half of twelve is six. So six is your estimation number, and you count off six cards as your estimation pile. Or, the spectator deals off seven cards. Seven is an odd number, so you subtract it from twenty-five. Seven from twenty-five is eighteen. Half of eighteen is nine. So there will be nine cards in your estimation pile. If your final number is in two digits, add the two together to get your estimation number.

Incidentally, with effects like these, the real trick is disguising the basic principle. So-called mathematical tricks should not appear to be so. After all, what credit accrues to the performer of a mathematical trick? He has not performed magic, but has presented a puzzle. The difference is this: With magic, you have a story.

The *Perfect Pile* trick could be presented as a puzzle. But it is far better to tell the story and act out the difficult estimation, pretending to gauge the number of cards held by the spectator. Of course it makes no sense. But it *is* magic.

FACE-UP, FACE-DOWN

Do-It-Yourself Discovery

This is one of the first impromptu card tricks I ever tried. The spectators' response told me that I had just performed real card magic. I was elated and determined to continue astonishing and mystifying.

The spectator shuffles the cards. Tell him to take half and give you the rest. "Now," you say, "while I turn my back, pick out a card, look at it, show it to the rest of the folks, and put it back on top of your pile."

Turn away and secretly turn two cards face up in your pile: the bottom card and the second card from the top.

When the spectator indicates that he is done, turn back, and tell the spectator to hold out his cards. Place your pile on top of his, even up the pile, and then direct him to place his arm behind his back, saying, "Now I want you to perform a little experiment with the cards behind your back."

Make sure of two things: that no spectator can see what goes on behind your assistant's back and that the assistant does not bring the cards forward until you are ready. To accomplish the latter, hover over the spectator, keeping alert to any premature disclosure. If he starts bringing the cards in front, say, "No, no, not until the completion of the experiment."

The position of the deck now: A card is face up second from the top, and a card is face up above the spectator's card in the middle of the deck.

"Take the top card . . . no, put that one on the bottom, so you'll know I'm not trying to fool you. Have you done that? All right. Take the *next* card, turn it face up, and stick it in the middle. Even up the cards."

Now you have the spectator bring the cards forward. Take the deck and fan through until you come to the face-up card. Ask the spectator to name his chosen card. Turn over the next card. "As you can see, you have located your chosen card yourself."

Once in a great while, the spectator will stick the card between your face-up card and the chosen card. You still have a decent trick. When you turn up the wrong card, simply say, "Oh my! You missed by one." Turn up the next card, showing that it is the selected one. When doing tricks like this, where you are trying to hide the presence of face-up cards, it is best to use a deck with a white border.

Behind My Back

This trick is clever, snappy, and mystifying.

You deal cards into a pile. When you reach twelve, tell the spectator to tell you when to stop. Wherever he says stop, make sure you actually stop on an *even number*. Call no attention to the number, however.

Set the rest of the deck aside. Pick up your even number of cards and rapidly fan through in groups of three, silently counting off half of them. Turn these face up and shuffle the pile. The pile has the same number of cards face up as face down, but in no particular order. Don't explain. Simply hand the pile to a spectator, saying, "Face-up and face-down cards. Would you shuffle them even more."

Turn away and have the spectator place the cards in your hand after he finishes shuffling. Turning back towards the spectators, quickly count off half the cards from the top and turn the bottom half over. Bring the two piles forward, one in the right hand, the other in the left. Say, "You will find the same number of cards face up in each pile." Fan through each pile, counting the face-up cards aloud and showing that you are correct.

The trick's effectiveness is dependent upon how rapidly you can do the counting behind your back, so let me offer some hints. Suppose you have a pile of eighteen cards. When you take the cards from the spectator, you must count off nine. Holding the pile in your left hand, push them from the top one at a time into your right hand, taking them one *under* the other. As soon as you have nine in your right hand, bring that hand to the front. At the same time, turn your left hand so that it is *back side up* and bring that hand forward. The hands are brought forward virtually simultaneously.

It takes a while to describe, but the actual counting and production of the cards takes only a few seconds.

The Rare Reverse

Until you try this one, you will not believe what an astonishing effect it has on spectators.

Hand a spectator the deck and tell him, "I'd like you to help me with an experiment. Please shuffle the cards. Now deal four cards face down in a row." Take the deck back.

"While my back is turned, select one of the cards and show it around."

Turn away from the spectators. Turn the top card and the two bottom cards of the deck in your hand face up. Say to the spectator, "Now I would like you to gather up all four cards on the table and mix them up a little."

Turn, holding the deck in the left hand (Illustration 43). Casually wave the hand, showing the top and bottom cards, as you say, "Now comes the difficult part of the experiment, the part where magic comes in."

Take the four cards from the spectator in your right hand. Turn the left hand over, apparently showing the bottom card of the deck. Actually, of course, it is one face-up card.

Place the four cards face-to-face with the "bottom" card, saying, "First, we need to place these cards face up in the deck. Four cards, so we must turn the deck over four times."

ILLUSTRATION 43:
Holding the deck in your left hand, casually wave the deck,
showing the top and bottom cards.

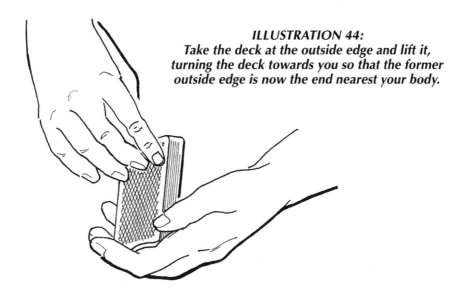

ILLUSTRATION 44:
Take the deck at the outside edge and lift it,
turning the deck towards you so that the former
outside edge is now the end nearest your body.

You count, "One, two, three, four," as, with your right hand, you turn the deck over four times in your left hand. Turn them over by taking them at the outside edge and lifting, turning the deck towards you so that the former outside edge is now the end nearest your body (Illustration 44). The object is to confuse spectators as to which cards are face up and which are face down.

"Now—four magical shuffles." Give the cards four brief overhand shuffles.

"Magic time! What is the name of the card you thought of?"

When the spectator names his card, fan through the face-down cards quite deliberately, tossing out each face-up card as you come to it. Fan all the way through the deck so spectators can see that there are only three face-up cards.

"The three *other* cards. And the card you thought of?" Turn the deck face up, fan through to the chosen card, and toss it out saying, "It has magically turned itself over in the deck."

My Favorite Card

When you run through this trick on your own, you may decide it is just too dumb to fool anyone. Believe me, it is effective and deceptive. What's more, although it's over in fifteen or twenty seconds, it leaves a lasting impression.

Have a spectator shuffle the deck. Take it back, saying, "I must find my favorite card. It's my favorite card, because it never lets me down."

Fan the cards, faces toward you, noting the top and bottom cards. They must be of different suits and values. If they are not, have the cards shuffled again, saying that you want them really well mixed. It is unlikely that you will need them shuffled a third time.

You have noted the top and bottom cards. They will tell you what your favorite card actually is. Suppose that the two cards are the king of clubs and the four of diamonds. Your lucky card will be a combination of these two; it will be either the four of clubs or the king of diamonds. Find one of these and place it face down on the table. "There it is," you say, "my favorite card."

Hold out the deck to the spectator and ask him to cut off a pile. After he does, turn the remaining cards face up in your hand and place your "favorite card" face down on top of the face-up cards. Don't rush it, but do it promptly to keep the spectators from getting a good look at the face-up card. Have the spectator place his pile face up on top of all.

Place the deck face down on the table. Now is the time to give the audience a chance to forget what you just did. Any story will do, but you might want to say something like this: "Why is this particular card my favorite? Years ago I was in a big poker game, and I was way over my head. Only one card would give me the winner—a straight flush. And I got it. Ever since, that has been my favorite card. Pause. "That's a lie. But I need practise with my patter."

Tap the deck for luck. Fan through the face-down cards to your "favorite card." Let us suppose that it is the king of diamonds. Set it and the card on either side of it on the table. Place the rest of the deck aside.

"My favorite card," you say. "And on one side, a card of the same suit. And on the other, a card of the same value." As you say this, turn each of the cards over.

"Now you know the *real* reason it's my favorite card."

Ups and Downs

With this trick, a selected card is found at the precise point a spectator tells the magician to stop dealing.

For years, I tried to work out a good way to do this. There are plenty of ways, but most require advanced sleight of hand and look pretty fishy. One day a few years ago, I stumbled on a very simple method. It is not so simple, however, that it doesn't astonish spectators. A chosen card must be brought to the top of the deck. A pro would use sleight of hand; we'll try subterfuge.

As I considered various sneaky methods, I recalled a device used in an old trick called *Card from the Pocket.* Combining a variation of this device with my new idea would produce a doubly astonishing trick. A spectator looks at a card at a chosen number down in the deck. The performer causes the card to move from that number to a spot in the deck chosen completely at random by the spectator. Best of all, the working is clean and there is no sleight of hand.

Turn your back and have the spectator shuffle the deck. Say, "I would like you to think of a number from five to twenty. Now count down to that number, taking one card under the other so that you don't reverse their order. Look at the card that lies at that number, show it around, and replace the cards on top."

Turn around and take the deck, saying, "We have a chosen card which lies at a freely selected number down in the deck. Now, quick as a flash, I'm going to move your card to a much more convenient spot."

Place the deck behind your back, move the top card to the bottom, give the ends a noisy riffle, and bring the deck forward. It should take no more than a few seconds.

"All set. But first, let's make sure I *have* moved your card. What number down in the deck was it?"

When he tells you, deal the cards into a pile, one on top of the other, until you get to the chosen number. Deal that card out face up. As you place the dealt pile on top of the deck, say, "Not your card, right?"

Naturally, it is not. Pick up the card and stick it face down into the middle of the deck. The chosen card is now on top.

"I would like you to watch for your card as I deal, but don't say anything if you see it." Deal the cards into a pile. The top card is face down, the second face up, the third face down, the fourth face up, and so on. After you have dealt ten or so, tell the spectator, "Please tell me when to stop."

When he says stop, offer to deal more if he wishes. If he chooses to have you deal more, go ahead. And at the next stop, again offer to deal more. It doesn't matter to you. Just remember to continue the face-down, face-up pattern.

When the spectator stops you, pick up the pile of cards and place them on top of the deck, apparently to straighten up the pile. But by no means comment on this. Fan quickly through the cards to the last face-up card and lift them off (including the last face-up card). Set the rest of the deck down with your left hand. The top card of the deck is, of course, the selected card. As you fan through the cards and lift them off, ask, "Do you see your card among these?" Of course, he doesn't.

"Then let's take a look at the face-down ones." Deal the packet into a face-up pile. Face-down cards are turned over and dealt face up; others are simply added to the pile as they are. "Seen your card yet?" He hasn't. "Are you sure you remember the name of your card?" When he assures you that he does ask him the name. Nod knowingly and say, "Of course." Tap the top card of the deck and turn it over. "See? I told you I was going to move your card to a much more convenient spot."

Here's a minor point which could make all the difference: When you deal the cards into a face-down, face-up pile, make sure that they overlap enough to conceal that first face-down card, which, of course, is the chosen one.

SPELLING

Impromptu Speller

With this trick, a card is chosen, shown around, and returned to the deck, which is thoroughly shuffled. Nevertheless, the performer spells out the name of the card (dealing one card from the top for each letter in the spelling), and it appears on the last letter of the spelling.

That's a fairly accurate description of most spelling tricks, including this one. Spelling tricks abound. Most require setups, and many others seem cumbersome. This is one of the best, because it is quick, direct, surprising, and—add to that, easy.

A card is selected by a spectator. You must know the name of this card. I suggest you use the *One-Cut Force* (page 38), or the *Double-Turnover Force* (page 39). Have the spectator show the card around, put it back into the deck, and then shuffle the cards. You also give the cards a good shuffle.

"I know what a suspicious person you are. You know how magical I am, and you think I have sneakily removed your card from the deck. I can assure you that nothing is farther from the truth. Here, I'll show you." Turn the deck face up and begin fanning through the cards, from bottom to top.

"I want you to notice that your card is still here, but don't reveal the card to me by so much as a word or gesture. Just observe that it's still here."

As you fan rapidly through the cards, one by one, watch for the selected card. When you come to it, begin spelling the name of the card to yourself, moving one card (to the right) for each letter in the spelling. Let us say the selected card was the jack of hearts. When you come to it, count it as J, the next card as A, the next C, the next K, until you have spelled J-A-C-K-O-F-H-E-A-R-T-S. Note the very next card. Suppose it is the three of clubs. Spell out that card in the same way. Separate the cards at the point where you complete the spelling. Tap the next card with the cards in your right hand.

"See that card? I can tell you this. That card is *not* your selected card." Cut the deck at the point of the division, bringing the indicated card to the bottom, and turn the deck face down.

"Want to see another trick?" Pause. "Just kidding. No need to get upset. Now I assume you saw your card." The spectator will probably admit it. "Okay. We're going to try to find your card by spelling its name. For example, if your card had been the three of clubs (name the second card you mentally spelled out), we would spell it like this."

Spell out the name of the card, dealing out one card from the top for each letter in the spelling. On the last card of the spelling, turn the card over. It is the card you spelled—in our example, the three of clubs.

"There you are—the three of clubs. We will try to find your card the same way. What was the name of your card?"

He names it, and you spell it out, revealing his chosen card on the last letter of the spelling.

Note: When you are going through the deck, showing the spectator that his card is still there, you will sometimes find that his card is near the top. Just continue the count from the bottom, saying, "Funny, I haven't seen your card yet," or something equally inane.

Quick Speller

Ready for a paradox? In performance, this is one of the shortest tricks in the book. Naturally, it has the longest description. Stick with me on this one. The trick will seem a little complicated at first—actually it is not. You may find that this will be one of your favorites.

The trick is old but still good. Unfortunately, some versions are complicated and unnatural. All versions seem to require considerable memorization. My variation is simple and natural, and you need to remember only a few things.

First, the simple explanation. Every card in the deck can be spelled out, one way or another, in twelve cards, either by turning over the last card of the spelling or by turning over the next card. So the performer simply arranges for the chosen card to be twelfth from the top.

Here's an easy way to get it twelfth down. Have the deck shuffled. Take it back and give four cards to each of three spectators. Have each one remove a card from his group of four. A fourth spectator takes one of these three cards, shows it to everyone but you, and places it on top of the deck.

"Thus," you say, as you gather up the eleven outstanding cards, "we guarantee a card choosen completely at random." Place the eleven cards on top and proceed with a false cut (*The One-Finger Cut,* on page 26).

You ask the spectator to name his card. He does. You spell it out, dealing off one card for each letter—and there's his card. It's not quite that simple, of course, but not as difficult as some card writers have tried to make out. I will tell you exactly how I taught myself to spell out all the cards.

The most important thing to remember is that the card is twelfth from the top. This means that if the selected card spells out in twelve letters, you turn over the last card of the spelling. If it spells out in eleven letters, you spell out the card and turn over the *next* card. Exactly twenty-seven cards spell out in eleven or twelve letters. Not bad—but others you have to work at a little.

How about cards that spell out in ten letters? There are only four, and they are all clubs. Obviously, when you finish spelling out the card's name, the chosen card will still be two down in the deck. No problem. Before you start spelling, you will lose a card from the top—it's easy, as I will explain later—and turn over the next card after completing the spelling.

Seventeen cards are spelled with thirteen or fourteen letters. We eliminate the two letters in "of" by spelling out the suit and then the value. Now they can be handled exactly the same as cards that spell out with eleven or twelve letters. With twelve letters (originally fourteen), you turn over the last card of the spelling; with eleven (originally thirteen), you turn over the next card.

Only four cards, all diamonds, spell out in fifteen letters. These require special handling, as I will explain later.

Does it all sound too complicated? Actually, you need remember very little of the above. The spectator names his card, and you have it twelfth from the top. Somehow you must get to that twelfth card. This requires a quick computation. While figuring out how I'm going to spell out the card, I usually make small talk, saying things like, "Oh, the king of spades. That's one of my favorite cards. I see no reason this shouldn't work out perfectly."

How do I compute? The easiest way, I have discovered, is to first figure the suit and then the value. Clubs count five, spades and hearts six, and diamonds eight. *That* you should remember. Values count three, four or five. That you *don't* have to remember.

Let's take a few examples. The spectator names the seven of hearts. Hearts is six, seven is five. That's eleven. Add two more for "of." That's thirteen. No good. We'll have to spell out H-E-A-R-T-S and then S-E-V-E-N, and turn up the *next* card.

The spectator names the jack of spades. Spades is six; jack is four. Add two more for the "of." That's twelve. Spell out J-A-C-K-O-F-S-P-A-D-E-S, and turn over the last card of the spelling.

I will make a suggestion soon that will make all of this second nature to you. First, let's go over how you handle the spellings. As I mentioned, with cards that spell out in eleven or telve letters, you simply spell out the card. With a card that spells in eleven letters, you spell out the card and turn over the next card. With a card that spells out in twelve letters, you turn over the last card of the spelling.

With cards that spell out to thirteen or fourteen letters, eliminate the "of." Then treat them exactly like cards that spell out in eleven or twelve letters.

Let's try thirteen. The spectator says the queen of hearts is his card. You see that hearts is six and queen is five. Add two more for "of." You have thirteen. Drop the "of" and you have eleven letters. Although you have already been told the name of the card, you now say to the spectator, "Let's see—what's the suit?" He will say, "Hearts." You spell it out.

"And what's the value?" you ask. He says, "Queen." So you spell it out *and turn over the next card.*

Suppose the number is fourteen. Diamonds is the only suit in which cards are spelled out in fourteen or fifteen letters. For fourteen letters, you follow the same procedure as with thirteen, only you turn over the *last card of the spelling.*

Only four cards are spelled out with fifteen letters. You follow a procedure similar to that used for thirteen- and fourteen-letter cards. Drop the word "of," spelling out the suit and then the value. But that means you will have dealt one beyond the card when you spell it out.

So you must get rid of one letter in the spelling. You do that by getting rid of the "s" at the end of "diamonds" with a little verbal trick. It will seem perfectly natural if you follow the precise wording. Suppose that the spectator says his card is the seven of diamonds. You note diamonds is eight, and seven is five. That's thirteen—already too high. You say, "Let's see. Your card is a diamond." Spell out diamond. "And the value is what?"

He says, "Seven." Spell out seven, turning over the last card of the spelling.

Just keep remembering the card is twelfth down; the rest is easy.

But how about the cards that spell out in ten letters? As I mentioned, there are only four, all clubs. You must lose a card from the top, bringing the chosen card eleventh from the top. Now you can spell it out and turn over the next card.

How do you lose a card from the top? I do it the easy way. After the spectator names his card, and I note that it spells out in ten, I show the top card, saying, "Your card is not on top," and I bury it in the middle. Immediately, as a smoke screen, I add, "And your card is not on the bottom," and I show it and bury it in the middle. Then I proceed with the spelling.

Now for the suggestion that will make all this second nature to you. Go through the entire deck, figuring out the spelling of each card. Here's the way I do it. I count off eleven cards, look at the bottom card of the deck and place it below the eleven cards, which I return to the top. The card is now twelfth down.

I proceed exactly as though a spectator were there. I make small talk while I compute the spelling of the card, *and then I spell it out.* I discard that one. Eleven cards are already counted off, so I look at the bottom card of the deck, place it below the eleven cards, place all on top, and proceed as before.

When I finish the deck, there are still eleven cards not spelled out. I set these aside, and then take the rest of the deck, count off eleven, take a look at one of the eleven I used in the preceding spellings, place it below the new pile of eleven, and place all on top of the deck. Then I spell the card out, as before. I do the same with the remaining ten.

Incidently, the spelling of some cards differently is *not* a drawback. Since the spectator doesn't know what to expect, and since you perform the trick only once, the effect is perfect.

Review of the actual spelling: The spectator's card is twelfth from the top. The card's name can be made up of ten, eleven, twelve, thirteen, fourteen, or fifteen letters.

Ten letters. Only four cards, all clubs, spell out in ten letters. Before spelling, you must lose a card from the top. You do this by showing that the top and bottom cards are not the chosen ones and then burying them in the middle. Now you spell out the card and turn over the *next* card.

Eleven letters. Spell the card out and turn over the *next* card.

Twelve letters. Spell the card out and turn over the *last* card.

Thirteen letters. Spell out the suit (including the "s" at the end) and then the value. Drop the word "of." Turn over the *next* card.

Fourteen letters. Only five cards, all diamonds, are spelled out in fourteen letters. Spell out the suit (including the "s" at the end) and then the value. Turn over the *last* card.

Fifteen letters. Only four cards, all diamonds, are spelled out in fifteen letters. You say, "Your card is a diamond." Spell out "diamond" without the "s" at the end. Then spell out the value. Turn over the last card of the spelling.

Why have I gone into such detail with this particular trick when others seem easier? Because it is the best, the fastest, and the most direct of all spelling tricks.

A Hot Spell

An old principle is used in this trick. In fact, I use a variation of this principle in *Tick Tock Trick;* but I felt there had to be at least one more good effect using the same principle—all it would take was camouflage. I came up with this spelling trick, which gets excellent audience response.

Have a volunteer shuffle the deck as you explain, "I am going to attempt a feat of mentalism. Would you please think of a number from one to ten. Do you have one? All right. Now change your mind. This is not psychological; we must be sure you have complete freedom of choice."

"In a moment I'll turn my back, and I would like you to count two piles of cards, both containing the same number of cards as the number you thought of. For example, if you thought of four, deal two piles of cards with four cards in each pile. Do this quietly so I won't be able to hear you." Turn away while the spectator follows your instructions.

"Now lift up either of the two piles, look at the bottom card, and show it around. Please remember that card. And now place that pile on top of the deck." After your assistant is done, continue, "Please place the deck in my hand and hide the other pile you dealt."

Turn around and face the spectators with the pack behind your back and say, "I am going to find your card *behind my back,* using nothing more than mental vibrations to guide me. What's your card?"

When the spectator names his card, spell it, removing one card from the top for each letter, like this: Suppose the spectator says his card was the nine of clubs. You mentally say "N" and take the top card in your right hand. For the letter "I", you take the next card on top of the first. The card for "N" goes on top of the first two. The card for "E" goes on top of the first three. Continue on, adding one card on top of those in the right hand for each letter remaining in the spelling: O-F-C-L-U-B-S.

Naturally, you do not want the spectators to *hear* you doing this, and you do not want to give away the fact that you are doing anything tricky with the deck. The counting of one card on top of the other must be done fairly slowly; otherwise, noise will give it away. So take your time. You can do what I do: Babble while spelling out the card.

I spell the card out in three chunks. With our example, I would spell the nine of clubs like this: While spelling N-I-N-E, taking one card in my right hand for each letter, I would say something like "Nine . . . nine . . . very difficult. Really think of the value nine, so that I can feel that card vibrating." By this time, I have four cards in my right hand. I add two more for O-F, while saying something like "I'm not sure. I may have it." Then, while spelling C-L-U-B-S, I might say, "Nine of clubs is very tough. Clubs, clubs, clubs. Particularly confusing." Notice that this sort of jabbering helps you keep track of what you are doing behind your back, while creating the illusion that you are either a mentalist or a lunatic.

Bring the deck forward and say, "Presto! Here is your card, right on top." Turn over the top card. It is wrong, of course. You place the card in the middle of the deck, declaring, "Of course that isn't your card. I know what's wrong. It's what people always say about me: 'He's not playing with a full deck.' Would you please put the rest of the cards on top. I won't look."

Avert your head while your assistant puts on top of the deck the pile of cards he had hidden. Take the deck and hold it to your forehead, saying, "Concentrate on your card, please." After a moment of intense thinking, say, "I know exactly how to find your card. We'll spell it out. What is your card, please?" Yes, he has told you the name already, but there is no need to stress that.

When he names his card, spell it out, dealing one card from the top for each letter in the spelling. Turn the last card of the spelling face up; it is the spectator's card.

GAMBLING

Impossible Poker Deal

"I'd like to demonstrate a poker deal," you say, fanning through the cards. "I'll need lower-value cards. Gamblers don't want aces and face cards when they make their big killings. Those cards are so obvious that people might suspect the gamblers of cheating."

Remove all the cards from two to seven, tossing them face up on the table. Set the rest of the deck aside. Pick up the low cards and fan them out, faces towards yourself, saying, "Let's get some pairs here."

The statement is a form of misdirection. Actually, you'll remove three threes, three fives, and three sevens—three trios of *odd* cards, but you'll collect these cards in pairs. First toss out two face-down threes. On top of them, toss a three and a five. On top of the pile. toss two fives. Finally, place *three* sevens on top of all.

Turn to spectator Hal and ask, "Would you please shuffle these while I get some more pairs?" Hal shuffles the nine odd cards while you proceed.

Now gather three trios of *even* cards, using the same misdirection. Toss out two face-down twos, a two and a four, two fours, and three sixes. Put the rest of the cards back on the deck.

Have Hal set his cards aside and shuffle the packet you just collected. When he's finished shuffling, say, "Hal, you can place either packet on top of the other." After he puts the packets together, proceed by having Hal deal two hands.

I prefer, however, to give the spectators some reason to feel that, in some way, I'm exerting control. I hold out my left hand and ask the spectator to place the packet in my hand. I place my right hand flat on top of the packet and give my hands a quick up-and-down movement. "A little shake does the job," I say. In fact, I do this "little shake" before each deal.

Let's assume that you've done the "little shake." Hand the cards back to Hal and ask him to deal two five-card poker hands face down, one to you and one to himself. Hal does so, alternately dealing a card to you and a card to himself.

When he finishes, say, "Remember, you shuffled the cards yourself." Turn over the two hands, showing that you have the winner.

The two hands are on the table face up. Place your cards face up on top of his. Turn the combined hands face down. Take the undealt cards and place them face down on top of the combined packet, saying, "You might as well deal the rest of the cards into two hands."

Perform the "little shake," and have him deal again.

Once more you win. Put your face-up cards on top of his, as before. Turn the combined hands face down. This time the combined hands go *on top* of the undealt cards.

Pick up the packet and give it a "little shake." Say to Hal, "The problem is, you don't get to make any choices. The cards are dealt, and you have to accept what you get." Deal a face-up card to him and one to yourself. "But now you'll have the advantage of choosing your cards. You can decide if you want each card. If you don't want it, I get it."

Turn over the next card on the packet. "Do you want this card?" If he wants it, deal it to him face up. If he declines the card, add it, face up, to your hand. Continue until each of you has five cards. (Once Hal has five cards, you get enough more to complete your hand).

Again, you're a winner.

Place your face-up cards on top of his, asking, "Now do you want to deal, or do you want me to deal?" If *you* are to deal, place the combined pile on top of the undealt packet and deal. If *he* is to deal, place the undealt packet on top of the combined pile, and hand him the cards. In either instance, don't forget that vital "little shake."

Naturally, you win again.

Note: How does the trick work? In an older trick, only ten cards were used: three sets of three-of-a-kind with one separate card. The separate card is always referred to as the "Jonah" card—with good reason. When the ten cards are dealt out, the person with the Jonah card cannot win. (Try it out.)

This trick is subtly set up so that the same system operates. In each deal, *you* get either all odd cards or all even cards. The *spectator* gets only *four* odd cards or *four* even cards. If he gets four odd cards, he always receives one even card, the Jonah. If he gets four even cards, he always receives one odd card, the Jonah. He *cannot* win.

Freedom of Choice

I hit upon the basic principle used here some time ago, but only recently developed a trick that takes full advantage of it. This trick has been well received by magicians and laypersons alike.

Since spectator Evan likes cards games, say to him, "Let's see how good a poker player you are. First, would you please shuffle the deck." After he finishes, take the deck back, and turn it face up so that all can see the cards. "Evan, I'm going to try to find you a really bad five-card poker hand. *But* I'll give you a bonus card. First, we'll take the bottom card." Name the card at the face of the deck. Suppose it is the two of clubs. Say, "So the two of clubs is your first card."

Proceed to fan through the cards, ostensibly choosing a five-card hand for Evan, along with a bonus card. As you do this, you will be placing five face-up piles onto the table. Unknown to the spectators, the second card from the bottom of each face-up pile will be a member of the spade royal flush (aces, kings, queens, jacks, tens). In other words, when each pile is turned face down, the second card from the top will be a member of the spade royal flush.

You have called attention to the two of clubs, the bottom card. "Let's find another good card for you." Fan through the cards until you come to a member of the spade royal flush. Fan off one additional card, calling attention to the card now at the face of those in your left hand. "Here's a really bad card," you say. "So this will be your second card" (Illustration 45). Even up the cards in your right hand and set them in a face-up pile on the table. In our example, the top card of this face-up pile is the two of clubs; the second card from the bottom of the face-up pile is part of the spade royal flush.

ILLUSTRATION 45

In the same way, fan through to the next member of the spade royal flush. Again, fan off one additional card. Name the card at the face of those in your left hand and make a comment about it. Even up the cards in your right hand and place them in a face-up pile next to the other pile on the table.

Do this two more times. Four face-up piles are in a row on the table. The face card of each pile is one you have selected for the spectator's hand. The second card from the bottom of each face-up pile is a part of the spade royal flush. The face card of those in your left hand is the fifth card you have selected for the spectator. "Now," you say, "I'll give you a bonus card."

Again fan through the cards, going one beyond the last card of the spade royal flush. Perform the same routine, placing a fifth pile face up on the table, next to the others. The second card from the bottom of this face-up pile is the fifth card of the spade royal flush. The "bonus card" is at the face of those in your left hand.

(If you've been following along with a deck of cards, you may have run into some trouble. I deal with this in the *Notes* at the end.)

Gesture towards the piles on the table. "These five cards are your poker hand. If you want, you can exchange one of those for the bonus card. What could be fairer?"

If Evan chooses to make the exchange, trade the card at the face of those in your left hand for the face card of the face-up packet he chooses. Set the cards in your hand aside face down. If he chooses not to make the exchange, simply set the leftover cards aside face down.

Place the top card of each pile above its pile. You now have five face-up piles in a row. Above this is another row, consisting of individual face-up cards (Illustration 46). "Now you can exchange any of your cards for any of the new cards here." Evan does so, probably enhancing his hand considerably.

ILLUSTRATION 46

"Now I'm *really* going to give you a break." Turn all five piles face down. Turn the top card of each pile face up on top of its pile. "You can exchange any of these cards to improve your hand." Now he should have an excellent hand.

Remove the leftover face-up cards from the five piles and toss them face down on top of the cards you set aside earlier.

"Do you have a good hand?" you ask Evan. Of course he does. "I agree. In fact, I think you'd win most card games with that hand. So let's see how *I* might do."

Turn over the top card of each pile. You win, for you have a royal flush in spades. "Not bad."

Notes:

(1) As you fan through the cards, two members of the spade royal flush may be close together. When you notice this, cut between the two cards and give the deck a quick overhand shuffle. Then hand the deck to a spectator and have him shuffle "so that everything is perfectly fair." The trick is not diminished, even if this occurs more than once.

(2) Sometimes you'll fan through fifteen to twenty cards without coming across a member of the spade royal flush. When this happens, comment, "I don't see anything I like here." Cut about twelve cards or so to the top and then continue the fanning procedure.

(3) Occasionally, in the fanning procedure, you'll provide the spectator some good cards—a pair of aces, for instance. When this occurs, say, "I'm feeling generous. I might as well give you a *few* good cards."

From the Land Down Under

Ken Beale created an unusual poker trick, to which I have added a strong climax and appropriate patter.

You must make a simple setup in advance. Place the four aces on top of the deck and a small straight flush on the bottom of the deck. A typical straight flush might be the five, six, seven, eight, nine of hearts. As you might know, a straight flush beats any other hand except a higher straight flush.

Look through the deck, faces towards yourself, and find the four jacks, tossing them face up onto the table. "Never play poker with a man from Australia," you say. "I met a fellow from Australia the other day. His name was Kangaroo Downs, and he invited me to play poker with him. The first thing he did was take the jacks from the deck. He said, 'In Australia, we always use the four jacks,'" Indicate the jacks on the table. "Then he said, 'In Australia, we play with just sixteen cards, so we'll need twelve more cards.' Then he counted out twelve cards like this."

Fan out the top three cards. Remove them from the deck and place them into a pile on the table, saying, "Three." Fan off two more cards and place them on top of the pile of three, saying, "Five." Deal single cards onto the pile, counting aloud: "Six, seven, eight . . . ." When you reach twelve, stop. Set the rest of the deck aside. Pick up the pile.

"Then Kangaroo Downs said, 'In Australia, we mix the cards like this.'" Turn the jacks face down so that they are in a row. Dealing from left to right, place one card on each jack. Repeat until all twelve cards are dealt out. Pick up the pile on the left. Place the pile to the right of it on top. Place the next pile to the right on top of the combined pile. And place the pile on the extreme right on top of all.

"Kangaroo said, 'In Australia, we always do a down-under deal, like this.'"

Deal the top card face down onto the table, saying, "Down."

Place the next card on the bottom of the stack in your hand, saying, "Under." Deal the next card onto the card on the table, saying, "Down." The next card goes under. Continue the deal until four cards remain in your hand. But you can stop saying "Down" and "Under" about halfway through.

"Kangaroo handed me the remaining four cards. He said, 'Here's your hand.'

"I said, 'But a poker hand should be five cards.'

"He said, 'Not in Australia. Care to make a bet?' I looked at my hand."

You are holding the four jacks. Place them face up onto the table. "A very good hand. So I makde a little wager. Kangaroo said, 'Now for my hand.'

Pick up the cards on the table and do the down-under deal until four cards remain in your hand. "I showed him my four jacks. And he showed me his four aces."

Lay the aces face up onto the table. "Then Kangaroo said, 'Let that be a lesson to you: Never play the other fellow's game.'

"I said, 'True. But in all fairness, we should play one hand of American poker, double or nothing.'

"Kangaroo said, 'Okay. You can deal, but I get to shuffle Australian style.' I agreed. He gathered up the cards like this."

Pick up the cards you dealt onto the table and put them on top of the deck. Place the four jacks face down on top of the deck. Place the four aces face down on top of them.

(You can leave out the following shuffle if you wish.) "Kangaroo gave the deck a really sneaky shuffle." You perform a riffle-shuffle as follows: Take the top half of the deck in your left hand and the bottom half in your right hand. Riffle off at least a dozen cards with your left thumb before you start interweaving the cards in your right hand. At the end, you will automatically riffle off on top a dozen or so cards from your right hand. This means that your small straight flush remains on the bottom of the deck and the four aces remain on top.

"Kangaroo said, 'Now we'll do the down-under shuffle.' "
Hold the deck from above in your left hand (Illustration 47).

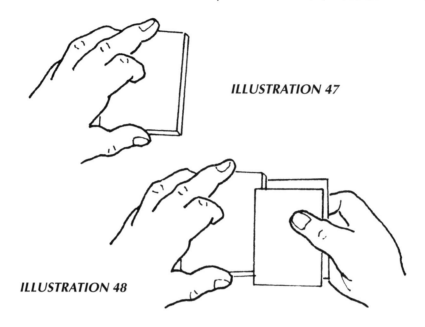

ILLUSTRATION 47

ILLUSTRATION 48

With the right thumb on top and the right fingers below, grasp the
top and bottom cards together and pull them sideways from the
packet (Illustration 48). Set the pair onto the table. Take the top
and bottom cards again in the same way. Set this pair on top of the
first pair. Continue until you have ten cards in the pile.

"Kangaroo said, 'Here are your ten cards. Deal 'em!' So I took
the ten cards and dealt them like this."

Deal out two regular poker hands. The first card goes to your
opponent, the second to yourself, and so on, until all ten are dealt.

"Kangaroo said, 'What do you know! I got the aces again.' "
Turn over his hand, showing the aces.

" 'Excellent hand,' I said. 'But I don't think it beats this.' "
Turn over your straight flush one card at a time.

"He was so angry, I figured the least I could do was offer some
advice. I said, 'Let that be a lesson to you: Never play the other
fellow's game. ' "

Two-Handed Poker

After doing a number of card tricks, you will frequently hear, "I'd sure hate to play poker with you," or, "Could you cheat at poker?" It's not a bad idea, then, to have a poker trick in your arsenal. This one is very easy and very clever.

You offer to demonstrate crooked poker dealing. But to make things easier, you will use only ten cards. Remove from the deck three aces, three kings, three tens, and a nine. Don't show them. Have the nine on top.

With an overhand shuffle, draw off the nine and shuffle the rest of the cards on top of it. Shuffle again, drawing off the last few cards singly so that the nine ends on top. If you cannot do the overhand shuffle, simply mess the cards around on the table and then gather them up, making sure that the nine ends on top. You may follow this procedure for all succeeding deals.

Deal the cards alternately to the spectator and yourself. Naturally, when the hands are turned over, you win.

This is one of the most ingenious poker effects ever devised. The fact is, the hand with the nine can never win. Is that cute, or what? Take the nine and try getting a winning hand with any four other cards of the nine cards remaining. If you take two pairs, the other hand will have three of a kind. If you take three of a kind, the other hand will be a full house. If you take a pair, the other hand will have two pairs.

Repeat the trick a few times. Then, with a shuffle, leave the nine on the bottom and let the spectator deal. He loses, of course.

Next, shuffle the nine to the top. Hand the deck to the spectator and tell him that you will try something different. "You may deal the cards one at a time to either hand in any order you wish—just so we both end up with five." If the spectator deals the first card to himself, he loses, so try the stunt again. Say, "Deal them in any order you wish."

If the first card goes to you, say, "Now *this* time, no matter what you do, *I* am going to lose."

If the spectator insists on dealing the first card to himself two or three times, you'd better hang up. You are simply destined to win. Gather up the cards, toss them on the deck, and shuffle. After all, we mustn't call attention to that nine. Don't be afraid to repeat this trick. Over the years, I've never had anyone catch on.

GAMBLER'S BONUS

Here is a routine of four gambling tricks, guaranteed to convince onlookers that you are one skilled prestidigitator. No sleight is ever involved.

When you do a gambling demonstration, you are in a pardoxical position. During most of your tricks, you are trying to convince spectators that it is all magic, that you use no sleight of hand. With a gambling demonstration, however, you attempt to show how skillfully you manipulate the cards. In the first instance, you may be using plenty of sleights; in the second, you will be using none.

When you do your tricks, what are the spectators to believe? At one level, they *know* that you are using all sorts of skullduggery, probably including sleights. But if they are to enjoy your performance, they must suspend their disbelief. In a sense, they *want* to believe in magic; often, the more skeptical a spectator seems, the more he wants to believe. To most spectators, you are Mr. or Ms. Magic; the fact that you have displayed apparent manipulative ability with the cards in a gambling routine will add to this allusion.

These tricks are arranged to facilitate going from one to the next; I recommend that you try the whole routine a few times before selecting a favorite or two.

Mind Control Poker

Ask for the help of an assistant. Tell the volunteer, "I am going to set up some cards and then attempt to control your mind in a little poker demonstration."

The setup takes very little time. Hold the card faces towards you and thumb through them, finding the appropriate cards. First, find a king; separate the cards at that point so that the king is the rearmost card of those in your right hand. Take the king behind the cards in the left hand, using the left fingers to grasp it. Thus, the king becomes the top card of the deck. Find an ace and place it on top of the king. Continue by placing on top two nines, two queens, two jacks, two tens, and a king.

From the bottom up, the eleven cards are K-A-9-9-Q-Q-J-J-10-10-K. The last king is the top card. Here is an easy way to remember this stack. I remember KANN, as in "I think I KANN." This gives me the first four cards I must put on top: K (king), A (ace), N (nine), N (nine). I have no trouble remembering the next three pairs—queens, jacks, tens—because they are in descending order. Last, a king goes on top.

Turn the deck face down and say that you're all set. "Obviously, we'll need some cards." Count off eleven cards from the top of the deck, taking them one under the other so that they retain the same order. Make no mention of the number. A good way to count them off is to take three groups of three and one group of two into the right hand. Set the rest of the deck down.

"Now you're going to choose from five sets of two cards," you say. Take the top two cards of your packet (a king and a ten) and spread them, showing them to the spectator. Make no comment about the values of the cards. Place these two cards together on the bottom of the packet, keeping them in their original order. Show the next pair in the same way. Continue on until you have shown the spectator five pairs of cards, each time placing the pair on the bottom.

"Now I am going to offer you a choice. But there really is no choice at all. I am going to control your mind so that you will end up with a *king high straight*. No doubt of it; you will choose a king high straight."

Take the top two cards and spread them slightly, face down, offering the spectator his choice of the two. "Take either one," you say, "and place it face down in front of you." After he chooses one, place the other card on the bottom.

If you have been following this with cards in your hand, take a look at your packet. You will notice that in each instance you are offering him the choice of a pair. His first choice, for instance, is from a pair of kings. Obviously, this is because you actually started with eleven cards, not ten. For whatever reason, spectators never suspect.

Again you take two cards from the top of the packet and offer the spectator his choice. Place the rejected card on the bottom. Continue on until the spectator has chosen five cards. Each time you have placed the remaining card on the bottom. This includes the last choice. Place your packet of six cards on top of the deck.

"Five different times you had complete freedom of choice," you explain, "but I still controlled your mind. Take a look at what you have."

When the spectator shows his cards, he reveals a king high straight, just as you had predicted. Give everyone a chance to verify this and then say, "That wouldn't do you much good, though. Look what you left me."

Take five cards from the top of the deck and show that you have an *ace high straight*. Before I display them, I generally adjust the cards so that they read in A-K-Q-J-10 order.

Flush of Success

You explain that you are going to demonstrate how easy it is to get a good hand when you have all the best cards to choose from. As you chat on, remove all the high cards from the deck: aces, kings, queens, jacks, and tens. You may fan through the cards and toss them out face up as you come to them. You may try this method, which is faster: Fan through the cards and when you come to one of the high cards, push it upwards about an inch so that it sticks out of the top of the deck. Do the same with all the other high cards. When done, turn the deck face down, grasp all the protruding cards at the side, and pull them from the deck.

Spread all the high cards out face up on the table. What you are about to do is lay out four hands, arranging it so that you will get a *royal flush in hearts* when the cards are gathered together and dealt.

As I will explain, you improvise with the spectators as you lay out the four hands face up. In the first hand, the second card must be a heart. Since the hands are laid out face up, we are talking about the fourth card down as the cards lie face up, or the *second card* if the hand were turned face down and dealt.

In the second hand, a heart must be placed third. In the next hand, a heart must be placed fourth. And in the last hand, a heart must be placed first and fifth.

In the first hand, a heart is second; in the second hand, a heart is third; in the third hand, a heart is fourth; and in the fourth hand, a heart is at both top and bottom.

Pick up the hands face up in this order: The fourth hand goes on the first hand; this pile goes on the second hand; that pile goes on the third hand. Turn the packet face down and give the cards a complete cut.

Spectators tend to believe that a complete cut disarranges the cards. Actually, the cards are in a never ending sequence, and a cut retains their order. If you were to cut the original top card back to the top, the packet would be in precisely the same order as before the cutting started.

Have various spectators give the cards a complete cut. For the trick to work, you must have a heart on the bottom. So after each cut is completed, grasp the deck edgeways, tilt it up so that you can see the face of the bottom card, and tap the cards on the table as though straightening them out. If the bottom card is other than a heart, have the cards cut again. Repeat this until you get a heart on the bottom.

Then deal four face-down poker hands, including one to yourself. Show the first hand, commenting on its value. Show the second and third hands the same way. Say, "It really doesn't matter. It's pretty hard to beat a royal flush." Turn your hand over and show it. Again, I like to arrange the cards from ace to ten before showing the hand.

How do you improvise with the spectators as you make up the hands? You might say something like, "Look at all these great cards. What would be a pretty good hand?"

If a spectator calls for a flush or a straight flush, you cannot oblige, for the first hand must have precisely one heart. So you might say, "Not *that* good!"

Chances are you'll be asked for two pairs, three of a kind, or a straight. Make up the hand from the spread-out cards, making sure that the second card is a heart, and that no other is. Put together the next two hands the same way. Spectators will probably want one of them to be a full house. If they again ask for a flush, say, "Sure, just watch my face if this doesn't work."

Take up the last five cards on the table; quite often they will make up a pretty good hand. Make sure you have a heart on top and a heart on bottom.

You'll have little trouble providing the hands called for; after all, the spectators must choose from the cards on the table. You can have a lot of fun improvising with the spectators.

You can also get some entertainment from the repeated cuts as you keep looking for a heart at the bottom of the stack before you deal. Sometimes the number of cuts can go to double figures before a heart finally shows up at the bottom. This can be turned to your advantage, as you say things like, "Let's try one more cut, just to make sure they're mixed." Or, "Let's try one with the left hand." You can ad-lib other equally inane reasons. When you finally get a heart on the bottom, you can say, "I don't know about you, but I'm getting sick of this." Take the cards and deal the hands.

Gambling Aces

A simple stack is required for the next trick. You can cleverly cover this up by saying, "I have to stack these cards . . . hope you don't mind." Thumb trough the cards and, following the procedure described in *Mind Control Poker* (page 118), place three nines on top. Place five spot cards on top of them. Now from the top down, you have five spot cards followed by three nines.

Mutter something like, "Now where the heck are those aces?" Find the aces and place them on top one by one in the manner described. "All set." From the top down you have four aces, five spot cards, three nines.

Commence your patter: "A cardsharp was attending a quiet party when he decided to liven things up a bit. He slapped a deck of cards down on a table . . . " Slap the deck down on the table. " . . . and said, 'Who wants to play three-handed poker?' "

"Naturally, everyone gathered around. A wise guy asked, 'Why three-handed poker?' The cardsharp told him, 'To make it easier.' The wise guy said, 'I've seen this before. Where are the four aces?' The cardsharp said, 'Right here on top—just in case I need them.' " Deal out the four aces face up.

"The cardsharp said, 'Now I'll deal a few sample hands before we start the betting.' " Put the aces back on top. Deal four hands of three cards each, including one hand to yourself.

"The wise guy said, 'You just stacked the cards so you'd get three aces.' The cardsharp said, 'Not at all. Look—one ace in each hand.' "

Pick up your hand and turn it over, showing that there is only one ace. Place the hand on top. Do the same with the third hand, the second hand, and the first hand, in that order—each time placing the hand on top.

"The cardsharp said, 'Let's try another deal.' " Again deal four hands of three cards each.

"The wise guy said, 'I've seen this. For sure, you've stacked them this time.' The cardsharp said, 'No way. Look—one ace in each hand.' " Show the hands in precisely the same way as you did the first time.

"The cardsharp said, 'Now let's get down to business. One more deal.' " Deal four hands of three cards each.

"The cardsharp asked, 'Now who wants to make a bet?' The wise guy said, "*I'll* make a bet. You stacked the cards, I'll bet you twenty bucks you hold three aces.' The cardsharp said, 'You're on, buddy. And you're dead wrong.' "

Move your three-card hand to one side. *Now this is important:* Place the third hand on top of the deck, followed by the second hand and the first hand.

"The cardsharp said, 'You're right about one thing—I did stack the cards.' " Turn over your hand, showing the three nines.

"The wise guy forked over the twenty and said, 'What about the aces?' The cardsharp smiled and said, 'I told you. Right here on top—just in case I need them.' " As you say this, deal the aces face up one by one. Just follow the directions; the trick works itself.

At the conclusion of the trick, replace the aces on top and give the cards a casual overhand shuffle, bringing them to the middle. You'll need them for the next trick.

Ace Surprise

You will need the four aces on top. At the end of *Gambling Aces* (page 123), you shuffled them to the middle. As you commence your patter, begin fanning through the cards, faces towards you. You will be looking for the four kings, but in your first move, simply cut the aces to the top and continue fanning through the cards.

"I'll need the four kings for this," you say as you begin going through the deck. "This is my last gambling demonstration and you may be able to catch me if you watch very carefully." Toss out the kings face up as you come to them. "Some gamblers can deal seconds, some can deal thirds, some can deal bottoms, and some can deal cards from the middle. And a good cheater makes it look as though they are all coming from the top."

You should have the kings face up on the table now. "I'm not going to tell you exactly what trickery I'm up to, but I urge you to watch closely."

Gather up the kings and place them on top. Even up the cards carefully and deal them out face down next to one another. "Are these the four kings?" Pause. "Of course they are."

As you show each one, place it back on top. Then deal the kings out again face down. "Four kings. Now watch."

From here on, do *not* describe what you are doing. Fan out four cards from the top of the deck, taking them in the right hand. Tilt the deck down slightly with the left hand and square up the cards against the base of the left thumb. Drop these four on top of the first king you dealt out, the one to your left. Even up the deck. Carefully deal the top card face down, well off to your left.

Again fan out the four top cards, taking them in your right hand and squaring them against the base of your left thumb. Drop these four on top of the second king you dealt. Even up the pile and place it on top. Square up the deck. Deliberately deal the top card face down on the one you already dealt to your far left. Follow the same procedure with the two remaining kings. Then set the deck down to your right.

"Were you watching carefully? I hope so. The question is, 'Where are the kings?' " Chances are that the spectators will say that the kings are on the pile you dealt to your left. If they do, say, "Oh, no. The kings are right here." Deal them face up one at a time off the top of the deck. "There's a much better hand over here." Deal the four-card pile face up one at a time, revealing the four aces.

If the spectators should indicate that the four kings are on top of the deck, show them that this is so by dealing them out face up. "You're right. These are the kings. But what good are kings . . ." Deal the four-card pile face-up. ". . . against four aces?"

GRAB BAG

Countdown

The principle used in this trick is old, deceptive, and applicable to any number of tricks. A card is selected and returned to the deck. The spectator locates his own card by counting off a freely selected number of cards. This is the general effect.

Actually a card is forced on a spectator. See *One-Cut Force* (page 38), *Double-Turnover Force* (page 39), or *Face-Up Force* (page 39). After the spectator shows the card around, he returns it to the deck and shuffles the cards.

Taking the deck back, you say, "Now watch how I do this." Fan through the cards, faces towards you. When you come to the selected card, count off nine cards beyond and cut the deck at that point. The selected card is now ten down from the top.

Show the spectators the bottom card, declaring triumphantly, "*This* is not your card." After the excitement dies down, add, "I could do that trick forever. But let's see how you can do."

Give him the deck and tell him to deal into a pile any number of cards from ten to twenty. Tell him to add the digits of his selected number and to deal that number back on top of the deck. For instance, if he dealt off thirteen cards, he adds one and three, and deals four cards back onto the deck.

"What is the name of your card?" you ask.

When he names it, you turn over the last card dealt back on the deck. Sure enough.

Clearly, it doesn't matter what number from ten to twenty is chosen. When the digits are totalled and the sum counted back onto the deck, the original tenth card down will be the last card dealt.

The Four Aces Again

This trick is based on the same principle as *Countdown.* The effect is so astonishing that I suspend my prejudice against setups. Besides, the setup can be done with the spectators watching.

The setup is this: You need the four aces to be tenth, eleventh, twelfth, and thirteenth from the top of the deck. If you're using your own deck, you can set up the cards in advance and make this your first trick. After I explain how the trick works, I will give you two impromptu methods of setting up the cards.

The strong point to this trick is that the spectator does it all. Tell him to think of any number from ten to twenty and to deal that number of cards into a pile. Then he is to add the digits in the number and deal that many cards back onto the deck. When he is done, take the cards remaining in his dealt hand and set them aside.

"Now I would like you to deal the remaining cards one at a time into four neat piles, just as though you were dealing hands."

The first four cards he deals are, of course, the aces; they will be at the bottom of the four piles. After he has dealt twenty or so cards, tell him, "You may deal as many more as you want and stop whenever you wish." When he stops, take the remaining cards from him and add them to the others you originally set aside.

At this point, a little review should add to the mystification. "You freely selected the original number you dealt off. And when you dealt the cards, you stopped wherever you wished. Right?"

Don't wait for an answer. Simply turn over all four piles, displaying an ace at the face of each.

As promised, here's a way to set up the cards while the spectators watch. Suppose you have just performed a four-aces trick, like *Easy Aces* (page 58). When you are finished, make sure the aces are together in the deck. Do a few more tricks, preferably ones which do not call for shuffling. Fan through the cards, faces towards you. When you come to the four aces, count nine cards beyond. Part the deck at this point and cut them. This brings the aces to the desired position from the top. Show the bottom card, saying, "This is *your* good-luck card. Let's see if it works."

Apparently, you have simply looked through the deck and found his good-luck card and cut it to the bottom. Take off the good-luck card and set it to one side. Before the climax, you can wave the card over the four piles to help bring about the magical result.

Suppose the aces are scattered through the deck. Again run through the cards, faces towards you. Tell the spectators that you must find *precisely* the right card for the experiment to work.

As you come to each ace, separate the cards and thumb each ace to the bottom. "No, no," you mumble, as you keep adding aces to the bottom. When all four are on the bottom, go back to fan through again. As before, count nine cards beyond the aces and cut the cards at that point.

Show the bottom card. "Here it is!" you declare, setting the card aside. "Without this bad-luck card, the experiment is bound to work."

Get Out of This World

When I was young (back in the olden days), this trick was called *Out of This World*. Many feel it is the best card trick ever invented.

With the deck face down, the spectator attempts to separate the red and black cards. To his amazement, he succeeds. The problem is that the trick requires a completely set-up deck. Lots of us worked out ways to set up the deck in the course of doing other tricks, but at best they were clumsy, and they were always a pain in the neck to the performer.

Here is an impromptu method that many lay claim to. All I have added are a few tips. The virtues to this method are:

1. There are no sleights whatsoever.
2. There is no prearrangement of the cards.
3. It is *snappy*. Furthermore, the effect is astonishing.

"For this experiment," you tell the spectators, "I need an assistant, preferably one with ESP or psychic powers. If we can't manage that, I'll settle for someone who's heard of ESP or psychic powers. Or I'll take someone who can *spell* ESP."

When you get your volunteer, have him shuffle the deck and hand it back to you. Fan the cards in your left hand, faces towards you, making sure that the spectators do not see the faces. Now you are going to eliminate all of one color from the top three-fifths or so of the deck. You will do this by taking them out one by one, as I will explain in a moment. This will leave you with a top section of approximately fifteen to twenty cards of the opposite color.

Look over the top section and see which color dominates. You must eliminate the opposite color. For example, if there are more reds than blacks in the top portion of the deck, you will want to take out all of the blacks and leave the reds. Let's assume that this is the case: You want to get rid of the blacks. Take a black card from the top portion and place it face up on the table. Next to it place a face-up red card that you get from the bottom portion of the deck.

"These are the markers," you explain. "If you think a card is red, we'll place it on the red marker. If you think it is black, we'll place it on the black marker. This way we'll discover whether you have any extrasensory perception."

Pick out a black card from the top portion of the fanned cards. Holding it face down, ask the spectator, "Do you think this one is red or black?" When he answers, place it face down on the appropriate marker. Continue in the same way, eliminating black cards from the top section of the deck.

Place the cards on the table in an overlapping column going away from you. From the spectator's view, the cards will look like Illustration 49.

ILLUSTRATION 49
This is the spectator's view of the two overlapping columns, with the two markers, one red, one black.

Pretend to study the cards as you pick one out for the spectator's decision. Playact. You are pleased with some of his choices; you frown slightly at others. Tell your assistant, "You're doing quite well for an amateur."

As an added fillip, you can do this: When the spectator calls black, smile, and show him the card before you place it on the black pile. Compliment him. Do this once only, of course.

When you have fifteen or more cards of the opposite color in the top portion of the deck (in our example, red), stop the deal. "I think your psychic vibrations are fading from boredom; we must try something a little different."

Hand the spectator the bottom portion of the remaining deck and keep the top portion (the cards of one color) for yourself. Tell him to shuffle his pile. While he does so, shuffle your pile.

Exchange piles with the spectator. Shuffle your pile and tell him to shuffle his. Since his are all of the same color, the shuffle will obviously not affect the outcome.

Take a red card from your pile and place it face up on the black pile. Take a black card from your pile and place it face up on the red pile. Set aside your pile without comment.

"From now on, black cards go here . . ." Indicate the new black marker. ". . . and red cards go here." Indicate the new red marker. "Now I'd just as soon you do you own dealing. I'm exhausted. Just go through one card at a time, dealing face down, and follow your instincts."

You may try another bit of byplay if you wish. When the spectator has dealt about half of the cards, stop him, saying, "Oh-oh!" Take the last dealt card from the black pile. It is, of course, a red card. Show the card and place it face down on the red pile saying, "I wish you'd be a little more careful." The cards should be lined up as in Illustration 50.

ILLUSTRATION 50
The cards should be lined up as shown above.
Two new markers have been dealt.

When the spectator finishes, one column of cards is perfect: The black cards are under the black marker, and the red cards are under the red. The other pile, however, has black cards under the red marker, and red cards under the black. In the original version, a sleight was recommended to enable the performer to show the second pile to be perfect. No sleight is necessary. The method of showing the piles given here is totally deceptive and has the added advantage of not appearing suspicious.

When the spectator finishes dealing, go to the "good" pile. Separate the reds from the blacks by leaving an inch or two at the middle marker. Remove the two markers and casually toss them aside, face down. Turn over the color group closest to the spectators, spreading the cards sideways to show they are all the same color. Then turn over the group nearest you and spread the cards sideways (nearer to you than your first spread), showing that they, too, are all of the same color (Illustration 51).

ILLUSTRATION 51
Turn over the group nearest you and spread the cards sideways
(nearer to you than your first spread).
Show that this group, too, is all of the same color.

Handle the other pile just as casually. Close it and pick it up. Turn it over so that the cards are face up and the two markers are face down. Casually discard the marker that was on top, putting it with the other two markers you have discarded. Fan the cards down to the next marker, showing them to be the same color. Remove this group, still fanned out, and place it next to the pile on the table closest to the spectators. The two groups nearest the spectators are of opposite colors (Illustration 52).

ILLUSTRATION 52
The two groups nearest the spectators are of opposite colors.

Discard the fourth marker, placing it with the other three markers. Fan the remaining cards, showing that they are the same color. Place this group, still spread out, next to the group nearest you. Everything is perfect. Reds are next to blacks, just as (presumably) they were dealt.

Pick up the markers, casually add them to the discarded pile. Give the pile a little shuffle; then congratulate the spectator on his extraordinary powers as you gather up the rest of the cards.

Go over this one several times before you try it out. You will be pleased with the reaction to "the world's greatest card trick."

The Process of Elimination

Ordinarily, I dislike tricks with a lot of dealing. But done snappily, this one has a tremendous effect.

You say, "I want you to observe how rapidly I deal these cards. It's well known that I'm among the top five percent of rapid card dealers. Which is a real money-making skill. Big call for that."

Rapidly deal six piles of five cards each, thirty cards in all. Have a spectator choose two cards from the remaining deck. set the rest of the deck aside. Take the two cards and show them to everyone, naming them and making sure to repeat their names at least twice, so that everyone will remember them.

Give the two cards back to the spectator. Tell him, "Please place one of your two chosen cards on top of one of the six piles." After he has done so, say, "Now place the other selected card on top of one of the other piles."

Take note of which two packets have the chosen cards on top. Place two other piles on top of each one. You now have two piles, sixteen cards in each one. In each pile, a chosen card is sixth from the bottom. Place either pile on top of the other.

Next, you will rapidly deal the cards alternately into two piles. Both chosen cards will be in the first pile you deal to.

You will eliminate the other pile, as I will explain later. You will repeat this procedure three times, leaving you with one pile containing two cards. They are, of course, the chosen ones.

Before we go into the elimination process, let us consider the dealing of the cards into two piles. It is not particularly deceptive if you *always* keep the pile on your left. Therefore, I recommend that on the first deal, you start with a card to your left, then one to the right, and so on. The next deal, place the first card to your *right*, the next to the left, and so on. On the third deal, start on your left; on the fourth, start on your right.

Clearly, the entire effect depends upon how you eliminate the piles. You ostensibly offer freedom of choice, while actually keeping the pile you want. Here is what I recommend.

After the first deal, tell the spectator, "Please pick up a pile." If he picks up the pile containing the two chosen cards, take the pile from him and, after brushing the other packet aside, deal the "chosen" pile into two new piles. If he picks up the other pile, take the one he leaves and rapidly deal that one into two piles. When you are done, casually take the pile from him and toss it aside.

After the second deal, tell the spectator, "Please hand me a pile." If he hands you the pile containing the chosen cards, brush the other packet aside, and deal the selected pile into two new piles. If he hands you the other pile, set it aside, pick up the pile with the selected cards, and deal it into two packets.

When you have finished the third deal, ask the spectator, "Which pile?" If he indicates the one containing the chosen cards, push the other packet aside, and deal the chosen pile into two new piles. If he chooses the other one, set it aside, pick up the pile with the selected cards, and deal it into two piles.

On the last deal, you have two packets containing two cards each. Tell the spectator to place a hand on each pile. Then direct him to lift up one hand. If he lifts the hand covering the chosen cards, take that pile and show the cards. If he lifts the other hand, take the pile he uncovers and set it aside. Then show the two selected cards.

The dealing and choosing actually take very little time. And the denouement is quite effective. But for the trick to work, I highly recommend that you follow my instructions for pile selection *precisely,* and please use the exact wording.

First: "Please pick up a pile."
Second: "Please hand me a pile."
Third: "Which pile?"

On the fourth selection, the wording is not critical. Simply tell him to place a hand on each pile.

I remember the order of selection for the first three picks with the words "pick, hand, which." Generally, I can remember the method of doing the last selection.

The Double-Match Trick

This one has to do with matches only in the sense of two things resembling each other. I wish I knew who invented this trick so that I could offer him my heartiest congratulations. It has everything: directness, cleverness, undetectability, and an astonishing climax. What's more, it's easy to execute. And since the spectator does all the work, he is completely mystified. I'm sure this trick will become one of your favorites.

Like most tricks, this one is enhanced by a little romance. "For this experiment," you say, "I need a kindred spirit, someone whose spiritual vibrations will correspond to mine." If no one volunteers, say, "I'll settle for someone who knows one card from the other."

Have your volunteer shuffle the deck. Take it back and fan the cards so that only you can see the faces. "Now I"m going to select two cards, and it's important that I concentrate." As you give the cards a casual fanning, indicating the importance of concentrating, note the top card. Find the card that matches it in color and value, and toss it out face up. For instance, if the top card is the six of clubs, find the six of spades and toss it out.

Now note the bottom card, find the card that matches it in color and value, and toss that one out face up. Have this one a little closer to you, so you'll remember to use it first.

"I would like you to look at these two cards and try to get a clear impression of them in your mind."

Hand the volunteer the deck and tell him to deal the cards into a face-down pile. After he has dealt a dozen or so cards, tell him to stop whenever he wishes. When he stops dealing, place the *second* card you took from the deck (the one matching the bottom card) face up on top of the pile he dealt from. Tell him to put the rest of the deck on top. You can also point to the second card you took and have the spectator place it face up on top of his dealt cards. This keeps the entire trick in his hands.

The position now is that in the lower portion of the deck your face-up card is face-to-face with its matching card. The bottom card of the deck matches the card on the table.

Again have the spectator deal cards from the top into a face-down pile. When he has dealt a dozen or so, tell him to stop when he wants to. Obviously, he must not deal so many that he gets to the face-up card. If he seems intent on dealing forever, simply take the cards from him and hand them to someone else to complete the deal.

When the spectator stops dealing, place the other face-up card on top of the pile he dealt, or have the spectator do so. The spectator places the rest of the deck on top.

"Now let's see if we are really *simpatico.*" Take the deck and very deliberately fan through the face-down cards. Take out the first face-up card along with the card above it and set them on the table. Fan through to the next face-up card; remove it and the card above it, placing them next to the pair on the table.

Turn over each of the face-down cards, showing how wonderfully *simpatico* you two really are. Be sure to tell the spectator, "You really did a great job. I have a feeling you must be psychic."

Note: If you have performed *Three-Card Surprise* (page 57) and spectators ask for a repeat, you can do this one. The effect is similar, but the method, as you can see, is quite different.

If you decide to do this, do *not* indicate that you are going to produce the same effect. Instead, say, "Let me show you something a little different." Then proceed with the patter above.

Astounding Appearance

This trick lives up to its title. It's as close to real magic as you're ever going to get. Occasionally you'll come across someone who knows the basic trick; don't let that hold you back. If someone says, "Oh, I know that one," or, "I do that one myself," simply give the person a conspiratorial wink and continue. The effect is worth it.

A spectator chooses a card and replaces it in the deck, which is shuffled. You show four cards individually; none is the selected card. Again you show the four cards and place them in the spectator's hand. You take away three cards, snap you fingers, and the remaining card is the chosen one.

Here's how. First, force a card. Use *One-Cut Force* (page 38), *Face-up Force* (page 39), or *Double-Turnover Force* (39). Have the card shown around and replaced in the deck. After the spectator shuffles the deck, fan through the cards, faces towards you, saying, "I'm not absolutely sure which one is yours, but I think I can locate it within four cards." Cut the deck so that the forced card is fourth from the bottom. The cut is done quite openly. "I'm sure you'll agree that narrowing it down to four cards is truly mediocre."

Before we proceed, check *The Glide* (page 15). Hold the deck in the glide grip and show the bottom card, asking, "Is this your card?" When the spectator says no, turn the deck down and deal the bottom card onto the table. Place the new bottom card on top of the deck without showing its face, remarking, "And we place the next card on top—for magical purposes." This is more effective than saying, "I place the next card on top because I feel like it." Or even worse, "I place the next card on top because if I don't, you'll soon be shown the same card twice in a row."

Tip the deck up, showing the new bottom card. "Is this your card?" Naturally, the spectator denies it. Turn the deck down and perform the glide, dealing the spectator's chosen card onto the one on the table. Place the bottom card (the one you just showed to the spectator) on top of the deck, repeating, "We place the next card on top—for magical purposes."

Show the bottom card and again ask if this is the chosen one. The spectator says no. As you place it on top of the two on the table, attempt to look crestfallen. This time, when you place the bottom card on top (to be consistent), pause after you say, "I place the next card on top . . ." Eye the spectators questioningly; they will be happy to explain that you are doing this for magical purposes.

Repeat the whole business, placing the bottom card on top of the three on the table and the new bottom card on top. When the spectator denies that the fourth one is his card, ask, "Are you sure?" Look puzzled, unless puzzlement is your natural look—in which case, look natural. "Now let's check to make sure."

There is now a pile of four cards on the table; the second one from the bottom is the chosen card. Pick up the pile and hold the cards in the glide grip. Ask the spectator to hold out his hand.

Show the bottom card. "This isn't yours?" you query. Of course he responds negatively. Turn the pile downwards and perform the glide, placing the spectator's chosen card face down on his extended palm. Place the next card on top for magical purposes.

Show the bottom card, repeating the query. Turn the pile down and place the bottom card on the spectator's palm. Do *not* shift a card to the top. Fan the remaining two cards, showing them to the spectator with the question, "And neither one of these is yours?" Add these to the face-down cards in the spectator's hand.

"Now let's check this again." Take the top card from the pile in the spectator's hand. Place it face up in your other hand, saying, "This isn't yours?" Quickly take the second card, place it face up on the first card you took, and repeat the question. And once more with the third card. Place the three cards to one side. Remaining in his hand is the chosen card.

To prevent premature disclosure, take his other hand and place it on top of the card. "Hold the card right there, please. Now tell me, what's the name of your card?" Gently hold his hand on the card so that he doesn't show it yet.

When he names his card, snap your fingers over his hands and then gesture to him, indicating that he should turn the card over.

Note: The key to this trick is performing it with some speed. No doubt you have noticed that when you place the cards in the spectator's hand, you show the same card twice. Don't worry about it—even when it is an obvious card, like an ace. If you proceed apace, no one will notice. I have done the trick for many, many years and nobody has ever called me on it.

Murder

Here's a very simple trick I came up with many years ago. It's one of those story tricks that spectators usually enjoy, and it has a surprise ending.

Put the four queens in a face-up row on the table. Also, lay the four aces, a king, and a jack to one side, also face up. A spectator selects a card and places it face up near the queens. Take the jack and place it next to the chosen card. Then use the following patter.

"I hope you all enjoy murder mysteries. The one I am about to present is challenging, thrilling, exciting, and preposterous. See if you can solve the murders. Yes, I said *murders;* this is going to be a juicy one. Now these four queens are rich, old spinsters living alone in a huge mansion. You, as symbolized by the six of clubs (name the chosen card), are their lawyer and in charge of their finances." Nod knowingly. Obviously, the spectator will be a prime suspect.

"One night you are visiting the four ladies. Also in the house is the tall, gaunt, old butler. Indicate the jack. You notice that from time to time he glares maniacally at the old ladies."

"Suddenly the lights go out, there is a shot (snap your fingers), and when the lights go on again, one of the ladies has been murdered." Turn one of the queens face down.

"You are a good friend of the chief of police (indicate the king), so you phone him and ask for help. He immediately sends out four of his best detectives to surround the house." Put the four aces in a face-up square around the queens, the jack, and the choosen card.

"If the detectives had been sensible, they would have gone *inside* the house. But that might have prevented any more murders, and would have spoiled this engrossing murder mystery. Somehow they must have known that.

143

"Sure enough, the lights went out, a shot was fired (snap your fingers), and another lady was murdered." Turn down another queen.

"Before the detectives could get to the house, the lights went out again, and two shots rang out (snap your fingers twice), and both remaining ladies were murdered." Turn the last two queens face down.

"The chief was infuriated when he learned of this, so he came to the house personally and gathered up all the suspects and took them to the station for a lie detector test." Gather up the cards so that they will read, from top to bottom: chosen card, ace, ace, jack, ace, ace.

"Yes, the chief was even suspicious of his own detectives. For the lie detector test, he decided to use the word 'murder.' Whoever reacted positively to his word would be the guily party. So let's spell out 'murder.' "

See *The Glide* (page 15). Hold the cards in your left hand in the glide grip and transfer one card from the top to the bottom for each letter as you spell out the word "murder." Show the ace at the bottom. Turn the cards face down and deal the ace face down on the table with the right fingers.

"We eliminate one of the detectives." Repeat the spelling, and the chosen card appears at the bottom. Show this card as before, but when you turn the cards down, perform the glide, drawing off the second card from the bottom and placing it face down on top of the ace you have eliminated.

"And—surprise!—you too are eliminated." Continue the elimination until only two cards remain.

"This leaves only two suspects: one of the ace detectives and the butler. Naw, it couldn't be the butler."

As you say this, separate the two cards, holding one face down in each hand. When you bring them back together, put the former bottom one on top. Spell out "murder" again. Show the bottom card, the jack, and deal it into the elimination pile.

"I *knew* it couldn't be the butler. So who do we have left? That rotten, vicious, conniving, sneaky, criminal . . ."

Look at the remaining card.

"Oh, no. There must be some mistake."

Turn the chosen card face up.

Quaint Coincidence

This one should be reserved for times when you have two bright, cooperative spectators, helpers who are capable of following directions.

This is similar in some respects to *Tricky Transpo* (page 64), so it would not be advisable to perform both in the same set, but it is different enough to include here, since it has an excellent climax.

Hand the deck out to be shuffled. Turn your back and have one spectator think of an odd number from five to twenty-five. Another spectator thinks of an even number from five to twenty-five. Each spectator is to count off the number of cards equal to the number he thought of. The rest of the deck is put aside. The two piles are put together and shuffled.

Turn around and take the pile. Tell the two assistants to note the two cards that lie at the numbers they thought of. Once they have noted the cards, they need not remember the number. Slowly deal the cards into a face-up pile, counting aloud as you do so. When you complete the deal, pick up the cards and turn them face down.

"Now don't forget your cards," you smilingly caution, "or this effect goes right up in smoke. We've dealt the cards only once, and, as you know, three is the magic number. So let's try deal number two."

Before you deal, give the cards a false cut—see the *One-Finger Cut* (page 26)—to throw off spectators.

Now hold the cards face down in the left hand and, starting at your left, deal them alternately into two face-down piles.

"Now for the third and magical deal." Take the left-hand pile face up in your left hand, and the other face down in your right hand. "Stop me immediately if either of you sees his card."

Simultaneously thumb off cards into two piles. Deal from the top of each pile. Make sure that you have exactly the *same* number of cards in each pile. Clearly, the pile on your left is dealt face up and the one on your right, face down. When one of the spectators tells you to stop, set the cards in your hands aside. Point to the face-up card and ask the spectator if he is certain that it is his. Then ask the second spectator to name his card.

When he does so, turn over the top card of the other pile, revealing the quaint coincidence.

MIND READING

A Word About Mind Reading

There are three ways in which the card artist can read minds:

1. *Force* the selection of a card on a spectator.
2. Learn the name of a card after a spectator has thought of it.
3. Actually use telepathy.

If you can do number three, you may as well skip this section. Most often the mind reader uses method one. Four of the five tricks in this section are actually *forces*. Some might be applicable to other tricks where it is necessary for you to know the name of a selected card, but the *forces* on pages 34 through 40 are quicker and more direct. Obviously, you can decide for yourself.

If you are going to do mind reading, I recommend that you program a number of tricks. Besides the tricks in this section, you might choose among the various prediction tricks.

If you are doing several mind-reading tricks, a spectator might naturally wonder, "Why can't I just think of a card and then you name it?" Before the issue comes up, I like to explain, "I am better able to see the card in your mind if you actually look at a card and then concentrate as you visualize it." Sure, it's nonsense. But if you *can* read minds, it's semilogical. There will be more tips on the techniques of mind reading as you go along.

In the Palm of Your Hand

Don't be frightened by this one. It's as close as you can come to real mind reading.

First, let's practise. Hold the deck in your left hand. Push off the top card and, with the aid of the left middle fingers, take it into the palm of your right hand, trying to conceal it (Illustration 53).

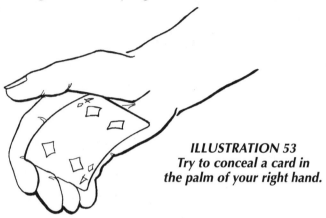

ILLUSTRATION 53
*Try to conceal a card in
the palm of your right hand.*

Don't worry; I'm not going to ask you to palm a card in plain sight. Put the cards behind your back and try the same palm. Now place your right hand on your left wrist as in Illustration 54. Practise this a few times. You're ready to roll.

ILLUSTRATION 54
*Place your right hand on your left wrist.
The card should now be completely hidden.*

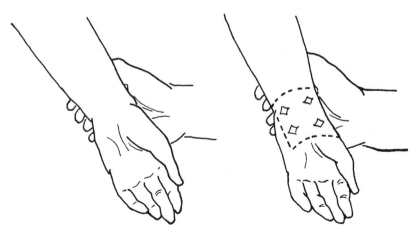

149

To start, you must know the top card. See *The Peek* (page 14). Now ask a spectator to come up and help you. For this trick, you cannot be surrounded by spectators, as you will see. Have the spectator stand by your side as you put your hands behind your back, deck in the left hand. Palm the top card and place your right hand on your wrist, as described above. Obviously, no one should be in a position to observe this.

Turn your back to the spectator, offering the deck, and say, "Cut off a pile of cards, please." After he has done so, turn towards him, add the palmed card to the top of the deck, and reclasp your wrist, saying, "Is that enough?" Again, no one can be behind you to observe.

The answer to your question is invariably yes. If he says no, say, "Sure, it is," and proceed. Turn you back to the spectator again and proffer the cards in your hand, saying, "Look at the card you cut to, show it around, and replace it."

After he has done this, say, "Now put the rest of the cards on top and take the deck."

Apparently, the spectator has cut the deck, looked at the card he cut to, and replaced the cutoff cards. What's more, he then took the deck into his own hands, eliminating the possibility of your trying any funny business.

Turn to face the spectator. It is time for a little psychological smoke screen. "I would like you to give the deck one complete shuffle." The spectator shuffles the deck.

"Aha!" say the spectators to themselves, "He must know the card above or below the selected card." They know a trick that works like that.

You continue to foster the misapprehension by saying, "Now if I go through the deck and find your card, would that be a good trick?" Usually the spectator agrees.

"Well, I don't want to do a trick. Instead, I am going to attempt to read your mind."

Take the deck from the spectator and hold it to your forehead. "Please concentrate on your card. I see red clouds. I would say your card is a red—a diamond. Let me see—it looks like a four—no, no—an ace. The ace of diamonds."

Equally, you could see dark clouds, of course, for a spade or a club. I like the idea of almost naming the wrong value, briefly mistaking a four for an ace, a queen for a jack, a three for an eight—any two cards that look somewhat alike. All of this enhances the illusion that you are actually mind-reading.

Crisscross

One piece of advice: Just because a trick is easy, don't give it short shrift. Just because the secret is simple, don't hurry through your presentation. A simple method of mind reading, for instance, can be just as effective as a complex one—maybe even more so. Consider this trick, which appears in most elementary magic books. When I teach magic, I use this to provide insight on presentation.

To begin with, you must know the top card of the deck. See *The Peek* (page 14). Set the deck down and ask a spectator to cut off a pile of cards. He is to set the pile down and put the rest of the deck on top of it crosswise.

The former top card of the deck is now on top of the lower pile; you know it, and if the spectators think about it, they know too. They aren't going to think about that, because you're going to do this absurdly simple trick like a real pro. You're going to take their minds and eyes off the cards.

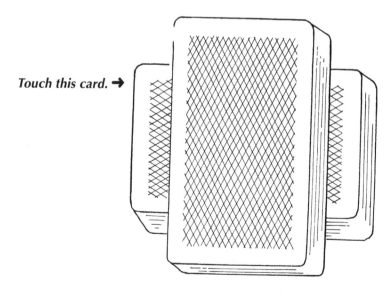

Touch this card. ➜

ILLUSTRATION 55
*The spectator cuts off a pile of cards, sets down the deck,
and then places the rest of the deck on top of it, crosswise.
Then, touch the top of the card of the lower pile with your forefinger.*

To do this, you merely speak for a moment. I usually say something like this: "You had complete freedom of choice as to where you cut the cards. You could have cut off a big pile, a little pile, whatever you chose. Now I want you to take a look at your card." Here you *touch* the card he is to look at so there will be no mistake (Illustration 55).

You do *not* say, "I want you to look at the card you cut to." This might bring up nasty thoughts, like, "Which one *did* I cut to?"

Have him show the card around. Now add more tinsel to the tree by having him replace the card from where he took it and even up the deck. He is to give the deck one shuffle of his choice, but only one shuffle.

Again, you hold the deck to your forehead and gradually reveal the color, the suit, and the value.

Yes, the trick is elementary. So what? Does it fool people? With proper presentation, it certainly does. Toss this in occasionally among the more subtle mind-reading tricks and check out the spectator reaction. I think you'll be pleased.

The Big Deal

To begin with, you must know the second card from the bottom of the deck. You may choose among the methods offered in *The Peek* (page 12). I recommend this variation of number four.

You say, "The vibes just aren't right. I'd better remove my bad-luck card."

As you fan through the deck, note the second card from the bottom. Continue on to the queen of spades, or some other "bad luck" card, and remove it from the deck. If you can, shuffle the deck, retaining at least the bottom two cards.

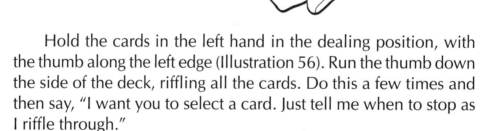

ILLUSTRATION 56
Hold the cards in your left hand, in the dealing position, with your thumb along the left edge.

Hold the cards in the left hand in the dealing position, with the thumb along the left edge (Illustration 56). Run the thumb down the side of the deck, riffling all the cards. Do this a few times and then say, "I want you to select a card. Just tell me when to stop as I riffle through."

Now the spectator is going to get the bottom portion of the deck, and you want him to have less than half the cards. So start your riffle just above the middle, and riffle *slowly.* Make sure you stop *exactly* where the spectator indicates. Keep the top portion and give the bottom portion to the spectator.

"Now let's deal them into piles, one card at a time." Deal your pile in front of you, as he deals his in front of him. Match him card for card. Stop dealing when the spectator runs out of cards. Set the rest of your cards aside.

Tell the spectator, "Place your top card in the middle. Now put your bottom card in the middle. Next, look at the new top card and show it around."

Suiting action to words, you have shown the spectator the way by placing the top card in the middle of your pile and the bottom card in the middle of your pile. You have also lifted the top card of your pile, *definitely not looking at it,* and returned it to the top. The card the spectator has looked at is, of course, the card which was originally the second card from the bottom of the deck.

Tell the spectator to shuffle his packet. Hand him your packet and tell him to shuffle it in with the others. It is a mistake, I believe, to simply name the chosen card. I like to stress the mind reading. Granted, there may be a hint of a twinkle in my eye. While it is true that the spectators, at one level, *know* you cannot possibly read minds, it is just possible that you may be able to. And how *could* you have done it if you had not read the spectator's mind?

I tell the spectator to concentrate on his card as he shuffles. Then, as with the other mind-reading tricks, I gradually reveal the suit and the value.

Pretend to concentrate. You might tell the spectator something like this: "You may or may not believe in mind reading, but I would like you to do as I ask. Please concentrate on the color of your card. Actually think of the color." Then reveal the color.

"Now please think of the suit." As you concentrate, tell the spectator that you are getting mixed signals, that you can't be quite sure. Then tell him the suit. Do something similar in revealing the value.

Believe me, all of this razzmatazz enhances the trick. The spectators are not quite sure whether you have actually performed mind reading. Regardless, they know you have done a great trick.

The Three Piles

I invented this trick by combining two well-known principles. You will like this one, I think, when, after you have finished, you hear spectators comment on how "you didn't even touch the cards."

Again, you must know the top card. You can use one of the methods listed under The Peek (page 14). Then, if you can, shuffle the cards, making sure that the top card stays there.

Hand the deck to a spectator and tell him to deal out a pile. After he has dealt seven or eight cards, tell him to stop when he feels like it. Ask him to deal another pile next to it. Again, after several cards have been dealt, tell him to stop when he wishes. Tell him to deal a third pile next to the second one. When the spectator has finished dealing to the third pile, take the rest of the cards from him and set them aside.

The spectator now has three piles in front of him. The *bottom* card of the first pile he dealt is the original top card of the deck.

Tell the spectator, "Put your hand on a pile, please."

1. If he places his hand on the first pile he dealt, gather up the two remaining piles, placing them on top of the deck. Tell him to look at the bottom card of his pile.

2. If he places his hand on a different pile, say, "And place your other hand on a pile."

Suppose he places his *other* hand on a different pile. Don't *say* anything. Gesture with your two hands that he is to hand you the two piles he is covering. If he doesn't catch on, say, "Hand me the two piles, please." Put the two piles on top of the deck and tell the spectator to look at the bottom card of his pile.

Suppose he places his *other* hand on the pile containing the force card. Pick up the uncovered pile. Tell the spectator, "Lift a hand, please."

If he lifts the hand covering the pile containing the force card, gesture that he is to hand you the covered pile. If his eyes glaze over, point to the covered pile and say, "Hand me the pile, please." Have him look at the bottom card of the remaining pile.

If he lifts his other hand, the covered pile is the one containing the force card. Pick up the uncovered pile and have him look at the bottom card of the remaining pile.

The above *sounds* complicated, but just run through it a few times and you will find that, in practise, it is quite simple.

After the spectator has looked at the bottom card of the pile and has shown the card around, have him place the pile (with the chosen card) on top of the deck. Even up the deck and set it aside. Then, as with the previous three effects, read the spectator's mind as convincingly as you can.

The Three Location

The previous mind-reading tricks were variations of forcing a card on a spectator. This trick, however, is quite different.

Since I first came across *The Three Location* many years ago, I have included it nearly every time I have displayed my so-called mental powers. In the original version, the spectator was offered only nine cards to choose from. As a slight improvement, I developed a method of offering thirteen cards.

Fan through the deck, saying, "I want to find a suitable card for you to choose mentally." Find a three, count six cards beyond it, and cut the cards at that point so that the three becomes the seventh card from the top.

"I'm going to show you some cards, and I want you to think of one. I won't watch your face, and I don't want you to say anything when you have thought of one."

Slowly show the cards one by one to the spectator, taking them one under the other so that they remain in the same order. Keep your head averted. Show the spectator exactly thirteen cards and return them to the top, saying, "Do you have one?"

If his answer is no, say, "I'll go slower this time", and go through the thirteen cards again. When the spectator has one, say, "Now I'll try to find your card."

Put the deck behind your back, count off six cards and turn the seventh card (the three you found) face up. Replace the six cards on top, cut the deck, and bring the cards forward.

"I have located your card in the deck. What's the name of your card?" If he names the three, you have a miracle. Show him that it is face up in the middle.

If it is another card, fan through the cards, faces towards you, saying, "Note that there is a face-up card in the middle." As you fan to the three, showing the face-up card, spread the cards on either side, so that you can see where the chosen card is in relation to it.

Turn the cards face down, leaving them spread out. If his card is either directly above or below the three, say, "And with the face-up card, I have located your card." Pull out the face-up three with the chosen card, either above or below it. "What's the name of your card?" you ask. The spectator repeats the name. Turn the two cards over, revealing the mentally selected card.

If his chosen card is second from the three on either side, say, "Note that the face-up card is a three." In fact, you make this statement in all ensuing instances. Now you start on the three and count to the selected card, like this: Touch the three, saying, "One"; touch the second card, saying, "Two"; touch the selected card, saying, "Three." Pull the selected card from the deck. As before, and in all other instances, ask, "What is the name of your card?" When he repeats the name, turn the card over.

If the thought-of card is three cards from the three on either side, count over three, as above, starting with the *next* card. Pull the selected card from the deck, and finish as before.

Suppose his selected card is four cards from the three. As before, say, "Note that the face-up card is a three." Then, starting with the three, spell out T-H-R-E-E, landing on his selected card.

If the selected card is five cards from the three, spell out T-H-R-E-E, starting with the card next to your face-up three, again landing on his selected card.

If it is six cards from the three, again spell out T-H-R-E-E, starting with the card next to your face-up three, but, at the completion of your spelling, pull out the *next* card.

Why do you ask the spectator to name his card twice? Nothing but good can come out of it. It helps build to the climax. Also, some spectators will forget that you asked the first time; thus, you have a genuine miracle. What's more, you create the impression that you paid no attention when the thought-of card was named the first time.

When you fan the cards, showing the face-up three to the spectators, they see only the backs of the cards and they are looking at the face-up card you are displaying. They do not realize that at the same time, you are looking at the faces of the cards.

Despite my labored explanation, this is quite a snappy trick. Need I add, do it only once?

Either/Or Force

You must know the top card. Deal cards into a pile, telling a spectator to tell you when to stop. As soon as he says stop, start dealing another pile to the right of the first one. Again, the spectator tells you when to stop. Immediately, start dealing a third pile to the *left* of the first one. Once more the spectator tells you when to stop. Place the remaining cards in your hand to the far right.

Four piles are in a row on the table. You know the bottom card of the second pile from your left. Cover the two piles on the right with your outstretched right hand and the two piles on the left with your outstretched left hand. Ask, "Right or left?" Whichever is chosen, push aside the two piles on your right.

"Pick up a pile, please." If he picks up the pile containing the force card, push aside the remaining pile and tell him to look at the bottom card. If he picks up the other pile, take it from him and place it aside with the other discarded piles. Tell him, "Please look at the bottom card of your chosen pile."

This business is called the *equivogue* or the *magician's choice*, of which there are many versions. Try it out; it's quite easy and totally convincing.

161

PREPARATION

Two-Faced Card Trick—1

For the next two startling tricks, you'll need a double-faced card. Such cards can be purchased at your local magic shop. But for our purposes, you can just as easily make up your own. Simply take two cards and glue them back to back, making sure they're precisely even.

This first trick was reported by Harry Riser in *MUM*, the publication of the Society of American Magicians.

Let's say that your double-backed card has the jack of spades on one side and the ten of hearts on the other. You'll also need a regular jack of spades and ten of hearts. Have the double-faced card in your pocket, with the ten of hearts side facing out.

To start, take the legitimate jack of spades and ten of hearts from your pocket and show both sides of both. "I'd like to try an experiment with these two cards— the jack of spades and the ten of hearts." Place the two cards back to back and square them up. Still keeping them squared, turn over the two, displaying first one side and then the other.

Ask spectator Sean to assist you. Place the two cards into his pocket, with the ten of hearts facing out.

"Sean, where's the ten of hearts?" Naturally, he replies that it's in his pocket. "And the jack of spades is in the same pocket, right?" Of course. "So if I take the ten of hearts from your pocket, like this . . ." Remove the ten of hearts from his pocket. ". . . then you would still have the jack of spades in your pocket. And now *I'll* have the ten of hearts in *my* pocket." Suiting action to words, place the ten of hearts *face out* into your pocket, *behind the double card.*

With a laugh, say "I think we all understand now that the jack of spades is in your pocket and the ten of hearts is in mine. But let's check to make absolutely sure." Remove the jack of spades from Sean's pocket and hand it to him. Remove the double-faced card from your pocket, displaying the ten of hearts side. (Make sure no one sees the other side of the card).

Holding the ten of hearts in the dealing position in your left hand, take the jack of spades from Sean with your right hand. Turn it face down and place it under the double faced card. Apparently the jack of spades and the ten of hearts are now back to back. Even up the cards and dispay both sides. Put both cards into Sean's pocket, with the legitimate jack of spades facing out. Behind it, of course, is the double card with the ten of hearts side facing his body.

Now comes a very sneaky piece of business based on an ambiguity in the expression "Pick a card for me." It can mean either "Do me a favor and pick a card," or "The card you name will become my card." So say to Sean, "Pick a card for me, Sean—ten of hearts or jack of spades." If he chooses the jack of spades, say, "Okay, you picked the jack of spades for me." If he chooses the ten of hearts, say, "You picked the ten of hearts, so I get the jack of spades."

Reach into Sean's pocket and remove the double-faced card, showing the jack of spades. (Practise this move. Needless to say, it's vital that no one see the other side of the card). Place the double card into your pocket behind the legitimate ten of hearts.

Pause a moment, staring into space. Shake your head. "I keep forgetting. What card do you have?" He says that he has the ten of hearts. Ask him to remove the card from his pocket. It's the jack of spades. You remove the legitimate ten of hearts from your pocket.

Casually show both sides of the two cards and put them away.

Two-Faced Card Trick—2

Let's try another stunt with a double-faced card. Reported by Martin Gardner, this was a specialty of Bert Allerton's.

Again, assume that the double-faced card has the jack of spades on one side and the ten of hearts on the other. You'll also need a regular jack of spades and ten of hearts. Place the jack of spades face up on the table. On top of it, place the ten of hearts face up. On top of all, place the double-faced card, with the jack of spades side up.

Place all three in your pocket with the two-faced card on the outside, jack of spades side facing out.

Start by removing the two outermost cards from your pocket, making sure that spectators don't see the other side of the double-faced card. Fan the two out, showing the jack of spades on top and the ten of hearts below it (Illustration 57).

ILLUSTRATION 57

The jack of spades, of course, is the double-faced card. "As you notice, we have the jack of spades and the ten of hearts." Close up the two cards and turn them over, showing the back. Ask, "Can you remember what the two cards are?" Turn the two face up once more. "That's right, the jack of spades and the ten of hearts." Move the jack of spades below the ten of hearts. Move it back on top again. Close up the two cards and turn them over, showing the back. "What are they again?" Turn them face up and fan them. "That"s right."

Ostensibly, you've shown the backs and fronts of both cards.

Place the double-faced card on the table; naturally the jack of spades side is up. Now perform an easy sleight known as *Wild Card Turnover.* With your right hand, hold the ten of hearts at the lower right corner with your thumb on top and fingers beneath. Place your left first finger on the lower left corner of the card on the table. (See Illustration 40, page 71). Slide the card in your right hand beneath the right side of the card on the table and, with a counterclockwise move, flip both cards over. Release your grip on the ten of hearts as you complete the move. Logic tells us that both cards should now be face down, but (as you'll discover) logic doesn't prevail. On the table now is a face-up ten of hearts (the other side of the double-faced card) and a face-down ten of hearts. In your pocket is the jack of spades, facing outward.

With your right hand, pick up the face-up ten of hearts (the two-faced card) and place it *behind* the card in your pocket. Make sure no one sees the other side as you place it in the pocket with the ten of hearts side out. In what seems to be an attempt to fool the spectators, as you place the card in your pocket, say, "Now I'll put the jack of spades into my pocket." As you say this, look as shifty-eyed and sneaky as you possibly can.

With your right hand, point to the card on the table. "So what's this card?" The group won't be deceived by your miscalling of the card you placed in your pocket. Someone's bound to say, "*That's* the jack of spades."

"No, no," you say, pulling the outermost card from your pocket and tossing it onto the table. "*This* is the jack of spades. The other card is the ten of hearts." Turn it over. Pick up the jack of spades, casually show its back and drop it face up onto the ten of hearts. Pick up the two and place them, faces outward, in the pocket *behind* the double-faced card. (You'll recall that the double-faced card has its ten of hearts side facing out).

Apparently, you're done. "Did you like that?" Pause. "Maybe you'd like to see it again."

Remove the two outermost cards from your pocket. This time, simply fan them face up without showing the backs. On top is the ten of hearts side of the double-faced card; below it is the face-up jack of spades. Drop the double-faced card on the table, ostensibly the ten of hearts. With the jack of spades, perform *Wild Card Turnover* (page 165). On the table the spectators see the jack of spades side of the double-faced card and a face-down card. Pick up the double-faced card, saying, "Now I place the ten of hearts in my pocket." Place the card *behind* the ten of hearts in your pocket. Point to the card on the table. "What's the other card?" You'll be told that the other card is actually the ten of hearts. Pull the outermost card from your pocket, saying, "No, no. *This* is the ten of hearts." Turn over the other card. "This one is the jack of spades." As before, casually show the back of the ten of hearts, drop it on top of the jack of spades, and place the two, faces outward, in your pocket behind the double-faced card.

Again, pretend briefly to be done. Then say, "Would you like to see how it's done?" They will. "Actually, I use three cards."

Remove the two outermost cards from your pocket and separate them on the table. Spectators will see a jack of spades and a ten of hearts. Actually, they're seeing the jack of spades side of the double-faced card.

Explain, "I actually use *two* jacks of spades." Pull the jack of spades about halfway out of your pocket so that all can see it. Push it back into your pocket.

Pick up the ten of hearts and turn both tabled cards over, using *Wild Card Turnover*. Spectators now see the ten of hearts side of the double-faced card and a face-down card. Pick up the double-faced card, apparently the ten of hearts, and place it in your pocket behind the other card as you say, "I actually put the ten of hearts in my pocket, but I call it the jack of spades to confuse you."

Pause a moment, saying, "It's really quite easy. You see, I just reach into my pocket and take out the *other* jack of spades." Take the outermost card, the jack of spades, from your pocket and toss it onto the table.

Someone's bound to say, "But what about the jack of spades that's still on the table?"

Shake your head. "I'm afraid you're really not paying attention. That isn't the jack of spades . . ." Turn the face-down card over. ". . . That's the ten of hearts."

Casually show both sides of both cards and put them away.

Lucky 7

I developed a slight variation of a Lin Searles trick.

There's an easy setup: You have a face-down seven on top, followed by seven face-up cards.

Spectator Charlene should be willing to assist. Say to her, "Charlene, I'd like you to choose a card, but let's make sure that you choose one completely by chance. When I give you the deck, I'd like you to place it behind your back." (If you're seated at a table, she should take the deck under the table). Give her the deck, making sure no one is behind her to see what goes on.

When the deck is behind her back, continue: "Now please cut off a good-sized pile from the top of the deck and turn the pile over so that it's face up on top."

Turn away and continue the directions: "Even up the cards. Now bring the deck forward and fan through the face-up cards to the first face-down card. Set down all the face-up cards for a moment. Next, look at that first face-down card, the one you cut to. This is your chosen card, so you must remember it. After you look, leave it face down on top of the packet. Now pick up that pile you cut off and place it *face down* on top of the deck." Make sure you give all the directions slowly and clearly so that Charlene understands every step.

Turn back and take the pack from Charlene. With your right hand, take off the top card, making sure no one sees its face. Say, "Behind my back, I'll stick this card face up somewhere in the deck." Your left hand takes the deck behind your back, while your right hand takes the card behind your back.

"Let's see. I'll put it in face up right about . . . there." Actually, you simply place the card face down on top of the deck. Bring the deck forward. Turn it face up. Start fanning through the cards.

"With the deck face up, the card I stuck in should now be face down." Fan through to the face-down card. Set aside all the cards you fanned through to arrive at the face-down card.

"Ah, here's my card. Let's see what it is." Turn it face up and drop it on the table. "Perfect! A seven. That's my lucky number. Let's count down seven cards. What was your card?" Charlene names it. You deal off seven cards, and hers shows up as the last card in the count.

Color Confusion

Don Smith created this trick; I adjusted the handling somewhat. You'll need a red-backed deck and a blue-backed deck. Remove seven cards from the blue-backed deck. Make sure there are at least three spot cards on the bottom of the blue-backed deck. Take eight assorted face cards from the red-backed deck. Place one of these in your pocket. The rest go on the bottom of the blue-backed deck.

The situation: You have a blue-backed deck from which seven cards have been removed. At the bottom of this deck are seven red-backed face cards. Directly above these are at least three blue-backed spot cards. In your pocket is a red-backed face card. Place the deck into the blue-card case. (Get rid of all other cards).

In performance, remove the deck from it's card case. Hold the deck face down and casually fan through about two-thirds of the cards, saying, "Let's try an experiment with these cards." Make sure you don't get to the red-backed cards. Don't call attention to the color of the backs. The fanning should be sufficient to establish this.

Close up the deck. Turn it over. "On the bottom, I have a group of face cards." Fan through them, showing them, and fan a few cards past them. As you close up the fan of face cards with your palm-up right hand, add a spot card at the back. Lift the packet off with your right hand as you set aside the balance of the deck face down. Even up the packet.

You're about to perform the *flustration count*, a sneaky maneuver attributed to Brother John Hamman. It isn't a difficult sleight. In fact, it's not a sleight at all, but an easy, subtle move which is totally deceptive. In performing the *flustration count*, you'll casually demonstrate that all the cards in the packet you're holding have blue backs, even though only one of the cards actually does have a blue back.

Now you're holding the packet from above in your right hand, fingers at the outer end and thumb at the inner end. (If you have shorter fingers, your right first finger may be resting on top near the outer end). Turn your right hand palm up, displaying the blue back of the top card. Turn your right hand palm down. With your left thumb, draw off the card on the face of the deck (Illustration 58).

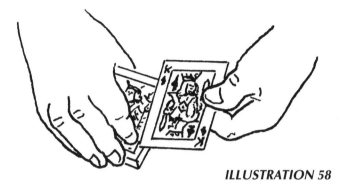

ILLUSTRATION 58

Hold this card in your left hand. Draw off another card from the face of the deck with your left thumb, letting the card land face up on top of the other card in your left hand. Casually turn over your right hand, showing the back of the top card again. Draw off two more cards individually. Once more show the back of the top card. Turn your right hand palm down and place the packet in your right hand face up on the table. Take the face-up cards from your left hand into your right hand and place these face up on top of those on the table. Pick up the packet with your right hand and place it face down in your left hand.

"Let's add a card." With your right hand, remove the red-backed face card from your pocket, showing only the back. "This one should be easy to tell from the others." Insert the card face down into the middle of the packet. Turn the packet face up and cut it several times.

Fan out the cards so that all can see the faces. Ask, "So what was the card we added?"

Spectators notice the spot card and name it.

"And do you remember the color of its back?"

The answer is "Red."

"Oh, how quickly we forget," you say. Take the spot card out and turn it over. It has a blue back. Pause a moment. "And you probably forgot that all these are red." Turn the packet over and spread it out, showing the red backs.

DISCOVERY

Discovery is the theme of some of the most imaginative card tricks, yet the basic idea is one of the simplest. A card is chosen, and the magician locates it.

No Touch, No Feel

Long, long ago, magician George Sands, came up with this superb, puzzling trick. I have added a few wrinkles.

Since spectator Ginny is quite bright, ask her to assist you. Hand her the deck of cards, saying, "Throughout this experiment, Ginny, I'm not going to touch the cards. To start with, I'd like you to give the deck a good shuffle." When she finishes, say, "Now I'd like you to deal the cards into a pile." Make sure you *don't* say, "Count the cards into a pile." At this point, you don't want her thinking about numbers. You, however, are counting the cards to yourself—as casually as you can. When she has dealt ten cards, say, "You can stop whenever you wish."

Continue to count the cards silently until she stops dealing. Turn away, saying, "Please set the rest of the deck aside. Now I'd like you to think of a number . . . say, less than ten. Remember that number. Next, look at the card that lies at that number from the top of your pile. For instance, if you thought of the number five, you'd look at the card that lies fifth from the top of your pile. Please remember that card and leave it at that number."

When she's ready, continue, "Ginny, set your packet down and pick up the rest of the deck. Remember that number you thought of? Please deal that same number of cards from the deck on top of your pile. So, if you thought of the number five, you'd deal five cards from the deck onto your pile. Then set the deck down again and pick up your pile."

"The first person to try this experiment was an Australian, so we must honor him by doing a 'down-under' shuffle. Deal the top card of your pile onto the table. Now put the next card underneath your pile. Deal the next card onto the table and place the next card underneath your pile. Continue like this until all your cards are on the table."

When she's done, say, "Pick up your entire pile and place it on top of the deck. Even up all the cards."

Turn back to the group. "Ginny, at no time have I touched the cards, and I'm not going to touch them now. Neither you nor I know exactly where your card is in the deck. Still, there is a certain aura which is attached to the card you've chosen, and I'm going to try to detect that aura. Please deal the cards slowly into a pile."

Ginny deals the cards down. "Slow down," you say, as she nears the selected card. "I feel that it's very close." Finally, you say, "Stop! What's the name of the card you thought of?" She names it; you point to the last card she dealt onto the pile. She turns it over and, of course, it's that very card.

You should be ashamed of yourself, bamboozling Ginny with a trick that's as easy to do as this one. As I mentioned, before you turn away, you note the number of cards that are dealt. With a very easy calculation, this number tells you at what number from the top the assistant's card will be when she slowly deals the cards out.

You divide by two the number of cards dealt out. If you end up with a number followed by one-half, you take the next whole number. This is the number at which the card will lie near the end of the trick. But if you divide by two and end up with a whole number, you divide *that* number by two. And you continue to divide by two until you do get a number that ends in one-half. When you finally get one-half at the end, take the next whole number.

For instance, suppose the assistant deals out fifteen cards. Divide fifteen by two, getting seven and one-half. Take the next whole number, eight. When the assistant deals out the cards at the end, the selected card will be eighth from the top.

Suppose the assistant dealt fourteen cards at the beginning. Divide this by two, getting seven. But you must get a number with one-half at the end, so divide the seven by two. This gives you three and one-half. Take the next whole number, which is four. The chosen card will end up fourth from the top.

Let's take an extreme example. The assistant deals out twenty-four cards at the beginning. You divide this by two, getting twelve. You divide the twelve by two, getting six. You divide the six by two, getting three. You divide the three by two, getting one and one-half. At last, a number with one-half at the end! Take the next whole number greater than one and one-half, which is two. At the end, the assistant's card will be second from the top.

Sheer Luck

This is my version of a trick of unknown origin. In some respects, it is similar to *No Touch, No Feel*, but the overall effect and the climax are quite different.

The trick works best when you display a sense of curiosity and wonderment throughout. You and the audience are participating in an experiment; heaven only knows what will happen!

"I'd like to experiment with something I've never tried before," you explain, smiling engagingly to prove that you're not lying through your teeth. "Mel, would you please help out."

Hand the spectator Mel the deck, asking him to shuffle the cards. "Now what? Oh, I have an idea. Why don't you cut off a good-sized bunch of cards and shuffle them up? I'll turn my back while you're doing it."

Turn away. Continue: "Let's see . . . maybe you should look at the top card of that bunch. Yeah, that's a good idea. In fact, show that card around and then put it back on top of the bunch.

"Hey, I've got an inspiration! Mel, set that bunch down and pick up the rest of the deck. Now we all know that seven is a lucky number, so think of a number from one to seven. Got one? Then deal that many cards from the deck onto your pile . . . right on top of your card." As he does this, you might mutter something like, "This is really getting good."

Continue: "Okay, Mel. Set down the rest of the deck and pick up the pile containing your card. Put that pile right on top of the rest of the deck and even up the cards." Turn back to the group and pick up the deck. "All I have to do is find your card. Now we're getting to the part that I haven't quite worked out yet." Casually fan off eight cards from the top of the group. (Don't count these aloud; you make it appear that any small number will do). Hold this packet of eight cards and set the rest of the deck aside. "Maybe it'll work better if we have fewer cards." Riffle the group of eight next to your ear. "Sounds like your card's here, all right."

Have Mel pick up the rest of the deck. Set the packet of eight on the table. "You know what might help, Mel? Remember that number you dealt on top of your card? I'll turn away again, and you deal that same number on top of the pile again." Point to the pile of eight cards so that he'll know exactly what to do. Turn away while he does his dealing. Turn back and have Mel set the deck aside and pick up the pile containing his card.

"It's pretty obvious what we have to try now, Mel. We have to eliminate lots of cards. Please put the top card on the bottom. Then deal the next card onto the table. Next, put the top card on the bottom. And again deal the next card onto the table." Have him continue this deal until only one card remains in his hands.

"What was your card, Mel?" He names it. It's the one he's holding.

Note: The deal used at the end of this trick is the opposite of the "Australian shuffle." In the latter, the *down-under* deal, a card is dealt onto the table and then one placed on the bottom, and so on. This is an *under-down* deal. The first card goes on the bottom, the next on the table, and so on.

Double Discovery

Whoever discovered the clever principle used here should be very proud, for it has been incorporated into any number of excellent tricks. This is my favorite.

You'll need a complete fifty-two-card deck and two willing assistants—Wendy and Grant, for instance.

Hand Wendy the deck. "We're going to have both you and Grant choose a card, Wendy. But we want to be absolutely fair. So each of you should have exactly half the deck. Would you please count off twenty-six cards and give them to Grant."

After she does so, turn your back. Give the following instructions, with appropriate pauses: "I'd like each of you to shuffle your cards. Look at the bottom card of your group and notice its value. Now very quietly deal off that many cards from the top of your group. Just deal them into a pile on the table. If the bottom card is a six, for example, you'd deal off six cards from the top of your group. A jack counts as eleven, a queen as twelve, and a king as thirteen.

"Once you've dealt off the cards, you don't need to remember the number. Just look at the top card of the pile you dealt off. Please remember it; that's your chosen card.

"Wendy, you're holding a group of cards. Please place this group on top of the cards that Grant dealt off.

"Grant, place the cards that you're holding on top of the pile that Wendy dealt off.

"One more job, Wendy, and then we're done. Put either pile on top of the other, and even the cards up."

When she finishes, turn back to the group. "It's pretty obvious that no ordinary human being could locate the two selected cards. But I am no ordinary human being. As a matter of fact, I'm from Krypton . . . or is it Mars? I can never remember."

Pick up the deck and hold it face down. You will deal the entire deck into a face-up pile, spreading the cards from left to right as you deal them (Illustration 59).

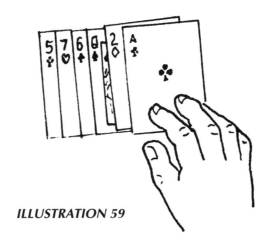

ILLUSTRATION 59

Deal out twelve cards face up. As you place the thirteenth card face up onto the pile, think to yourself, "King." As you deal the next card onto the pile, think, "Queen." As you deal the next, think, "Jack." Continue all the way down to ace. As you do this, at some point the card you're dealing will match the card you're thinking. For instance, you might think to yourself, "Six," and the card you're placing onto the pile is a six. Don't stop or pause at this point, but continue on as though nothing had happened. The fact is, however, that six tells you everything you need to know about the two chosen cards. The card following it is one of the chosen cards. Furthermore, the six tells you that the other chosen card is sixth from the bottom of the deck.

So you have dealt a six, and it matches the number you were thinking. Deal the next card (one of the selected cards) slightly out of line to mark the position of the six. This is important, as I will explain later.

You now continue dealing the rest of the deck face up. Spread out the cards. As you do this, mentally count backwards from the face of the deck to the sixth card from the bottom. Pass one of your hands back and forth over the cards. Let your hand fall on the first chosen card that you noticed, the one that followed the six. Push this card forward. "I believe that this is one of the chosen cards. Whose is it?"

Let's say that Grant admits that it's his. "Good. Now I must find Wendy's card." Again you pass your hand over the cards. This time, let it fall onto the sixth card from the bottom. Push this card forward. "And this must be your card, Wendy."

Another Example: You deal twelve cards one at a time into a face-up pile. When you deal out the thirteenth card face up, you think to yourself, "King." You continue the sequence, mentally counting one card lower each time you deal a card. Suppose that you're thinking, "Nine," and you deal out a nine at the same time. This means that the next card you deal will be one of the chosen cards, and that the other chosen card will be ninth from the bottom of the deck.

Sometimes, as you go through the backward sequence from king to ace, more than one card will match up. Suppose, for instance, that you mentally match both jack and three. The card after the jack might be one of the chosen cards, but so might the card after the three. What do you do?

After you come to each match, you move the next card a bit out of line. This eliminates the possibility of any later confusion. After you finish dealing out the entire deck, you can easily go back and look at the two possibilities. So a jack matched, and suppose that right after it came the seven of clubs. And a three matched, and let's say that right after it came the ace of diamonds. You'll have to eliminate one of the possibilities. The best way is the most direct way. Simply say, "Did one of you choose an ace?" If the answer is no, say, "I didn't think so." You now know that one of the chosen cards is the seven of clubs (the one that followed the jack), and that the other chosen card is eleventh from the bottom.

If one of your assistants *did* choose an ace, you say, "I thought so." Push the ace of diamonds forward. "I think it's this one." The matching card just before the ace was a three, so you now know that the other chosen card is third from the bottom.

Four Times Four

Years ago, I read a trick in a magic magazine in which four spectators each think of a card, and the magician discovers all the chosen cards. Unfortunately, I couldn't figure out the explanation. Either something was wrong with the write-up, or I was extremely dense. Since I preferred the former theory and I very much liked the plot, I worked out my own method.

Ask a spectator to shuffle the deck, take four cards for himself, and distribute four cards to each of three other spectators. The rest of the deck is set aside.

Tell the four spectators, "Please look through your cards and figure out one card that you like. Remember that card. Then mix up your four cards so that even you don't know which one is your card."

Mentally number the spectators from left to right as one, two, three, and four. Take Spectator Four's packet. Place Spectator Three's packet on top of it. Spectator Two's packet goes on top of the combined packets. And Spectator One's packet goes on top of all.

"If you don't mind, I'll mix the cards a bit. In fact, I'll give them the famous *holy-moley-what-the-heck-kind-of-a-shuffle-is-that?* shuffle."

Take the top card into your right hand, just as though you were going to deal it. Take the next card on top of that card, grasping it with your right thumb. Push off the next card with your left thumb. Grasp it with the right fingers, taking it below the two in your right hand. The next card goes on top of those in your right hand. The next card goes on top of those in your right hand. Continue alternating like this until all the cards are in your right hand.

"Let's try that again."

Perform the same peculiar shuffle. "That should do it."

With your right hand, take off the top four cards of the packet, dealing them *one on top of the other*, so that their order is reversed. Set the rest of the packet down. Fan out the four cards so that the four spectators can see the faces. "Does anyone see his card here?"

Whatever the answers, close up the cards and deal them out from left to right—in a special way. From your left to right, consider that there are positions one, two, three, and four on the table—matching the positions of the four spectators. When any spectator sees his card displayed, that card is dealt face down at the appropriate position; the others are dealt face up. Suppose that, on your first display, Spectators One and Four have seen their cards. Deal the top card (signifying Spectator One) face down at Position One. Deal the second card (signifying Spectator Two) face up at Position Two. Deal the third card (signifying Spectator Three) face up at Position Three. Deal the fourth card (signifying Spectator Four) face down at Position Four.

Since Spectators One and Four saw their cards, you dealt the first and fourth cards face down at Positions One and Four; the others were dealt face up (Illustration 60).

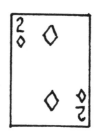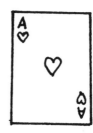

ILLUSTRATION 60

Pick up the packet, which now contains twelve cards. Fan out the top four cards of the packet. Take them from the packet, *retaining their order.* Set the rest of the packet down. Hold the four cards so that the four spectators can see them. Again ask if anyone sees his card. Let's suppose that Spectator Three sees his card. Deal the first two cards face up on top of the cards at Positions One and Two, respectively. Deal the third card face down on top of the card at Position Three. The fourth card is dealt face up on top of the card at Position Four. In other words, since Spectator Three saw his card, it is dealt face down; the others are dealt face up (Illustration 61).

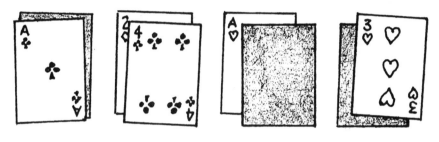

ILLUSTRATION 61

Pick up the packet, which now contains eight cards. With the right hand, take off the top four cards, *one on top of the other,* reversing their order. Set the remainder of the packet down. Show the four cards you counted off, as before. If a spectator should see his card, that card would be dealt face down at the appropriate number; the others would be dealt out face up on their respective piles. But no one sees his card, so all four are dealt face up on the appropriate piles.

Pick up the remaining four cards and fan them out, showing them. In this instance, you know that Spectator Two will see his card. So, as you go ahead and deal the cards onto their piles from left to right, you deal the second card face down on the pile at Position Two. The others are dealt face up.

With your right hand, pick up the face-up cards at Position One and place them, still face up, into your left hand. Pick up the face-down card at Position One. Ask Spectator One for the name of his chosen card. When he names it, turn the card over and hand it to him.

Do the same for the remaining three spectators, working from left to right. You have managed to identify all four chosen cards.

Note: You show a group of four cards four times. The first and third times, you take the cards one on top of the other, reversing their order. The second and fourth times, you fan out four from the top and take them in the right hand, retaining their order.

Sixes and Nines

Are you ready for a trick that has fooled some of the most knowledgeable card experts in the world? This is it. And Wally Wilson is the performer. He says that the basic trick is very old. But I was not familiar with it. Of course Wally has added a few wrinkles, along with his own special performance magic.

Preparation: Take the sixes and the nines from the deck. Place the sixes on top and the nines on the bottom.

Start by giving the deck a casual riffle shuffle. Let's assume you have the bottom half in your left hand and the top half in your right hand. Riffle off at least a half dozen cards with your left hand before you start meshing in the cards. This pretty much guarantees that a half dozen or so cards from your right hand will fall on top. It also guarantees that the sixes will still be on top and the nines on the bottom.

Spectator Lana will be delighted to assist you. Hand her the deck and say, "Lana, I'd like you to deal out the entire deck into four piles, going from left to right. Just deal them as though you were dealing out four hands in a card game—only neater."

When she finishes, continue: "Please pick up any one of the piles. Fan through the cards and take out any one you want. Put it aside for a minute while you set the pile back down. Now look at your card and show it around, but don't let me see its face."

After everyone but you has had a chance to see the card, go on: "Lana, put the card on top of any one of the piles." She does so. "Now if you want to, you can cut that pile. Or, if you prefer, place one of the other piles on top of it." If she cuts the pile on which her card sits, have her then stack all four piles in any order she wishes. If she does not cut that pile, have her proceed directly to the stacking of the piles.

The deck is now given at least two complete cuts. "You're the one who's been handling the deck, Lana, so it's certain that I have no idea of where your card is." Spread the deck face up onto the table so that all the cards can be seen. "Nevertheless, some people suspect that I sneak cards out of the deck. I want you to notice that your card is still there. I'll look away while you check it out." As you say this, spread through the cards as though further separating them to provide a better view. Actually, you're looking for the sixes and nines. In one instance, you will find a six and a nine separated by one card. That card is the one chosen by the spectator; remember it.

Mostly you'll find a six and a nine side by side. If Lana cut the packet before stacking the cards, you'll find a lone six and a lone nine somewhere. Just keep in mind that you're looking for the card that separates a six and a nine.

After you note this card, which will take just a few seconds, avert your head. "When you're done, Lana, gather up the cards, please, and give them a good shuffle."

At this point, you can take the deck from Lana and reveal the card any way you wish. You could read her mind, for instance. Wally Wilson prefers this startling conclusion that includes an easy sleight I'd never seen before:

Fan through the cards, faces towards yourself. Cut some to the top. Fan through more cards and cut another small group to the top. Eventually, cut the cards so that the chosen card becomes the third card from the top. As you do all this, mutter things like, "It has to be here somewhere. I don't know. I should be able to figure this out." After the last cut, turn the deck face down. "I think I have it, Lana. But this is very difficult, so I want four guesses. I probably won't need all four guesses, but you never know . . ."

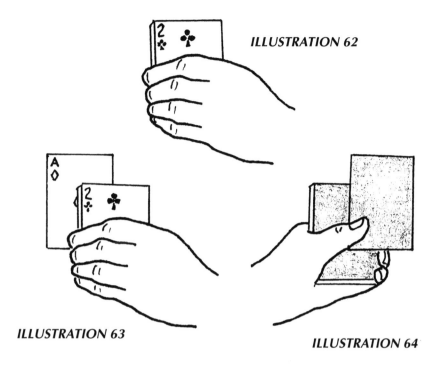

ILLUSTRATION 62

ILLUSTRATION 63

ILLUSTRATION 64

The deck is in your left hand in the dealing position. Lift your left hand so that the bottom card faces the group (Illustration 62). With your right thumb, pull up the top card diagonally. Move your right hand away so that about half the card is displayed (Illustration 63). The left thumb holds the bottom left corner of the card (Illustration 64). "Here's my first guess. Is this your card, Lana?" No, it isn't.

With the right hand, push the card back so that it is even with the others. At this point, you're still holding the cards in a vertical position. Lower the left hand to the regular dealing position. Deal the top card face down onto the table to your right.

Again raise the deck to a vertical position. Show the next card in the same way as before. Wrong again! Push the card back, turn the deck to a horizontal position, and deal the top card onto the table to the left of the first card.

Once more raise the deck to a vertical position. This time, you'll perform a deceptive move that I call the *thumb glide.* Move the right hand up to the deck, as though to display the next card. As you chat with the spectators about your hopes for your third guess, move the top card down about half an inch with your right thumb. This is easily accomplished by using *very light* pressure (Illustration 65). Then pull up the *second card from the top* and display it as you did the others (Illustration 66). You're wrong again, of course. Push the card back with the right fingers and push the actual top card back into position with the right thumb. *Now* lower the deck and deal the top card onto the table to the left of the other two cards. You have cleverly and successfully managed to switch the card you showed for the chosen card.

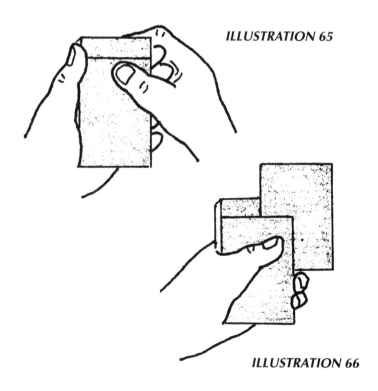

ILLUSTRATION 65

ILLUSTRATION 66

You want to show a fourth card, but the spectators just saw the present top card. So you say, "Lana, this doesn't seem to be working. Maybe I'll have better luck if you cut the cards." Place the deck on the table and let her cut it. Pick the deck up and show a fourth card in the same way as you did the first two. Failure! Give Lana a look of mock disgust, saying, "Thanks a lot, Lana." The fouth card goes face down to the left of the others.

Place your right hand on the two cards on the right, and your left hand on the two cards to the left. Say, "Left or right, Lana?" Whatever she replies, lift your left hand. Pull the two cards beneath your right hand towards you. Turn one of them over. "So you say that this is not your card, Lana." Right. Turn the other card over. "And this isn't your card." Again, right.

"Hand me one of these cards, please." Indicate the two face-down cards on the table. If she hands you the card on your left, turn it over, saying, "And this isn't your card."

If she hands you the card on your right, take it, and set it in front of her. Turn over the other face-down card, saying, "And this isn't your card."

In either instance, the chosen card remains face down on the table. "So, what is your card, Lana?" She names it. Make a few magical gestures over the chosen card and then ask Lana to turn it over. At last you've located the chosen card.

189

SETUP

These tricks, in one way or another, require some preparation. In some instances, only a card or two must be placed in position. In others, a number of cards must be set up in advance. I believe that a really good trick is worth the bit of extra trouble.

Blind Chance

I have seen versions of this principle used by both Nick Trost and Ed Marlo, so it's hard to know whom to credit. Regardless, it's a wondrous trick. My variation differs somewhat in order to create what I think is a stronger climax.

You may make the necessary preparation ahead of time, but I find it just as easy to do this: Turn away from the group, saying, "Excuse me for just a moment. I have to pick out a proper prediction card, and this requires extreme concentration." Turn over any card about sixth from the bottom of the deck. Find its mate—the card that matches it in color and value. Remove this from the deck. Turn back to the group, the deck face down in one hand and your prediction card face down in the other.

Let's say that you have turned the ten of spades face up so that it's several cards from the bottom of the deck. Your prediction card, then, is the ten of clubs. Place this face down on the table, saying, "Here's my prediction. But its accuracy will depend on someone else." Single out spectator Dorothy. "Will you help me, Dorothy? If we're on the same wavelength, this should work perfectly."

Hand her the deck. "Please place the cards behind your back. I want you to be able to choose a card without being influenced by me or anyone else in any way at all."

Make sure that Dorothy stands so that no one can see the cards.

"Reach into the middle of the deck, Dorothy, and take out any card. Turn it face up and set it on top of the deck. Now give the cards a cut and even them up."

When she is done, have her hand you the deck.

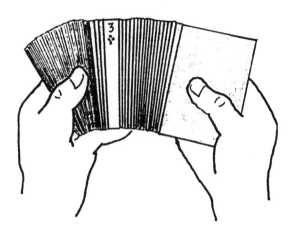

ILLUSTRATION 67

Fan through the cards so that all can see. When you come to a face-up card, fan a few cards beyond (Illustration 67). Next, fan back so that the face-up card is on top of the face-down cards in your left hand. Separate your hands; the face-up card remains on top of those in your left hand, while the balance of the deck is in your right hand. Place all the cards that are in your right hand *below* those in your left hand. You are now holding a face-down deck with a face-up card on top. "So your card is . . ." Name it. Naturally, it's the card that *you* previously turned face up. Place the card face up next to your prediction card.

Turn the deck face up. Murmur, "Let's see if you accidently turned over more than one card." Casually fan through about four-fifths of the deck, showing the faces. "No, I guess not." Close up the deck and set it aside.

"Dorothy, we'll now find out whether we're on the same wavelength. If we are, these two cards should match each other in color and value." Turn over your prediction card, showing that it matches her choice.

Note: At the end of the trick, you have a face-up card near the top of the deck. You have several options. You could make this your last trick, and simply put the cards away. Or you could do a few tricks where the face-up card will not show up. Then, at a break in the action, step aside and turn the card over. My favorite is to do a "take-a-card" trick. Turn away while the assistant shows the card around. Naturally, while your back is turned, you turn the face-up card over.

The Ideal Card Trick

Here's the ideal card trick: A card is selected, you do something miraculous with it, and no skill is required. Here we have the invention of U. F. Grant, a creative giant in the field of magic.

Preparation: Place any four face-up fourth from the bottom of the deck.

Spectator Daphne may have a funny name, but she sure is a good sport, so fan the cards out and ask her to select a card. Make sure, of course, that you do not spread the cards out near the bottom; no need to disclose the face-up four. Have her show the card around and then replace it on top of the deck. Give the deck a complete cut and set it on the table.

"Daphne, I am going to attempt a feat that is nearly impossible. I am going to try to turn a card face up in the middle of the deck. Will it be your card? Oh, no, that would be too easy. Instead, I will try to turn over a card that will tell us where your card is. I can't believe how tough this is going to be."

Pick up the deck and give it a little riffle at the ends. "I hope that works." Fan through the cards until you come to the face-up four. "Ah, here we have a face-up card, a four." Set the cards above the four onto the table. Lift off the four and place it, still face up, on the table. "So let's count off four cards." Deal off four cards, counting aloud. Place your finger on the last card dealt off. "What was the name of your card, Daphne?" She names it, and you turn it over.

193

Seven for Luck

Len Searles created this superb trick. Here's my variation.

Preparation: Place a seven on top, followed by seven face-up cards.

Address spectator Richard: "I'd like you to select a card completely by chance, so we should follow a certain procedure." Extend the deck towards him on the palm of your hand. "Richard, please cut off a substantial group of cards, turn the group face up, and set it back onto the deck."

When he finishes, even up the cards, and hand him the deck. "Now just fan down to the card you cut to and take a look at it . . . I'll look away." Avert your head while he looks at his card. "Done? Okay, then turn those face-up cards face down again and put them back on top of the deck, right on top of your chosen card."

Take the deck from Richard and show that the cards are all evened up. Take off the top card with your right hand, but don"t let anyone see it. Glance at it. It doesn't matter what the card is because you're going to miscall it anyway. Put the deck behind your back with the left hand and the card with your right hand, saying, "Okay, I'm going to stick this seven face up into the middle of the deck and hope for the best." Actually, you simply place it back on top of the deck and bring the cards forward.

"Seven! That's definitely good luck. Let's see where the seven is, and then we'll count from there." Turn the deck face up and fan through until you come to the face-down card, which, of course, is a seven. Take the cards you fanned off and set them aside. Pick off the seven and turn it over so that all can see. "There's the seven," you declare, for those who are farsighted. Set the seven aside. "So we'll count off seven cards. Richard, what was your card?" He names it. You count off seven cards and there it is . . . on the seventh card.

What Do You Think?

A spectator merely *thinks* of a card and, in practically no time, you—with your incredible magical powers—locate it.

Preparation: First, unknown to all, put all the eights and nines on the bottom of the deck. The order of these placed cards doesn't matter.

Ready? Say to spectator Greta, "I'd like you to think of a number *between* one and ten." (Be sure to say "between," because you don't want her to choose one or ten). "Now I'll show you ten cards one at a time. Please remember the card that lies at the number you thought of."

Avert your head as you hold up the top card, face towards Greta. At the same time, say, "One." Take the next card in front of the first and show it to Greta, saying, "Two." Continue through the tenth card. Replace the ten cards on top of the deck. They are, of course, in the same order.

"Greta, I'm going to put these cards behind my back and perform an astonishing feat. I'm going to put your chosen card in a position where you yourself will locate it with a randomly chosen card."

Put the deck behind your back. Take off the top card and put it on the bottom. Turn the deck face up. To yourself, *very quietly* count off the nine bottom cards, one on top of the other. Place this packet on top of the deck. Turn the deck face down and bring it forward. You now have an indifferent card on top, followed by the eights and nines.

"Okay, Greta, everything is ready. All I need to know is the number you thought of." She names the number. Let's say the number is six. Count aloud as you deal five cards onto the table. When you say "six" aloud, lift off the sixth card, turn it over, and continue to hold it. It will be either an eight or a nine. Whichever it is, announce its value, and say, "Let's hope that this card will help us find your card."

If the card is an eight, place it face up onto the pile you dealt off. In another pile, deal eight cards, counting aloud. Ask Greta to name her card. Turn over the last card dealt. It is the one she thought of.

If the last card you lift off is a nine, call attention to it, and then turn it face down on top of the deck. Deal off nine cards, counting aloud. As before, the last card will be the one chosen.

Summary: When the spectator gives the number she thought of, you deal off one less than this number, counting aloud. When you name the last number of the count, you hang on to the card. Turn it over, still holding it. If it's an eight, drop it on top of the pile you just dealt; deal off eight cards from the rest of the deck and turn over the last card. If it's a nine, replace it face down on top of the deck; deal off nine cards from the deck and turn over the last card.

A Face-Up Miracle

Doug Maihafer developed an astonishing trick which would ordinarily require considerable skill at sleight of hand. His trick, however, requires only a bit of preparation.

Aheads of time, note the bottom card of a blue-backed deck of cards. Go through a red-backed deck and find the duplicate to this card. Place the red-backed duplicate *face up* second from the bottom.

So the situation might be this: You have a blue-backed deck. The bottom card is the blue-backed jack of hearts. The second card from the bottom is a red-backed jack of hearts, which is face up.

In performance, approach spectator Hector, fanning the cards face down from hand to hand. (Make sure you don't get too close to the bottom and tip off the red-backed card.) "Hector, I might spread the cards like this and have you choose a card. But this might give you a better choice."

Place the deck on the table and do the *Crisscross Force* (page 40). There's a difference, however. After the spectator cuts off a portion and places the other portion on top crosswise, you stall for a moment. Then you pick up the *top pile* of the crisscrossed cards. Take off the bottom card of this group and, without looking at its face, hand it face down to Hector. In our example, this is the blue-backed jack of hearts. "Take a look at your card, Hector and show it around."

Meanwhile, put the pile you're holding on top of the other pile. Even the cards and pick them up. Hold the deck in the dealing position and tell Hector, "Push your card into the deck, please." He probably won't be able to push it all the way in, so you might have to push the card even with the others.

"I will now attempt an almost impossible feat. I'm going to try to make your card turn face up in the deck. What was your card, Hector?" He names it. Riffle the ends of the deck. Fan through to the face-up jack of hearts. "There it is—face up!" Take it from the deck and place it face up on the table. When the murmurs of approval die down, say, "What more could a magician do?"

Spread the deck face down next to the face-up jack of hearts. "Maybe I could change the color of the back!" Snap your fingers and turn the jack of hearts over, displaying its red back in contrast to the blue-backed deck.

Immediately pick up the deck; you don't want anyone going through it just now. Pick up the red-backed jack of hearts and put it into your pocket. Proceed with other tricks. If, as you're doing your routine, someone points out the blue-backed jack of hearts, say, "Oh, yes, I brought it back. *And* I changed it back to a blue-backed card." Then move right along.

FOUR ACES

It's Out of My Hands

How about yet another trick in which the spectator does all the work? Sprinkled among others, such tricks seem to be especially magical.

Spectator Edgar is an excellent card player, so you might ask him to take the deck and shuffle it. Continue: "Please go through the cards and take out the four aces."

When Edgar turns the deck face up, take note of the bottom card and remember it; this is your key card. Then you banter with the group, paying no particular attention as he tosses the aces out. (If he somehow manages to change the bottom card, however, take note of the new bottom card. This is your key card).

The aces are face up on the table. Ask Edgar to turn the deck face down. "Now, Edgar, put the aces in a face-down row, and then deal three cards on top of each ace." When he finishes, say, "Gather the piles up, one on top of the other, and put them on top of the deck."

Then: "Please give the deck a complete cut." Make sure that, as he begins the cut, he lifts off at least sixteen cards. Usually, the completed cut will leave the aces somewhere around the middle of the deck.

"In a moment, we're going to make some piles, Edgar. Which pile would you prefer—pile one, pile two, pile three, or pile four?" Whatever he replies, repeat his choice so that everyone will remember.

"Please deal the cards slowly into a face-up pile. If all goes well, I'll get a strong feeling as to when you should stop."

At a certain point (described below) you tell him to stop. Then: "Deal the next four cards into a face-down row. Then deal the next four cards into a row, right on top of the first four cards. Do the same with the next four cards, and then four more." Make sure he deals the cards across in a row each time. As he deals each group of four, count, "One, two, three, four."

Call the group's attention once more to the number of the pile that Edgar chose. "Don't forget. At no time have I touched the cards. Would you please turn over the pile you picked." He does so, and there are the four aces.

How you do it: When Edgar deals the cards out face up, you know exactly where to stop him. You watch for your key card, the original bottom card of the deck. To make sure the aces get into the proper pile, you simply subtract the number of the chosen pile from four. For instance, if Edgar chooses pile four, you subtract four from four, getting zero. After he turns over the key card, you allow no more cards to be dealt out face up. He immediately begins forming the four piles.

If he chooses pile three, you subtract three from four, getting one. So you let one more card be dealt face up after the key card.

If he chooses two, you subtract two from four, getting two. Therefore, two more cards are dealt after the key card.

If he chooses one, you subtract one from four, getting three. So three more cards are dealt after the key card.

An Ace Collection

I particularly enjoy tricks in which the "dirty work" is over before you've barely begun. This old four-ace trick, which I have modified somewhat, is a good example.

Fan through the deck, faces towards yourself, looking for the aces. "I'll need four aces for this experiment," you explain. As you find each ace, slip it to the face (bottom) of the deck. Spread out the aces on the bottom, showing them. "Here are the aces. And I can assure you that these are the only aces in the deck." Continue fanning through the cards. After you fan off three more cards, hold all seven cards slightly apart from the rest with your right fingers (Illustration 68). Don't pause, but continue fanning through several more cards.

ILLUSTRATION 68
*Seven cards are held apart
from the rest of the deck.*

Casually close up the cards, letting your right fingers slide under all seven cards at the face of the deck. Immediately lower your left hand and flip the rest of the deck over with your left thumb.

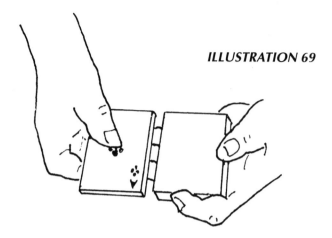

ILLUSTRATION 69

Place the left side of the face-up packet that's in your right hand on the tips of the left fingers (Illustration 69). Flip this packet over with the tips of your *right* fingers, so that it falls face down on top of the deck. This whole casual sequence takes just a few seconds.

As you go through the moves, say, "Now what we're going to do is . . ." By this time you should have completed the sequence. ". . . mix the aces . . ." Tap the top of the deck. ". . . throughout the deck."

Set the deck on the table and turn to spectator Hedda. "I'll need your help, Hedda. Would you please cut the deck into two fairly even piles. But don't forget which is the top bunch."

She cuts the deck into two piles. Point to the original top group. "And this is the top group, right?"

Right. "Now would you cut each of *those* piles into two fairly even piles." She does. Again, point to the original top group. "And this is the group that was on top."

Pick up that pile. "Now let's distribute the aces." Deal one card from the top of the pile you're holding onto each of the other three piles. (Presumably, an ace is now on top of each pile; actually, all four aces are on top of the pile you're holding). Set this pile down, alongside the other three.

"Let's make sure those aces are separated. Hedda, I'd like you to put these piles together in any order you wish. Just put one pile on top of the other until you have one pile."

After she finishes, have Hedda, or other spectators, give the deck any number of complete cuts.

Pick up the deck, saying, "It's magic time!" Riffle the ends of the cards. Turn the deck face up and fan through the cards, showing that the aces are all together.

Double or Nothing

I believe that the basic principle used here was developed by Stewart James, and Ray Boston adapted it to a four-ace trick. My version creates great spectator interest and has an extremely strong climax.

Start by tossing the four aces face up onto the table. "Here we have the four aces, as you can see. Now I'm about to play a game of *Double or Nothing*. I'll give out real money to the winner. Whoever volunteers will risk nothing whatever. Do I have a volunteer?"

You choose Hannibal from the multitude of eager volunteers.

"Congratulations, Hannibal. Just by volunteering, you have already won. To win even more, you'll have to keep track of the aces."

Arrange the aces in a face-down row. Fan off three cards from the top of the deck and place them on top of one of the aces. Tap the pile of four cards. "For double or nothing, keep track of this ace, Hannibal."

Place the pile of four cards on top of the deck. As you do so, get a break with your left little finger beneath the top card of the four. Double-cut this card to the bottom of the deck. (See *Double-Cut,* page 17).

"Where's that first ace, Hannibal? Is it on the bottom?" Turn the deck over, showing the bottom card. "No. Is it on top?" Turn over the top card, showing it, and then turn it face down again. "No. So where is it?" You coach Hannibal by saying, "Somewhere in the mmmm . . . somewhere in the mid . . ." Whatever he responds, you say, "Right! Somewhere in the middle of the deck. You've doubled your money! You now have *two* . . . pennies." This should get a chuckle. "Double or nothing, Hannibal. Let's try four pennies." Fan off the top three cards and place them on another ace. Pick up the four cards and place them on top of the deck. Double-cut the top card to the bottom of the deck.

"Where's that ace, Hannibal? Is it on the bottom?" Show the

bottom card, as before. "No. Is it on top?" Show the top card and replace it. "No. So where is it?" Hannibal should have no trouble this time. "That's right," you say, "somewhere in the middle of the deck. You now have eight pennies. Let's try for sixteen."

The procedure this time is a little different. Fan off three cards from the top of the deck and place them on top of one of the two remaining aces. Pick up the four-card pile. Carefully even it up; you're going to turn the pile face up and you don't want anyone to get a glimpse of the other aces in the pile. *Now* turn the pile over, showing the ace on the bottom. Place the pile face down on top of the deck. "You *must* know where that ace is. Obviously, it isn't on the bottom." Show the bottom card of the deck, as before. "And it isn't on top." Show the top card and return it to the top.

At this point, double-cut the top card to the bottom. "So, for sixteen pennies, where is it?" As usual, it's somewhere in the middle of the deck.

"The last double-or-nothing." Fan off the top three cards and place them on the last ace on the table. Place the four cards on top of the deck. "For thirty-two pennies, Hannibal—where are all four aces?"

Chances are he'll say, "In the middle of the deck." If he does, say, "Not exactly. They're right here." Deal off the top four cards face up. They are the aces. (Whatever he responds, proceed the same way).

Pause a moment for audience appreciation. "But that was close enough, Hannibal. You still win the thirty-two pennies." Take out your wallet. "Do you have change for a big bill?"

Wally's Wily Ace Trick

Wally Wilson was kind enough to give me permission to use his simplified and surprising version of an excellent four-ace trick. What's unique about this effect is that no one knows it's a four-ace trick until the very end.

In the original version, some preparation was necessary. I have changed things a bit so that the trick can be done impromptu. (You may prefer to do the other version, which I fully explain in the *Note* at the end). We will assume that some time earlier you performed a four-ace trick so that the four aces are together somewhere in the deck. Casually fan through the deck and cut the four aces to the top.

Spectator Estelle enjoys a good card trick, so approach her, saying, "Believe it or not, Estelle, I've just memorized the position of every single card in the deck. Let's see if I can prove it to you." As you say this, fan the cards face down from hand to hand, counting them. When you reach the twelfth card, hold it, along with the cards above it, separate from the rest; continue fanning through the cards. "Please pick one out, Estelle." After she takes a card, close the cards up, getting a break with your left little finger beneath the twelfth card. (It's best to count the cards in groups of three, thinking to yourself, "Three, six, nine, twelve.")

"Show the card around, please."

Grip the deck with the right hand from above, transferring the left little-finger break to the right thumb (Illustration 70). The thumb break is on the right side of the deck. The first finger of the right hand is holding the cards down so that no separation will be apparent to the spectators.

Riffle your left thumb down the left side of the deck all the way to the bottom (Illustration 71). Start to riffle the cards again, but stop when your thumb reaches a point about a third down in the deck. Lift off the top twelve cards with your right hand.

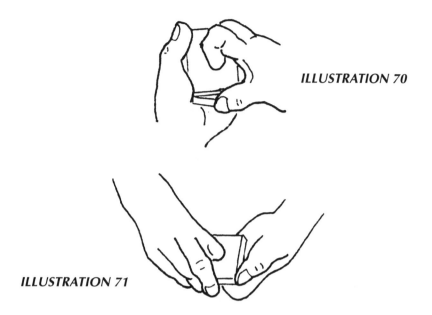

ILLUSTRATION 70

ILLUSTRATION 71

Hold out the lower portion with your left hand for the return of the chosen card. If Estelle hesitates, say, "Just put it right there, please." After she places her card on top of the pile, replace the twelve-card packet. This time you don't hold a break. Her card is now thirteenth from the top of the deck.

"Contrary to what you may have heard, Estelle, I'm a very observant person. For instance, I happen to know that your card is in the top half of the deck. So we won't need all these cards."

Deal three cards from the top of the deck, one at a time, into a pile. To the right of these, deal another pile of three cards, also one at a time. Go back to the first pile and deal a card on top of it. Do the same with the pile on the right. Continue alternating until you have two thirteen-card piles. (Count silently, of course.) At the end, you are holding half the deck. Turn over the top card of these. Let's say that it's a red card. If you choose, you may now use one of Wally Wilson's clever lines. Say to Estelle, "Your card was a red card, was it not?" If she says yes, fine. If she says no, say, "Well, I said it was not."

Regardless, replace the card face down and set down the half deck you're holding so that it's well out of the way.

At this point, the pile on your left has three aces on the bottom; the pile on your right has one ace on the bottom. You must arrange it so that the left pile has *two* aces on the bottom and an ace second from the top. And the right pile must have its ace on top. Here's how you manage it: Point to the two thirteen-card piles. "So, Estelle, I know that your card is in one of these piles." Pick up the pile on the left. Hold it from above in the left hand (Illustration 72). With the right thumb on top and the right fingers below, grasp the top and bottom cards together and pull them sideways from the packet (Illustration 73).

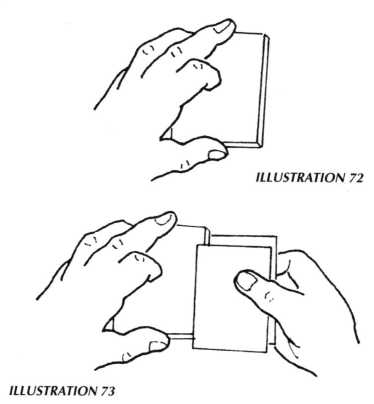

ILLUSTRATION 72

ILLUSTRATION 73

"Your card could be the top or bottom card of this packet," you say. *"Apparently*, I have no way of knowing." Place the two cards on top of the deck. Fan the cards out. "More than likely, your card is somewhere in the middle. *If* it's in this pile." Close up the packet and set it onto the table. That pile is set. What's more, the chosen card is in proper position.

Pick up the packet on the right. Casually give it an overhand shuffle, shuffling off the last few cards singly so that the bottom card ends up on top. "Of course, your card might be somewhere in here." Fan the packet out. "Who knows?" Close the packet up and return it to the table. This pile is also set.

Place one hand above each pile, twitching your fingers and staring into the distance. Pick up the pile on the right and place it to one side. Indicate the pile under your left hand. "It must be in this pile."

Pick up the pile and, going from left to right, deal it one card at a time alternately into two piles. The pile on the left contains seven cards, and the pile on the right six cards. Toss in appropriate patter about trying to sense which pile contains the chosen card as you again place your hands over the two piles. Eventually, you pick up the pile on the left and place it right next to the first pile you discarded. Indicate that the small pile remaining under your right hand contains the chosen card.

Pick up this six-card pile and deal it into two piles, as before. This time each pile contains three cards. This time, you eliminate the pile on the right. Place it near the other two discarded piles.

"So we're down to three cards." Deal them out alternately from left to right. On your left is a two-card pile, which, after the usual rigmarole, you place aside with the other discarded piles. On your right is one card. "This must be the one you chose, Estelle. What's the name of your card?"

She names it, and you turn it over. You're absolutely right. But you may not receive the praise and applause you're entitled to. After a pause, you say, "Well, if you didn't care for that demonstration, perhaps you'd like to see something with the four aces."

Turn over the top card of each of the discarded piles. They are, of course, the four aces.

It's easy to remember which pile you must set aside: The first time, you set aside the pile on the right; next, the pile on the left; then the pile on the right; and finally the pile on the left. In other words, you first discard the pile on the right, and then alternate.

Wally's Setup Version: You may prefer to have the deck set up in advance. If so, the four aces must be distributed like this: on top of the deck, third from the top, twenty third from the top, and twenty sixth from the top.

Approach Estelle, fanning the cards and saying, "I could offer you the choice of a card by letting you pick one from the deck, Estelle. But let's do something a little different." As you fan the cards, count off the top *eleven*. When you reach the eleventh card, close the cards up, getting a break with your left little finger beneath that card. (Count the cards in groups of three, thinking to yourself, "Three, six, nine, and two more.")

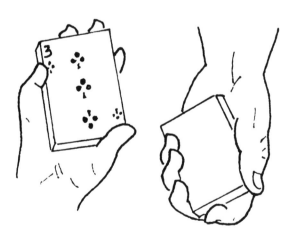

ILLUSTRATION 74

Still holding the break, grasp the deck with the right hand from above (refer to Illustration 70). Riffle your left thumb down the left side of the deck all the way to the bottom (refer to Illustration 71). "Just tell me when to stop, Estelle," you say, starting to riffle your thumb down again, slowly this time. If she says stop somewhere in the top third of the deck, fine. If not, riffle rapidly all the way down. "Let's try again," you say with a smile. When Estelle does stop you in the top third of the deck, lift off the top eleven cards with your right hand. Show the card to her (Illustration 74), saying, "Please remember this card, Estelle." Replace the packet on top of the deck. This time you don't hold a break. All the "dirty work" is done.

You do not shift the aces around as in the first version. Simply deal the cards into two piles of thirteen cards each, alternating from left to right. As in the first version, first eliminate the pile on the right, then the pile on the left, and so on, alternating.

Sneaky Aces

This is another trick shown to me by Wally Wilson, who felt it was the invention of Harry Lorayne.

Unknown to the spectators, you have the four aces on top of the desk. False-shuffle the cards, leaving the aces on top. Set the deck on the table. Ask spectator Myra to cut the deck in half, and then to cut each half in half.

There are now four piles on the table. Make sure you keep track of which pile has the aces on top. Pick up that pile.

Say to Myra, "Let's see how you did." One by one, take the top card of ech of the other piles and place it face down on top of the packet in your hand.

"We have to build suspense here. You cut to four cards." Count aloud, as you deal off the four top cards onto the table, one on top of the other. Pick up the four and place them back onto the packet, getting a break beneath them with your left little finger.

You should be holding the packet quite close to the pile which is on the table to the right. Turn over the top card and set it squarely on the packet. "Ah, an ace!"

With your palm-down right hand grip the top four cards, fingers at the front, thumb at the back. Lift off the four cards and place them on top of the pile which is on the right on the table. Apparently, you've placed only the ace on the pile.

Turn over the next card on top of the deck. "Another ace!" In precisely the same way as you gripped the four-card pile, grip the ace and place it face up on top of one of the other piles.

Do the same with the next ace. Finally, turn over the top card of the deck. Evidently, Myra has cut to all four aces. Gaze at her in wonder and say, "My, I'd hate to play cards with you!"

Grand Illusion

Fr. Cyprian is credited with the subtle move used in this trick.

Start with two aces on top of the deck and two on the bottom. (You might do this: After performing a four-ace trick, make sure the four aces are together somewhere in the deck. Perform a few more tricks. Then casually fan through the deck and cut between the aces, bringing two to the top and two to the bottom.) Give the deck a riffle shuffle, keeping two aces on top and two on the bottom. Set the deck on the table.

Spectator Joe's a good sport, so ask him to help out. "Joe, would you please cut the deck in half."

After he does, pick up the packet with the aces on top and give it a false shuffle, retaining the aces on top. (See *Controlling a Group of Cards,* page 32.) Set the pile down.

Pick up the other packet and shuffle the bottom two aces to the top. (See *Bringing the Bottom Card to the Top,* page 31.) Set this packet down near you, at a diagonal from the other packet. The positions of the two halves on the table:

A

    B

Cards will be cut from these packets and placed on the table. Packets will then be at these positions:

A **C**
D **B**

This is how it comes about: Have Joe cut off some cards from the packet at A. Point to position D and have him place the cards there. Have him cut off some cards from the packet at B and have him place these at position C.

213

The situation: Two aces are on top of the packet at position D and two aces are on top of the packet at position C.

Say, "Joe, I wonder how well you did."

Simultaneously grasp the top card at position C with your right hand and the top card at position D with your left hand. Grasp the card at position C at the *far end*, and the card at position D at the *near end*. Turn these aces face up at the same time. Place the ace from position C face up on top of the packet at B; place the ace from position D face up on top of the packet at A.

Again you'll grasp the top card at position C with your right hand and the top card at position D with your left hand. This time, however, you grasp the card at position C at the *near end* and the card at position D at the *far end*. Simultaneously turn these aces face up and place them on the piles from which you just lifted them.

This entire business of turning over the aces takes but a few seconds. If you follow with the cards, you'll see how simple it actually is. The illusion is that the top card of each packet was an ace.

"Good job, Joe! You cut the aces."

MISCELLANEOUS

I Guess So

Wouldn't it be wonderful if you could tell exactly how many cards a spectator cuts from the deck? Of course. But surely it would take years of practice. Yes. *Unless* you're willing to resort to treachery and deceit. Certainly *I* am.

I derived this trick from one by Norman Houghton, which required a trick deck. My method can be done impromptu with any deck. But it must be a complete deck of fifty-two cards.

Ask spectator Lauren to shuffle the deck. Take the cards back. Hold them face down as you begin fanning them from hand to hand. Count the cards in groups of three as you fan them. When you have fanned out twelve cards, push one more into the right hand. Hold this packet of thirteen separate from the rest as you continue slowly fanning the cards. Say to Lauren, "I'd like you to take any three cards from the deck. It doesn't matter which three you take. As you'll see, these are just 'confusion cards.' " Make sure she takes the cards from below your packet of thirteen.

"The values don't matter," you say. "Just set the three cards face down onto the table." While saying this, close up the deck. But with the tip of your left little finger get a small break below the thirteen cards.

Grasp the deck from above with the right hand, transfering the break to the right thumb (Illustration 75). Casually, with your left thumb, riffle down a dozen or so cards on the left side of the deck (Illustration 76). With your right hand, lift off the thirteen-card packet and hand it to Lauren. "Shuffle these, will you, Lauren?"

Since spectator Bret isn't busy, hand him the rest of the deck. "And you might as well shuffle these, Bret."

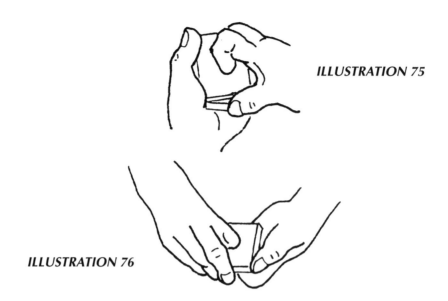

ILLUSTRATION 75

ILLUSTRATION 76

Have Lauren set her pile onto the table. When Bret is done shuffling, have him set his pile down also. "Bret, would you cut some cards off that pile that you just shuffled and set them down on the table."

The situation: Three piles are on the table. One pile contains thirteen cards, and you know which one. Three other cards are face down on the table.

"Lauren, I'd like you to place the 'confusion cards' on any piles you wish. Place them all on one pile, or two on one pile and one on another, or one on each pile—whatever you want."

These really *are* "confusion cards." You're using them to confuse the spectators as to what you're really up to.

It doesn't matter where Lauren places the three cards. All you have to do is keep track of the original pile of thirteen cards. If Lauren adds cards to it, remember the new number.

"Over the years, I've developed some skill at estimating the number of cards in a pile. Let me show you what I mean. Bret, pick any one of the three piles."

If Bret chooses the first pile you handed out, simply stare at the pile for a few seconds and then say, "The pile contains exactly thirteen cards." Or name the new number if Lauren added any cards to it. Have either of your assistants check the count. Gather up the cards and proceed to do something else.

ILLUSTRATION 77

If, however, Bret chooses one of the other two piles, have him pick it up. "I'd like to demostrate something. Bret, would you please count those out." He counts them aloud. "Now do you see how long that took?" Hold out your two hands palm up and flat. Have Lauren place one of the remaining piles on your right hand and Bret place the other remaining pile on your left hand (Illustration 77). You eye the two piles, and then give your estimate for each pile. "In this hand, I have (so many), and in this hand I have (so many)." Be sure to repeat your estimate. When Lauren and Bret count the piles, they discover that you were exactly right.

Let's assume that in your right hand is the original pile you handed out, the one containing thirteen cards. Further, let's assume that Lauren added one of the "confusion cards" to this pile. You know that the pile now contains fourteen cards.

When Bret counted his selected pile aloud, he came up with say, twenty-one cards. You add twenty-one to fourteen, getting thirty-five. So the cards on the table and the cards in your right hand add up to thirty-five. There are fifty-two cards in a full deck. Clearly, you subtract thirty-five from fifty-two to get the number of cards in your left hand—seventeen. You need not be a lightning mathematician. Most of the figuring can be done as you stare at the piles resting on your palms, ostensibly trying to make an accurate estimate.

Oily Water

There are probably more four-ace tricks published than any other type. I would guess that a close second would be the old-time trick "Oil and Water." The reason for the title is that oil and water don't mix, and neither do red and black cards. No matter how you mix them, black cards gather together, and so do red cards. Every version I've come across requires a fair amount of sleight of hand. My version depends on a swindle and bare-faced lying.

Hand the deck to a spectator, saying "Please remove four red cards and four black cards from the deck. Then arrange them so that they alternate black and red." The rest of the deck is set aside.

Take the eight cards from the spectator and fan them out face up, showing the alternating order. "You've probably heard the ridiculous theory that oil and water don't mix. Here we have red and black cards alternating. The black cards are oil, and the red cards are water. As you notice, they certainly do mix."

Turn the packet face down. "What happens if I move one card to the bottom?" Move the top card to the bottom. Turn the packet face up and fan it out. "Nothing. The cards still alternate." Turn the packet face down.

"How about two cards?" Move two cards to the bottom, one at a time. Turn the packet face up and fan it out. "They still alternate." Turn the packet face down.

"How about this?" Lift off two cards from the top, hold them to one side so that all can see that there are two, and then place them together on the bottom. Again turn the packet face up and fan it out. "Same thing." Turn the packet face down.

"What if I deal off a bunch of cards?" Take off five cards with the right hand, dealing them one at a time and one on top of the other. Do *not* count them aloud. Place this bunch on the bottom of the packet. Turn the packet face up and show it, as before.

Still holding the packet face up, say, "What happens if I remove a pair together from this group?" Pull two cards out. "Obviously, I always get a red and a black. And notice that the *remaining* cards still alternate red and black."

Replace the two cards in their original position. Pull out another pair, again demonstrating that a pair taken together from anywhere in the group will consist of a red and black. Again, point out that the remaining cards alternate red and black. Replace this pair in their original position. "So, obviously, oil and water *do* mix."

Turn the packet face down. "Now a little demonstration." Take off *four* cards with the right hand, dealing them one at a time and one on top of the other. Don't count them aloud. Casually fan out the group so that all can see that it consists of alternate colors. Place this bunch face down on the bottom of the packet. "What happens when we deal off a bunch of cards? You know the answer." Make a motion as though to turn the packet over.

"Does it matter if we transfer them one at a time?" Move three, one at a time, from the top to the bottom. "Of course not." Take off the top two cards together and place them face down onto the table at your left. "And here's a pair of red and black."

Move two cards, one at a time, from the top to the bottom. Take off the top two cards together and place them face down onto the table at your right. "Another pair of red and black."

Move one card from the top to the bottom. Take off the top two cards together and place them face down onto the two at your *right*. "Another black and red pair." Drop the last pair onto the pair at your left. "And the last pair of red and black.

"So here we have proof positive . . ." Turn over the pile on the left and spread out the cards. Turn over the pile on the right and spread these out. "Hmm . . . Don't tell me that everybody else is right . . . that oil and water *don't* mix."

More Oily Water

T. S. Ransom adapted an old principle to the "oil and water" theme. I have added the ideas I developed in *Oily Water*. The trick may be done separately, but let's assume you're doing it as a follow-up to *Oily Water*.

"Let's try that again," you say, still skeptical. "First, we alternate the colors." Hold the four reds in a face-up packet in the left hand and the four blacks in a face-up packet in the right hand. Thumb off the card at the face of each packet so that it falls face up onto the table. On your right, a black card lies face up on the table; on your left, a red card lies face up on the table. Cross your hands so that the left hand can thumb off a card onto the card on the right, and vice versa (Illustration 78). Uncross your hands. Thumb off a card from each hand onto the piles where you started. Cross your hands and thumb off a card from each hand, as before.

ILLUSTRATION 78

Clearly, each pile alternates red and black cards. Place either pile on top of the other. Pick the combined pile up and turn it face down. Apparently, the packet alternates reds and blacks. Actually, the fourth and fifth cards from the top are of the same color.

You now go through the same procedure as in *Oily Water*, except that you do not count off the four cards at the beginning.

Fill in with appropriate patter as you proceed:

Move three, one at a time, from the top to the bottom. Take off the top pair and place them face down onto the table at your left, saying, "A pair of red and black."

Move two cards, one at a time, from the top to the bottom. Take off the top pair and place them face down onto the table at your right. "Another pair of red and black."

Move one card from the top to the bottom. Take off the top pair and place them face down onto the pair at your right. "Another black and red pair." Drop the last pair onto the pair at your left. "And the last pair of red and black.

"*Now,* let's take a look." Show that each pile consists of the same color. Shake your head. "I guess I'm just not a good mixer."

Most Oily Water

In this final "oil and water" demonstration, we have another T. S. Ransom idea. I have changed it slightly to make it less obvious.

Feeling brave? This swindle works perfectly when done rapidly and with aplomb. If, however, you feel less than confident, don't bother trying it.

This works best as a follow-up to the previous trick, More *Oily Water.*

Turn the four red cards face down and hold them in the left hand. Turn the four black cards face down and take them in the right hand.

Now proceed rapidly! Cross your left hand over your right and thumb off each top card face down onto the table. Uncross your hands. *Immediately* cross your right hand over your left and thumb each top card onto the card already there. Uncross your hands. Repeat your first move, in which you placed your left hand over your right. You now have three cards of the same color in each pile, and you are holding one card in each hand. As you uncross your hands this last time, turn the two cards face up. One is red and the other is black. Take them in one hand and proudly display them, saying, "See? Oil and water *do* mix."

Toss the two cards to one side. In eager anticipation, turn the three-card piles over. Each pile contains the same color. Shake your head ruefully. "Or not!"

Big Turnover

A card is chosen. The magician causes it to turn face up in the middle of the deck. This is one of the strongest tricks you can perform. Tom Ogden developed a patter theme, which makes the trick even more entertaining. I have expanded on the theme somewhat.

Fan through the deck, asking spectator Troy to choose a card. When he returns the card to the deck, fan one card on top of it. Get a small break with your left little finger at this point. The chosen card is now the second card below the break. Perform one of the moves listed under *Control* (starting on page 17). The selected card is now second from the top of the deck.

"Troy, I will now magically cause your card to turn face up in the deck."

Tap the top of the deck. Tip the deck down so that all can see as you fan through the face-down cards. Clearly, no card is face up.

"But it may take a minute. I know what I did wrong. I should have riffled the cards." Riffle the ends of the deck. Fan through the cards as before. Again, failure.

"Okay, Troy, then I'll do it the easy way." Tap the top card. "I'll just turn your chosen card over . . . like this!"

Grasp the top card at the outer end with your right hand and turn it over so that you're holding it a few inches to the right of the deck. As you do this, push off the next card slightly with your left thumb. As you draw this card back onto the deck with your left thumb, get a small break beneath it with your left little finger. Immediately place the face-up card in your right hand squarely on top of it.

The situation: You have a face-up card on top of the deck. Beneath it is the chosen card. And below this card, you're holding a small break with your left little finger.

As you place the card face up onto the deck, say, "That *is* your card, isn't it, Troy?"

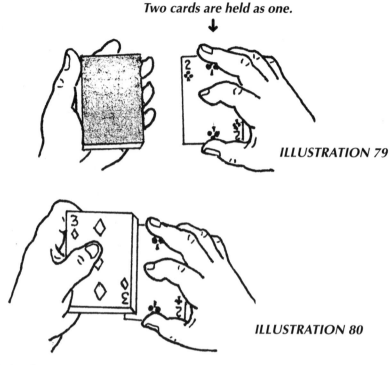

Two cards are held as one.

ILLUSTRATION 79

ILLUSTRATION 80

No, it isn't.

With your right hand, lift off the top two cards as though they are one. Your first finger rests on top, the other fingers are at the outer end, and the thumb is at the inner end (Illustration 79). With your left thumb, flip over the remainder of the deck so that it is face up. Slide the double-card under the deck as though you are replacing the face-up card on top (Illustration 80). Raise the right first finger to facilitate the placement.

The entire deck is now face up, except for the chosen card, which is face down at the rear of the deck. Since the deck is apparely face up, it's perfectly logical for you to say, "Now I *know* that your card is face up. It *has* to be one of these face-up cards." Tip the cards down and fan through about half of the face-up deck. Close up the cards and casually give them a cut. Turn the deck face down.

"See, Troy? I told you I'd turn your card face up." To the rest of the group: "Thank you so much. I hope you enjoyed that little demonstration."

Pause, looking slightly angry. "Did I hear someone say the word 'putrid'?" Since spectator Francine is very good-natured, you turn to her, saying, "Was that you, Francine?" Don't give her a chance to answer. "Shame on you. Do you think it's easy doing magic? Let's see you give it a try."

Make her take the deck. "What was your card, Troy?" He names it.

"All right, Francine, let's see *you* be magic. Tap the top card of the deck and then fan through the cards."

She does. And of course, the chosen card is face up.

"Good heavens! She got it!" Pause briefly. "You know, Francine, I could really use a good assistant . . ."

Easy Match

Simple is good. In this instance, simple is not only good, but extremely deceptive. This fine trick by Cy Keller has fooled some of the best.

The original trick called for two decks. I have arranged a one-deck version which is totally impromptu.

Spectator Rex will be delighted to assist you. "In this experiment, Rex," you say, "we'll each need about half the cards." Turn the deck faces towards you and note the bottom card. You're going to fan through the deck, looking for its mate—the card that matches it in color and value. Fan through several cards and place them *face down* in front of yourself, saying, "Some for me." Fan through several more. If the mate is not in sight, place these cards face down on your pile, saying, "Some more for me."

Fan through to the mate of the original bottom card. Lift off this batch, including the mate. Even up the group and place it *face up* in front of Rex, saying, "And some for you." You now have a small face-down packet in front of you, the bottom card of this pile being the original bottom card. In front of Rex is a face-up pile; the lowermost card is the mate to your bottom card.

If the pile in front of Rex is fairly small, add cards from the deck to his pile and to yours until each consists of about half the deck. Naturally, the cards go on his pile face up and on yours face down. As you add cards to the piles, keep saying, "Some for you" and "Some for me."

If the pile in front of Rex is quite large, put the rest of the deck onto your pile. If his pile is still larger than yours, take some cards from his, turn them face down, and put them onto your pile.

It sounds a little complicated, but the bottom line is this: Once you've put down the first two piles, you make sure that each consists of about half the deck.

Pick up your pile and casually give it an overhand shuffle as you tell Rex, "Please pick up your pile and turn it face down." Near the end of your overhand shuffle, draw off the last few cards singly, bringing the bottom card to the top. The top card of your pile now matches the top card of Rex's pile.

"Now for the experiment. Rex, let's see what happens when we perform the identical actions. Please do exactly what I do."

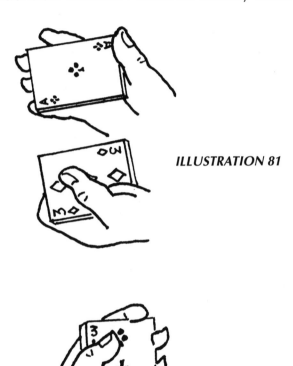

ILLUSTRATION 81

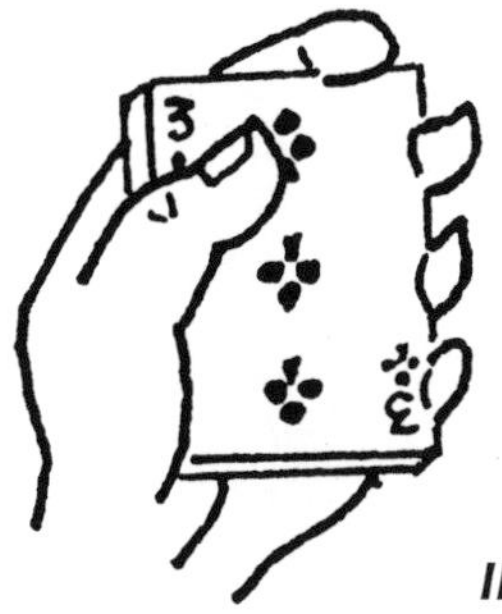

ILLUSTRATION 82

With Rex following your example with his cards, you cut off the top half of your packet. You place this top half face down onto the table. Turn the cards in your hand face up and give them several overhand shuffles (Illustration 81). Even up these cards and hold them face up in your left hand in the dealing position (Illustration 82). Lift off the top card of those you placed on the table and place this card face down on top of the face-up packet you're holding. Turn this packet face down and place it on top of your pile on the table. Rex, of course, has gone through the identical routine with his cards.

In case Rex and others are not sufficiently disoriented, you now use a bit of "time misdirection" so that they will forget precisely what has occurred. "Very often, Rex, when two persons perform identical actions, they get similar results. When this happens, some people call it coincidence, others call it fate. I think of it as good luck, especially if I'm conducting the experiment. So we performed the same actions; let's see the result."

Spread your cards out face down and have Rex do the same. His face-up card matches yours.

List to One Side

Time is hanging heavy on your hands. Why not telephone Nola and perform a card trick for her?

All you need is a pencil and paper, along with enough persuasive power to convince Nola to cooperate.

Start by asking her to get a deck of cards. When she returns to the phone, ask her to shuffle the deck. Then: "Nola, deal the cards from the top of the deck into a face-up pile. Please name the cards as you deal them out."

As she names the cards, jot down the name of each one, using this conventional shorthand:

9C

10S

JH

QD

(These stand for nine of clubs, ten of spades, jack of hearts, and queen of diamonds.)

After Nola deals ten-plus cards, tell her that she can stop whenever she wishes. Have her set the deck aside. "Pick out any card you want from those you dealt off. Remember that card and stick it into the middle of the main deck. Now shuffle up the main deck."

When she's ready, say, "Shuffle up the rest of the cards that you dealt off and put them on top of the main deck. When you're ready, give the deck a complete cut."

These are your final instructions: "Again, would you deal the cards from the top into a face-up pile and name the cards as you deal them." As she names the cards, keep your eye on the card names you jotted down. As soon as she names one, put a check mark by it. Continue checking off cards from the group. (Because she shuffled these cards, they will not be in order. But the checked-off cards *will* be together in a bunch.) Eventually, you will check off all the cards in the group except one. That is her chosen card. Stop Nola and tell her the name of her chosen card.

Sometimes the spectator will name a card from the group you wrote down but then will name cards that are *not* in the group. That first card she named from the group is her chosen card.

Note: When Nola names the cards for the second time, you might want to make a second list which you can use after she gets well down in the deck. This eliminates the possibility of your failing to check off one of the cards on your initial list.

Pop-Up Card

While chatting with the spectators, hold the deck in the dealing position in your left hand. Grip the deck from above with your right hand, fingers at the front, thumb at the rear. With your right thumb, riffle the top few cards slightly, separating the top two cards from the rest of the deck. Hold a break below these two with the tip of your left little finger.

Even up the cards at the ends with your right hand. Now simply *lift off* the top two cards with your second and third fingers at the front and your thumb at the rear. Hold the double card straight up so all can see it; then bend it almost in half so that the top of the face of the double card almost meets the bottom. Replace the double card on the deck, holding the center down with your left thumb. Take the top card in your right hand, thumb on top and fingers below. Hold this card sideways so all can see that it's bent downwards at the ends. Slide the card into the middle of the deck. Incidentally, as you take off this card, make sure your left thumb continues its pressure, holding down the center of the next card.

Grip the deck from above with your right hand, curling your first finger under so that it, rather than your left thumb, is now holding down the top card at the center. Move up the deck in your left hand, holding it at the sides between thumb and fingertips. Squeeze at the sides to prevent the top card from popping up, Take your right hand away and hold the deck up sideways so that all can see.

Say, "One, two, three." On "three," release the pressure of the fingers and thumb on the sides, and the card will visibly pop up at the middle about a quarter-inch or so. As I say, "Three," I usually snap the fingers of my right hand to add emphasis. With your right hand, carefully lift off the card, showing that it's risen from the middle of the deck.

Don't repeat the trick.

Those Mysterious Ladies

A card is chosen and replaced in the deck. Four queens are dealt out face down. The spectator chooses one, and it mysteriously changes to his chosen card.

"I'm going to need four mysterious cards," you say. Fan through the deck and remove the four queens, placing them face down in a pile on the table. Do this without showing their faces. First remove a red queen, then another red queen, followed by the black queens. So, from the bottom up, the pile on the table consists of two red queens and two black queens.

Have spectator Evan select a card as you say, "You need to choose a card to represent you." The card is taken, shown around, and replaced in the deck. You cleverly bring it to the top. The way I cleverly do it is with a double-cut (see *Double-Cut,* page 17), but you may use any other method. (See *Controlling a Card*, starting on page 17.)

Turn the deck face up and fan the cards from the bottom somewhat (not revealing the top card, of course), saying, "You could have chosen any of these cards to represent you." Close up the fan. "Now it's time to examine the mysterious cards." Place the deck face up on the queen pile. Pick up all the cards with your right hand, turning them over and placing them in your left hand.

"Four mysterious cards," you say. "And what could be more mysterious than four lovely ladies?"

Fan out the four face-up queens with your right hand, pushing off an additional card below them. As you push the queens back, obtain a little-finger break beneath the fifth card. With your right hand, from above, take the cards with your thumb at the near end and fingers at the outer end. Draw off the top queen onto the deck with your left thumb. Using the left edge of the remaining cards in your right hand, flip it face down. "Here we have a lovely redhead," you say. Turn the next queen the same way, saying, "And another gorgeous redhead." Flip it face down as before. Turn

232

over the next queen, saying, "A mighty pretty brunette." As you flip this queen face down, drop the two cards remaining in your right hand (presumably one card) on top of the deck. "And yet another attractive brunette." Push this last queen to the left with your left thumb and then, with your right fingers, flip it face down.

From the top down, the top four cards are black queen, chosen card, black queen, red queen. (The other red queen, irrelevant to the rest of the trick, is the fifth card down.) Spread out the top four cards and take them from the deck in your right hand. Set the rest of the deck aside.

Say to Evan, "Now you're going to have to choose one of these beautiful young ladies."

You're about to perform an easy maneuver known as *The*

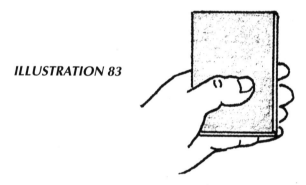

ILLUSTRATION 83

Olram Subtlety. Place the packet of four cards into your left hand so that they're considerably forward of the regular dealing position (Illustration 83). (This is so that when you turn your left hand palm down, the bottom card can be easily seen.)

ILLUSTRATION 84

Draw the top card off the front end of the face-down packet with your right hand. The instant it clears, turn both hands over. Your right hand displays the card just drawn off (a black queen), and your left hand displays the bottom card of the three card packet (a red queen) (Illustration 84). Turn both hands palm down, immediately dropping the card from your right hand face down and—*at the same time*—thumbing off the top card of those in your left hand, letting it land to the left of the card that comes from your right hand.

With your right hand, draw off the top card of the two remaining cards. Again, turn both hands over, displaying the faces. Turn your hands palm down. Simultaneously drop the card in your right hand to the right of the two on the table while dropping the card in your left hand to the left of those on the table.

Apparently, you've shown all four queens. Actually, you've shown a red queen twice. From your left to right, the cards on the table are red queen, chosen card, black queen, black queen. Let's assume that the chosen card is the seven of clubs. The layout could be this, as you look at it:

QH   7C   QC   QS

You now do an *equivoque* or *magician's choice* similar to that described in *Either/Or Force* (page 161). Say to Evan, "Pass your hands over those cards, and when you feel ready, let each hand fall onto a card." He covers two of the cards with his hands.

234

If one of the two is the chosen card, pull the other two cards towards you, saying, "Now please hand me one of those." If he hands you the chosen card, say, "So this is your free choice." Set the card face down directly in front of him. If he hands you the other card, drop it down with the others which you pulled out of line. Point to the card under his card, saying, "Your choice."

Suppose he covers two cards other than the chosen card. Indicate that he is to lift his hands. You pull the two cards towards you. As before, ask him to hand you one of the remaining two.

In all instances, Evan gets his chosen card. Turn the queens face up one by one, saying, "Here we have the poor ladies who weren't chosen." Toss them face down onto the deck.

"So you've chosen a red-haired lady. The question is, would she choose you? What was the name of the card representing you?" Evan names it, and you have him turn it over. "Excellent. You *were* chosen, and everyone lives happily ever after."

If performing the trick for a woman, use the four kings. In the patter, they become two redheaded men and two darkhaired men. When you pick up the kings so that they are face up on the face-down deck, fan them out, as with the queens. The patter changes slightly, however. "We have four mysterious men."

Good Choice

Here's a fast, clever trick requiring only nerve and a bit of practice.

In your pocket, you have four kings. The king of spades and the king of clubs have blue backs. The king of hearts and the king of diamonds have red backs. The order doesn't matter.

ILLUSTRATION 85

Remove the four cards from your pocket, making sure spectators cannot see any of the backs. Hold them face up in your left hand. Spread the kings out and ask spectator Ted to name one (Illustration 85). After he does so, say, "You can change your mind if you want to, Ted—it doesn't matter." When he finally decides on one, remove it from the group, saying, "This one." Replace it so that it's the lowermost of the face-up cards. Maneuver the other cards about so that the king that's of the same color as the one chosen is at the face of the packet. As you do this, say, "You could have chosen this one, or this one, whatever one you wished." Tell him that he can still change his mind. If he does, maneuver the cards so that they're in the appropriate position described.

You are about to perform a variation of the *flustration count,* previously described in the trick *Color Confusion,* page 170.

236

Close up the face-up packet and hold it from above in your right hand, fingers at the outer end and thumb at the inner end. Turn your right hand palm up, displaying the back of the top, chosen, card. Let's assume he has selected the king of clubs. Say, "It's amazing that you should choose the king of clubs, which has a *blue* back." Turn your right hand palm down. With the left *fingers*, draw the king of clubs from the back of the packet into your left hand. (This first maneuver differs from the standard *flustration count.*) Turn your right hand palm up again, displaying a red-backed card. Turn your hand palm down and, with your left thumb, draw off the card at the *face* of the packet so that it comes to rest on top of the king of clubs. (This is the standard move in the *flustration count.*) Perform the action again. Then display the back of the last card, turn your right hand palm down and drop the card face up on top of those in your left hand.

Ted has chosen the only card with a different-colored back.

Note: If you wish, repeat the trick several times. Simply put the cards into your pocket. Chat for a moment about what a coincidence has occurred. Then say, "I have another set of kings in my pocket." Dig into a different pocket. "No luck. Maybe they're here." Take the same set of kings from your pocket and repeat the trick. You might even put the kings away again and then go through the same routine. The basic trick is so deceptive that there's little danger that spectators will catch on, and it becomes quite amusing when spectators suspect that you're using the same kings.

Spin-Out!

Reinhard Muller created this quick, simple, startling effect.

Remove from the deck the two red aces, setting them aside face down without showing them. Have a card chosen and bring it to the bottom of the deck. The easiest way is to secure a little-finger break below the chosen card and then do a double-cut. (See *Double-Cut*, page 17.)

Hold the deck from above in your left hand, fingers on one side, thumb on the other side. Pick up one of the aces, show it, and place it face up on the bottom. As you reach out with your right hand to pick up the other ace, draw back the ace on the bottom slightly with your left fingers (Illustration 86).

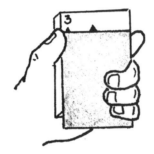

ILLUSTRATION 86

Bottom View.

Place the second ace face up on top of the deck. Still retaining the left-hand grip, grasp the front of the deck with your right hand. Your right thumb is on top, your right first finger on the selection, and your right second finger on a red ace (Illustration 87).

ILLUSTRATION 87

Bottom View.

The following move sounds a bit difficult; in fact, you'll master it after a few tries. Let loose of the left-hand grip. Simultaneously, with the right hand revolve the deck forward, and, in a snappy dealing motion, toss the cards onto the table, but not *all* the cards. You cling to the three cards you're gripping with your right thumb and first and second fingers—the two aces and the selected card.

ILLUSTRATION 88

Fan the three cards with your right hand (Illustration 88). Turn the fan over, showing that "the selected card, hidden in the middle of the deck, has been captured by the aces!"

GOTCHA!

Most so-called "sucker" tricks should be reserved for times when you have an obnoxious spectator. You can do only one sucker trick for a particular group, obviously, because your victim is unlikely to take the bait twice.

"Second Deal"

For this one, you must have an odious onlooker who's eager to catch you. Apparently you show the top card and then deal off the second card from the top in an extremely sloppy "second deal." The victim *knows* that the card on the table is not the card you claim it is.

The method is quite simple. You apparently show the top card. Actually, you perform a double-lift. (See *Double-Lift,* page 42.) You name the card. Then you make sure full attention is paid to your sloppy deal by saying, "I will now deal the card onto the table."

Very obviously push off the top card with your left thumb and pull the second card out with your right thumb (Illustration 89).

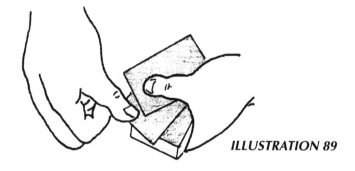

ILLUSTRATION 89

Pull the top card back with your left thumb. Actually, you're performing a "legitimate" second deal, only you're making it as sloppy as possible.

Look as smug as you can. Turn to the obnoxious spectator and say, "Can you remember what this card is?

Don't let anyone turn the card over. Put your hand over it if you have to.

The intended victim will probably say that it's not the card you claim it is. But if he doesn't, simply say, "Does everyone agree that this is the seven of hearts?" Or whatever card. If no one disagrees, say, "You're right." Show the card and continue with something else.

But it's your lucky day. The victim caught it all; he knows exactly what happened. This is definitely not the card; you dealt a second. Show the card and pause for a few seconds before the next trick so that you can enjoy the other spectators complimenting your dupe on his perspicacity.

No Wonder

Have spectator Karen select a card, show it around, and return it to the deck. Bring it to the top. (See *Controlling a Card,* page 17.)

Say, "Let's see if we can locate your card, Karen."

Double-lift, showing the second card from the top. (See *Double-Lift,* page 42.) Suppose this card is the three of hearts. Say, "Let's use the three of hearts to help us." Turn over the double card on top of the deck. Take the top card (the chosen one) and hand it face down to Karen. Say, "Just stick it face down partway into the deck."

After she does so, fan through to the partially inserted card (the one selected). Set aside the cards above it, remove the inserted card, and put it face down near Karen. Turn over the next card, asking if it's the one selected. Naturally, the answer is no.

Have Karen pick up the face-down (selected) card and insert it partway into the deck face down again. Once more it fails to locate the chosen card. You might even do it a third time. Finally, hand Karen the face-down card and say, "What was your card?" When she names it, say, "Well, no wonder it didn't work." Indicate that she is to turn the card face up.

If Karen should turn over the card sometime during the procedure, ask her why she seems startled. When she points out that it is her card, say sardonically, "Wonderful! Now this will *never* work."

Spectators will be amused by either conclusion.

Dunbury Delusion

Your potential victim, Mervin, has been trying to spoil your every trick. Have him select a card and show it around. Mervin is quite capable of lying about his chosen card just to goof you up, so it's vital with this trick that all spectators know the name of the card. When the card is returned, bring it to the top. (See *Controlling a Card*, page 17.)

Now give a lengthy speech. Near the end, you'll prepare for a sleight.

"This is the only experiment I do with cards which never fails. *Never* fails. And why? Because I've learned to tell when a spectator is lying and when he's telling the truth. Now, Mervin, I am going to cut the cards three times. The first time I'll cut a card of the same suit as your card, the second time a card of the same value, and the third time a card that will help us find your card.

"When I cut the cards, Mervin, I'll ask you a question which you are to answer yes or no. Nothing more. You may lie or tell the truth. It doesn't matter, because I'll be able to tell if you're lying or not. That's why this experiment never fails. If something has gone wrong, I'll be able to tell and can make an adjustment. Remember, just yes or no. And you can lie or tell the truth."

As you near the end of the speech, casually perform an overhand shuffle, in-jogging the first card and shuffling off. The card above the chosen card is now in-jogged. (See *Controlling a Group of Cards*, page 32.)

You're about to perform *Drop Sleight* (page 41). The preparation is slightly different from that described, however. Hold the deck in dealing position in your left hand. Grip the deck from above with your right hand, fingers at the front and thumb at the rear. Lift up at the jogged card with the right thumb so that you're holding a break above the chosen card with the tips of your left fingers along the right side and your right thumb at the rear (Illustration 90).

The cards above the break should be bent up slightly at the rear with your right thumb, letting a card drop off. With the aid of the third and fourth fingers of your left hand, adjust the cards so that your right thumb grips the top section along with the card which has been dropped at the rear (Illustration 91).

ILLUSTRATION 90

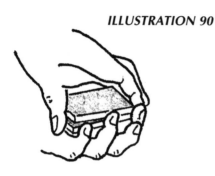

ILLUSTRATION 91:
For clarity, the left hand isn't shown.

You say, "Now the first card I cut will tell me the suit of your card."

Lift off the cards above the break with your right hand. Shove over the chosen card with your left thumb. (Let's assume the card is the four of hearts.) Flip it face up with the left edge of the cards in your right hand.

"See, the four of hearts."

As you continue talking, perform the drop sleight.

"This tells me that your card is a heart. Yes or no?"

As Mervin answers, thumb the card face down onto the table. Place the lower packet on *top* of the pile in your right hand, lifting the first finger to permit passage. The chosen card, presumably on the table, is now on top.

Chances are, Mervin's answer will be yes. It doesn't matter. If he says no, smile confidently and say, "Sure."

Cut the deck at random and flip over another card (the eight of clubs). Name the card and flip it face down. Thumb it face down next to the first card, and return the packet *below* the one in your right hand, so that the chosen card remains on top.

244

Meanwhile, comment, "This means that your card is an eight. Yes or no?" If he says yes, say, "Of course it is." Chances are he'll say no, to which you respond, "I can tell you're lying by that almost undetectable, sneaky little smile." In either instance, reassure him that this is the one trick you do which never fails.

Again you cut off a pile of cards and flip over the card you cut to. Name it, flip it face down, thumb it off onto the table next to the other two. The pile in the left hand is returned below the one in your right so that the chosen card remains on top.

Let's assume that the third card you cut to was the seven of spades. "Ah, here we have the seven of spades. This means that your card is seventh from the top. Yes or no? No need to answer. Of course it is. Now watch this as I magically move it from the seventh position to the very top of the deck." Give the cards a false shuffle or a false cut.

Lift off the top card and hod it face down. "And now the key question. Here we have your chosen card. Yes or no?"

Whatever the response, ask, "What is your card?" When he names it, turn the card over, announcing, "See? The one effect I achieve that never fails."

Watch them dive for that first card you dealt on the table!

Notes: Sometimes when you cut the second card, it's the same suit or value as the chosen card. This won't do. If it's the same suit, you're saying that this *is* the chosen card. If it's the same value, you're saying that you know that the first card you ostensibly placed down is the chosen one. So simply say, "Whoops, wrong card!" Continue cutting until you get one of a different suit and value.

Save the "sucker" tricks for severe cases. The best response to most irritating spectators is simply to perform your tricks well.

RECOVERY

An Out

The spectator names his selected card; you turn over the one in your hand, and it's the wrong one. Here's a way out.

Show the card and return it to the deck, asking, "Are you sure the five of spades was your card?" Fan through the cards so that no one else can see the faces. "It must be here somewhere."

What you want to do is bring the chosen card second from the top. Fan several cards from the bottom and transfer them to the top in a bunch. Continue doing this until you come to the chosen card. Fan one card beyond it and put that group on top. Confess, "No luck."

Turn the deck face down in the dealing position in your left hand. Take the top card and turn it face up. As you do so, push off the second card (the chosen one) slightly with your left thumb and then draw it back, taking a slight break under it with your left little finger.

Immediately place the card in your right hand face up on the deck. Square the ends of the deck with your right fingers and thumb. The two cards are now as one, separated slightly from the rest of the deck by the tip of your little finger.

"Obviously your card isn't on top." Grasp the double card with your right hand from above, thumb at the rear, second finger at the front, and first finger resting on top. Dig your left thumb beneath the deck and flip the deck face up. Place the double card underneath, presumably replacing on top the card you've just shown (Illustration 92). Carefully even up the deck, saying, "And equally obviously, your card isn't on the bottom. Watch for your card."

Fan ten or so cards from the bottom. "It's not among these." Turn these cards face down and put them on the back of the deck (Illustration 93). Continue this way all through the deck.

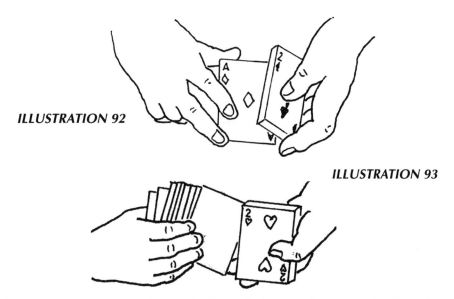

ILLUSTRATION 92

ILLUSTRATION 93

The last group you take includes all the cards up to the first face-down card. Presumably, you've shown every card in the deck, and the chosen card isn't among them. Actually, it's at your disposal on top of the deck.

How do you reveal it? You might do *Sneaky Slide*, in which you double-lift the top card, showing that the chosen card is still not there. Then you lift off the top card, slide it through the deck edgewise, and turn it over, showing that it has changed to the chosen card.

A second possibility is one which is also a good trick on its own merits. Put the deck into your pocket. Remove a card from the bottom and place it on the table. *Rapidly* continue doing this, saying, "Tell me when to stop." Make sure you get your hand back to your pocket when the spectator says stop, so that you can pull out the top card and flip it over face up.

A third possibility is to force the chosen card on your assistant, causing him to choose the same card again. You may use the standard force or one of the surefire forces. (See *Forces*, page 34.)

PARTING THOUGHTS

Write It Down

Go through the tricks again and jot down the page numbers of the ones you particularly like. When you finish, try out your selections—first on yourself, and then on others. It is easy to get into the habit of performing certain favorites, and letting other excellent tricks fade from memory. You can prevent this by keeping a record right from the beginning.

When you find a good card trick, perhaps you should make a memorandum of it—jot some notes down on a file card or in a notebook. From time to time, you can consult your notes and freshen up your routines.

Simplify

Some say that the perfect trick is one that has been simplified to the point that it requires no sleight of hand. I don't know about that, but I believe that you *should* try to simplify every trick as much as possible. Do you really need all those sleights? Can you substitute subtlety for a sleight, or simply drop one altogether? Think it through. At least in some respect, every trick you do should be uniquely yours.

Stay Within Yourself

You have heard the expression, usually in sports, that a certain person should "stay within himself." For instance, if a player tries to do too much, he will probably mess up altogether. Similarly, when you do card tricks, you should stay within yourself. Don't try tricks you haven't mastered. Don't experiment with sleights in public. Practise in private until the sleight is perfected. Why risk exposure when there are so many tricks that you do perfectly?

Be Prepared

Should you carry a deck of cards with you wherever you go? Although this may not be a bad idea, what you should *definitely* know is what you're going to do when someone hands you a deck.

It's quite simple, really. It doesn't matter whether you're at a party, in a small group, or with an individual—your response is the same. Have in mind three or four tricks that are particularly effective and that you perform especially well. The tricks need not be related or sequential—just *good*.

Suppose these tricks are well received and you are encouraged to do more. *Now* you're ready to perform a routine. The makeup of this program is your choice, of course. It can consist of all gambling tricks or all mental tricks, for example. Personally, I prefer variety. Whatever you decide, perform no more than five or six tricks, closing with one of your best, a guaranteed eyepopper.

AFTERWORD

You're interested in card magic. Let's suppose you do all the right things. You learn a dozen really good card tricks. You practise them till you have them down perfectly. You toss in some superb, imaginative patter. Then you try them out on susceptible, trusting friends and relatives—with great success! Now what? Where do you go from here?

It depends on how interested you are. Do you aspire to become one of the all-time greats, or would you prefer to dabble in magic? Do you want to become a professional, or remain an amateur? Nothing wrong with any of these.

Obviously, if you plan to make money performing magic, you'd better be prepared to practise a great deal. Furthermore, you'd better be creative, because very few spectators are interested in stale patter or ordinary tricks. Are there jobs? Yes. Probably more jobs than ever before. But there are more magicians than ever before, too. So you'd better be good. And dedicated. Furthermore, you'd better realize that very few magicians make their living solely doing magic. Most have a full-time job and perform magic as a sideline.

On the other hand, being an amateur magician has its rewards. There is certainly less pressure. No one expects you to be as good as a professional, so when you do a trick especially well, you hear things like, "You're a regular professional." It's much more gratifying than being a professional and hearing the reverse. Also, as an amateur, you view magic as a hobby. You can devote as much time to it as you choose, attaining perfection in your own good time.

Whatever your aspirations, you should get together with fellow magicians. They are a surprisingly helpful and friendly lot.

Check your phone book to see if there's a magic shop in your area. If so, you can drop in and get all the information you need about local organizations. Furthermore, you might just meet other magicians who can help you out with advice.

What if there is no magic shop in your area? Again, check the phone book. If any professional magicians are operating in your area, they will probably be listed. Feel free to give a call. Explain your situation and ask about any local group, formal or informal. Chances are, you'll get all the information you need about local magicians and organizations.

INDEX